Many Mansions

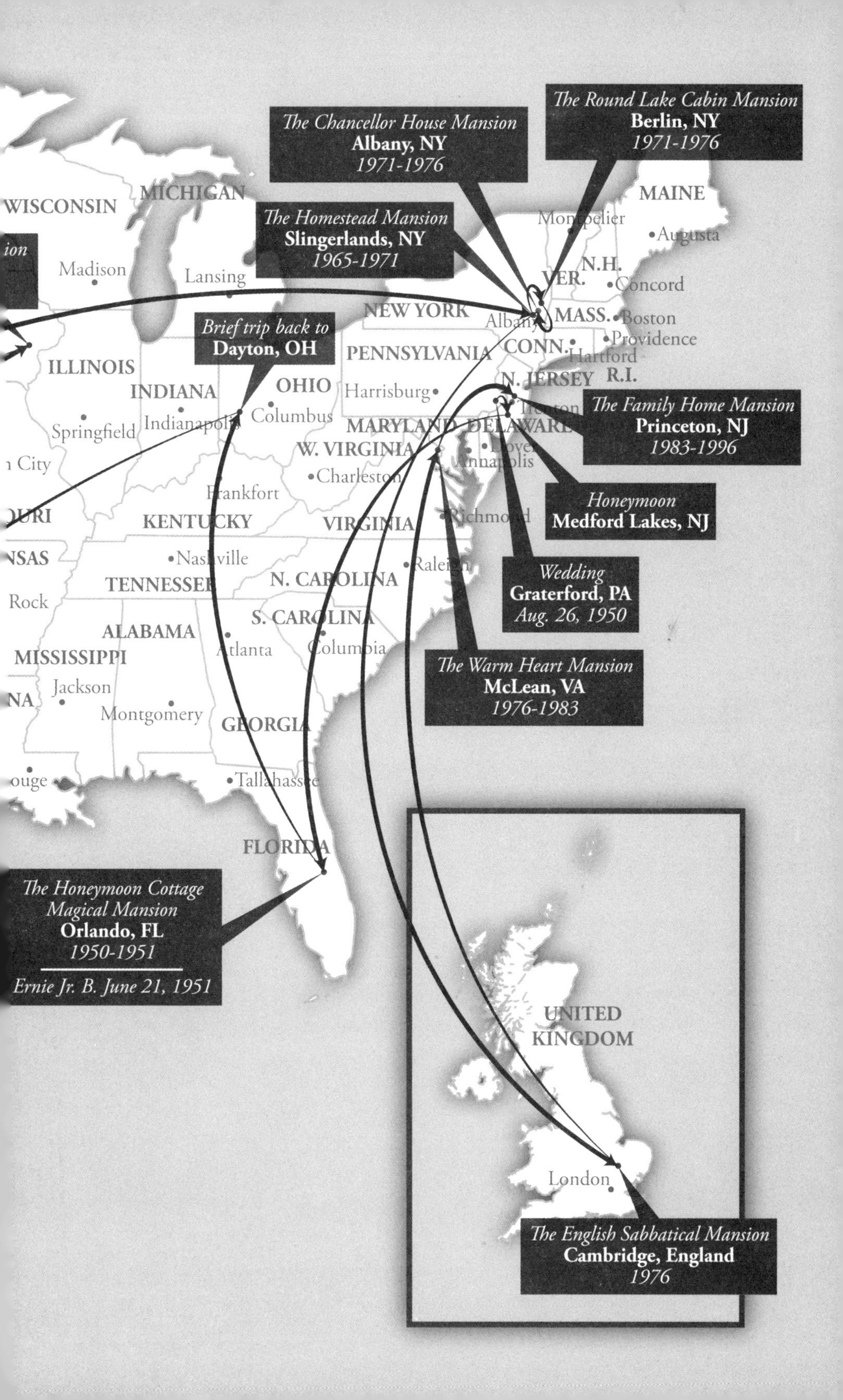

The Chancellor House Mansion
Albany, NY
1971-1976
The Round Lake Cabin Mansion
Berlin, NY
1971-1976
The Homestead Mansion
Slingerlands, NY
1965-1971
Brief trip back to
Dayton, OH
The Family Home Mansion
Princeton, NJ
1983-1996
Honeymoon
Medford Lakes, NJ
Wedding
Graterford, PA
Aug. 26, 1950
The Warm Heart Mansion
McLean, VA
1976-1983
The Honeymoon Cottage
Magical Mansion
Orlando, FL
1950-1951
Ernie Jr. B. June 21, 1951
The English Sabbatical Mansion
Cambridge, England
1976
UNITED
KINGDOM
London
WISCONSIN
MICHIGAN
MAINE
NEW YORK
PENNSYLVANIA
ILLINOIS
INDIANA
OHIO
N.H.
MASS.
CONN.
R.I.
N. JERSEY
MARYLAND
DELAWARE
W. VIRGINIA
VIRGINIA
KENTUCKY
TENNESSEE
N. CAROLINA
S. CAROLINA
ALABAMA
MISSISSIPPI
GEORGIA
FLORIDA
Madison
Lansing
Springfield
Indianapolis
Columbus
Harrisburg
Charleston
Frankfort
Nashville
Raleigh
Richmond
Atlanta
Columbia
Jackson
Montgomery
Tallahassee
Augusta
Concord
Boston
Providence
Hartford
Albany
Trenton
Dover
Annapolis

Many Mansions

Lessons of Faith, Family, and Public Service

Kathryn Boyer

In Memory of Her Husband, Ernest L. Boyer

Abilene Christian University Press

MANY MANSIONS

Lessons of Faith, Family, and Public Service

ACU PRESS

ISBN 978-0-89112-407-8

Printed in Canada

Cover design by Jennette Munger
Interior text design by Sandy Armstrong, Strong Design

For information contact:
Abilene Christian University Press
1626 Campus Court
Abilene, Texas 79601

1-877-816-4455 toll free
www.acupressbooks.com

14 15 16 17 18 19 / 7 6 5 4 3 2 1

ACKNOWLEDGMENTS

For some years I have had a nagging in my spirit that I needed to write about the life Ernie and I shared. I felt like I should take the responsibility to pass on to our four children, and the generations that follow, the full story of our shared life—with the focus centered on my beloved husband, Ernest L. Boyer. He was the constant strength of the family, and the spiritual, moral, and intellectual force on whose wisdom we all relied. I felt compelled to show the hand of God in Ernie's life.

I knew many experiences and circumstances would always remain unknown unless I told them. I felt that the story should be passed on, so that others, including colleagues and friends, would understand.

However, I questioned if I was ready emotionally to sort through the past to be able to tell the simple and innermost stories. Another very big question was "How could I organize the facts and the sequence of events into some logical and cohesive form?"

Then something remarkable happened when I was talking with our dear friend, Carolynn Reid Wallace, the former president of Fisk University who had also been a member of the board of trustees at the Carnegie Foundation for the Advancement of Teaching. In our conversation, I mentioned the house where we lived while Ernie was chancellor of the State University of New York System. Carolyn gave a surprising response, "Kay, you need to write a book about the houses where you and Ernie lived." The next day she gave me the title, "There Are Many Mansions." It was like a gift to me.

A book about the many houses where we had lived suddenly seemed like a manageable and exciting idea. I then started counting the houses—one, two, three, four, five, six, seven, eight, nine, ten, eleven. . . .

But weeks and months passed into years. The nagging feeling that I should write our story continued in my mind, but I was fully engrossed and fulfilled in teaching a weekly class in my home for international young ladies in English language practice and Bible study. Also, I did not want to give up the regular class I conducted for adults with special needs. I had no time to write, I reasoned.

Finally, I felt roused into action by the persuasive yet kindly conviction of Ernie's cousin, James Pawelski. In our hours of conversation, he would ask many questions about Ernie's basic concepts, educational philosophy, and his guiding principles for life. He would take pages of notes as I answered his questions. He repeatedly told me that I needed to be the one to write all the answers and give a complete account. His strong encouragement had much to do with my will to move forward in my effort to quiet my nagging spirit.

In November of 2009, I broke my hip and was forced into a time of quiet contemplation. At the same time, I was blessed with the precious gift of living with my family in New Hampshire for recuperation. During this time, I felt an unexpected peaceful completion of my grieving heart being healed, and I then felt ready to record whatever I could remember about the life Ernie and I shared.

The family gave suggestions on how to proceed. Ernie Jr. did not like the idea of hiring someone to write the book for me or recording the story. He gave me a simple plan—set aside at least two hours each day, six days a week to write. Decide on the best two hours and use those same hours each day. As much as possible, let nothing interfere.

I had very little knowledge about how to write my story on a computer. I contacted a graduate student, Manoj Shrestha, who skillfully preserved every chapter after I finished writing it. This plan allowed me to steadily move toward the completion of a book. Each time I sat down at my computer to write, I would ask God to do the writing for me. God was always by my side, and I pray He is beside you too as you read through these pages.

TABLE OF CONTENTS

INTRODUCTION

Ernie felt confident he had inherited strong genes. His beloved grandfather, Rev. William Boyer, lived to be one month short of his hundredth birthday, and both of his parents lived long lives. Furthermore, we trusted that I had long-life genes. So he and I told each other we could count on growing old together.

I was so confident of those genes that I even disregarded a vivid memory from my childhood. My mother was clearly feeling sad that day as she kneaded the bread. I looked at her, and in my young mind, I too felt sad. As a tear rolled down her check, I asked, "Is this the day that Papa died?" I had never known my father; he had died when I was three months old, leaving my mother to raise me and my five siblings. She nodded, "Yes." With determination I said, "I will never get married because it only means sadness." Her expression immediately changed. She stopped kneading the bread as she firmly replied, "Oh, never say that. I would never give up those almost ten wonderful years with your Papa."

Somehow, I knew my mother was right, and many years later, her words helped me accept my own husband's death. I remember heaving a sigh of relief as the first decade of our marriage slipped by—we had made it beyond my own parents' ten years of marriage. Then when we passed our fourth decade and celebrated our fortieth wedding anniversary, I breathed another big sigh of relief. We were both healthy. Surely, we were going to grow old together.

Then how could it be, that only a few years after that fortieth anniversary he was diagnosed with lymphoma? In our perfect plan, we would have grown old together, but he died when he was only sixty-seven years. I was the same age and now a widow. I grieved for him then, and I continue to miss him. But each day I feel deep gratitude for our forty-five years and three months of marriage and for the gift of my treasured garden of memories. Now years later, at eighty-two years old, I will try, with help, to draw from those past years' memories, as best I can to tell Ernie's story, my story, our story.

CHAPTER ONE

HOUSE 1

The Honeymoon Cottage Magical Mansion

Orlando, Florida

1950–1951

"By wisdom a house is built,
and through understanding it is established;
through knowledge its rooms are filled
with rare and beautiful treasures."

—Proverbs 24:3–4

The house and church addresses do not matter because neither the house nor the church are there any longer. Because Disney World has taken over much of Orlando, Florida, the narrow street may also be gone. But in 1950, there was a short street called Cook Street.

The one-story, two-bedroom bungalow parsonage for the Orlando Brethren in Christ mission church was on that street, and in July of 1950, Ernie was asked to serve as the pastor for that church.

He had just graduated from Greenville College, a small Free Methodist college in Illinois, and I had completed my three-year nursing education program in Norristown, Pennsylvania. We had been engaged and planning our wedding for the three years that I was in nursing school and he was earning his degree. We were both only twenty years old when we graduated and when we got married on August 26, 1950, so young that we had to have the signed consent of our parents to get married on our long-awaited wedding day.

The wedding took place at my home church, a "plain" church in Graterford, Pennsylvania. No musical instruments were used in any of our churches, so there was no organ to play the wedding march. Instead, I walked up the short aisle in step to the a cappella singing of a quartet of four men who were Ernie's friends from Messiah College. Ernie's Grandfather Boyer performed the marriage ceremony, preaching a moving sermon on love, and my minister brother, Irvin, spoke the prayer of blessing on our lives together. My whole nursing class had reserved seats near the front. The only little fancy touch that I included without criticism from the bishop was my white, satin wedding dress. My mother designed it and made it with a short train that flowed from the back as I walked. During my whole journey up the aisle, I kept my eyes on my smiling, waiting groom.

After the wedding and reception, we drove from my home in Pennsylvania to Orlando, Florida, in a maroon 1948 Chevy, a wedding gift from Ernie's parents. But first we stole away to a charming resort spot in Medford Lakes, New Jersey, for a two-day honeymoon. The day after our wedding was a Sunday, so we went to a small log cabin chapel service. Ernie often talked about that Sunday morning sermon. In fact he never forgot the sermon outline and how much it touched his heart.

We stayed at a lovely inn next to a lake, but the place was a bit out of the range of our simple and thrifty lifestyle. Shocked by the prices listed on the menu, we would order only one meal for the two of us to share. I recall that Ernie was too embarrassed to ask for an extra plate, but I found courage and shyly asked.

As we then drove on to Florida in our maroon Chevy, we were unclear about what we would find at the Orlando mission assignment. However, we were just so happy to be married and were too preoccupied with each other to concentrate on anything else. We were oblivious to the fact that this uninterrupted time together was a rare treat that would not be repeated very often in the future.

Our Own Lovely and Cozy Space

We arrived in Orlando on Saturday, exactly one week after our wedding day, as we were expected to be there in time for Ernie to preach and take charge on Sunday. The former minister had resigned after some kind of disagreement with the mission board, and all but two of the families in the congregation had left. Ernie's assignment was to build up the remaining church.

When we arrived, unlocked the door, and walked into the parsonage, we thought it was beautiful. It was our first home and our first joy of sharing our life together. How we had dreamed and planned for this during our long, three-year engagement and our almost-constant separation when we would write letters of sweet endearment to each other every day. To us, the newly married, blissful bride and groom, this house—regardless of how small—was a magical mansion. Only well after our arrival did we even notice the worn linoleum in every room and realize the furniture looked like someone else's cast-offs.

After a quick tour, I said to Ernie, "I'll cover the worst worn spots in the linoleum with the pretty throw rugs." The rugs, along with all our other wedding gifts, were in the trailer that we had hauled behind the car. I knew I could cover the used couch and the scarred tables, dressers, and stands with the things I had crocheted or embroidered and placed in my hope chest to use at this very time. I visualized finding some flowers to put in our gift vase and placing them on the coffee table. It was to be our own lovely and cozy space. And so it was—to our eyes!

Our first impression of the little, white, traditional-looking church with the small steeple was surprisingly agreeable. I guess we expected it to be worn down like the parsonage. I don't mean to depict anything the least bit grand, but it was quite pleasant, and it felt of God's presence. This worshipful atmosphere helped to prepare our hearts to focus on our mission and not on ourselves.

The side walls had tall, plain glass windows. Rows of comfortable, polished wood benches filled the sanctuary, and the center aisle led to a raised platform and the altar railing. The pulpit was set back into a lighted alcove.

Ernie immediately tested the acoustics and announced they were more than satisfactory. He had spent the past two college years on debate teams that won state and regional awards, and the experience had made him aware that good sound quality was of utmost importance when speaking publicly. Of course, this was a very different setting, but the concept was clearly in his consciousness.

The next day, Ernie and I stood at the church entrance door waiting to greet people as they arrived. Eight people came and seemed very glad to see us. They were all members of the two families who had made the decision to remain and support the Brethren in Christ Church.

That Sunday, Ernie went behind the pulpit and honored that tiny congregation and the Lord with a simple and inspiring sermon. He spoke from Exodus chapter 4 where God asked Moses, "What is that in your hand?" "A staff," Moses answered. That staff wasn't much, but what Moses had was enough for God to use to show His power. Ernie pointed out that everyone in that small group had something God could use. With a united and prayerful effort, what they had would be enough to meet the challenge of reviving this church, Ernie told them.

I don't remember the list of qualities Ernie said were available for us to hold on to and let God use, but I do remember that I, along with the eight people seated in the two front rows, was moved and inspired. We sang and prayed together, and we felt bonded with a purpose. Ernie and I understood that God had placed us at this church to serve Him, and we undertook the task determined to give our all regardless of how many—or how few—people were in attendance on that first Sunday.

Growing in Love and Numbers

Ernie was never without solutions, and he immediately started to make plans to revitalize this suffering church. He focused on the young people who lived in the area, and we made home visits and discovered some eager teenagers who said they would be happy to attend the church just around the corner. The two families who stayed with the mission church had several young folks, and they joined together with the four or five eager teens we met to form a willing core. Others soon joined as Ernie wrote and directed simple Bible dramas for the young people to perform at the Sunday evening services.

In addition, I made colorful but simple drawings as I stood next to the bright lights Ernie had installed while the youth group sang and gave readings. I quickly taught my methods to one of the eager teens, and she took over the chalk drawings so that I would be free to join the singing group.

The teenagers loved being involved, and Ernie tried to find parts for each one of them. He had a talent for making them feel at ease and capable of doing more than they thought possible. Their personalities seemed to develop and mature as they enjoyed feeling part of something where their unique talents could be recognized and cultivated. They began to learn many things from the gospel lessons, and lives were beginning to change. They started to attend Sunday morning services, and other family members soon followed, and our Sunday school program grew as a result, meaning we soon needed more teachers. A family from Ohio decided to buy a small grocery store in our neighborhood and move close to the church as mission workers. The father became the Sunday school superintendent; the mother taught a class and played the piano; and their two children were active in the youth group.

The church group quickly grew and became a loving and friendly Christian community of dedicated workers for God's kingdom. Sunday morning services, Sunday school classes, and the evening youth programs were filled with joy from God's Spirit, and the people kept coming. By April the pews were filled, and on Easter Sunday we had to bring in folding chairs to place along the aisles for more seating.

I should mention that the youth were naturally inclined to some mischief and figured out how to carry out a playful trick on us. Ernie suggested to me that we should burn our big pile of endearment letters we had written during our three-year engagement period. He questioned why we should carry those boxes of letters around with us since we now had each other. I dearly loved those letters, but I also could understand his reasoning and so reluctantly agreed that we should set them on fire. When no one was around, we emptied the boxes on a big pile in the middle of the gravel driveway. I felt sad when the match ignited and all of those meaningful words went up in smoke.

At that moment, the wind came up and lifted bits and pieces of those words into the sky. We had not even considered this possibility, but it was too late to rescue the letters and within a short time, some pieces of our endearment letters fell into the hands of some of our church teenagers. Being as mischievous as they were energetic, they tried to match some of the pieces and then fill in the blanks with their own love adjectives. They then giggled sheepishly as they showed us their own invented endearing words from those half-burned pieces. It was good fun, and we hoped that they learned from us that true love comes from our loving Father.

Lessons in Manners

We were paid a small stipend but mostly had to live on the Sunday morning offerings. The people who attended the little church were hard-working laborers, and their offerings were small. However, the offerings increased a little as the congregation grew, and by carefully checking the grocery store prices and sales, I managed to prepare meals for a steady flow of visitors, mainly retired couples from the Pennsylvania and Ohio churches who came to sunny Florida during the winter months to escape the northern cold.

It could be rather discouraging to see another couple pull up in our driveway with a Northern state license plate, knowing they would be expecting a home-cooked meal and a free bedroom, oblivious to our plans to spend the evening visiting a new family who had just started to attend church. Furthermore, I only had a scant food supply. It completely shocked us that professed Christians could have such uncouth manners to appear at our door with their suitcases without having the grace and politeness to notify us that they were coming. We had no idea when we accepted the Orlando assignment that it would include running a bed and breakfast during the winter months. Neither did we know that some strangers, who were church people, could be so ungracious.

I'm still shocked by one couple who showed up one late afternoon with no warning at all. Because of our frugal grocery budget, all I could afford to prepare was a casserole of rice, ground beef, and tomatoes, that I called Spanish rice. When the platter was passed to the husband, he took the serving spoon, stirred the food with his rough farmer hand and asked, "Are there tomatoes in here?" When I said there was, he gruffly replied, "On our farm up north we feed tomatoes to the pigs." His poor, sweet, little and round wife blushed a bright pink and replied that she was sure they would enjoy the food. We were young and had much to learn about how to handle the insults of difficult people. In this case we managed by trying to figure out an appropriate dinner conversation—which was not easy to do.

There were many other situations that made us realize a pastor's life is certainly not all perfectly delightful. It is however, a life of dedicated, caring service, and the experience made us keenly aware of how much we should appreciate, favor, and generously support our pastors.

Honoring God and Each Other

I made friends with the young mother who lived next door, and we visited while she hung out diapers and I hung out the bed sheets that I used for the continual flow of the northern visitors. I considered these opportunities to visit with her over the clothesline the bright spot in the extra duty required to constantly keep up the guest bedroom. One day Ernie was working on a sermon at the desk beside the open window, and he heard the two of us talking. I was going on, actually bragging about him—my wonderful husband—and I remember saying he had the art of doing a common thing extraordinarily well. But Ernie was quite embarrassed as he listened.

When I went into the house, he told me I should never have to brag about him because his life and aptitudes should be able to speak for themselves. Perhaps he was also thinking that my bragging about him may have made my friend think I was trying to prove that my husband was more wonderful than hers. That would be very unkind. I understood what he was asking of me, and at the same time I knew I would never belittle him. For the next forty-five years I tried to honor his wish, although I know I failed when I was alone with my mother, and maybe on other occasions too. I continue, however, to be mindful of his request as I recount this personal story.

The days were very full, but on weekdays the two of us would walk from our house across the lawn to the empty church, kneel together at the altar rail, and earnestly pray for God's direction for this growing church and for our lives. Long after we left that little house and quiet church, we continued to ask for God's wisdom and direction throughout the course of our marriage.

Saying Hello—and Good-bye

The biggest event, the greatest joy, and the sweetest memory of this house, our Honeymoon Cottage Magical Mansion, was the birth of our first child. Our darling, Ernest Leroy Boyer Jr., was born at Orange Memorial Hospital in Orlando, Florida, on Thursday, June 21, 1951. I had a short labor, but we were disappointed that Dr. Pohlman did not permit Ernie to be with me for the birth. During that era, hospital and doctor rules were rigid, and our requests were not even considered. But we had our own perfect baby. We were as proud and elated about this miracle as we could be. Ernie was a most doting father and loved to fall asleep while holding his baby across his chest. Of course, from the teenagers to the elderly grandmothers, our church family smothered our baby with love and admiration.

It was at this little mission church, a church we had grown to love, that we dedicated our baby, Ernest Jr., as we called him, to God for His service. The pews were full, and together the congregation rejoiced and prayed the dedication prayer with Ernie and me. We prayed that God would direct the life of our precious three-week-old baby boy so that he would grow up to love and serve Him.

One month after Ernest Jr.'s birth, and after a year of fully dedicated service at the Orlando Brethren in Church mission church, we repacked the little trailer. Our lives were now being led in a different direction as Ernie did not feel that his life's work was to be a pastor. During his undergraduate studies in psychology and history, Ernie never felt called to be a pastor; instead, he had a deep longing to continue his studies and felt that was what he should do.

The opportunity to take that step came when a friend at Upland College in California wrote that there was an opening for the next school year on the college staff. Employment at the small Christian college and the opportunity to enroll in a master's program at California State University in Los Angeles was a very strong attraction. Ernie wrote a letter of acceptance to Upland College, and we said a prayer of thanks to God for answering those prayers we had said while kneeling at the altar rail.

It was difficult to say the many sad farewells to our beloved church family. I doubt they ever fully understood why we felt led by the Holy Spirit to leave. But Ernie had fulfilled the Mission Board's assignment to help a stricken church to heal, and the church was now prepared to receive someone who had been trained for that work and was ready to take on a long-term appointment.

We left knowing we would not be losing friends but looking forward to gathering new ones in a delightful college setting. Ernie and I had a deep sadness to leave our Honeymoon Cottage Magical Mansion. We were still honeymooning, but the time had come to enlarge our horizons.

CHAPTER 2

HOUSE 2

The Minuscule Mansion

Upland, California
1951

"Give us a little home. The smallest places are roomiest, when peaceful joy is guest."

—Mary Caroly Davis

After much ado, we drove away from our first house and the place where our son, Ernest Jr., had been born. We drove away from dear friends and away from the mission church that had become so close to our hearts. It was a sharp, wrenching departure accompanied by many tears.

Ernie pointed our little Chevy north toward Dayton, Ohio, where his family lived. From there we would head for California and the unknown. The decision to leave Orlando had been made prayerfully, and Ernie had a clear vision about the next phase of our life together. His dream of the future became my dream, even if uncertainty made the dream a bit scary. We were courageously moving ahead by faith.

We put in several long days of driving. One night we stopped at a motel where I washed diapers in the bath tub; we spread them out in the car the next day to let them finish drying. Because there were no infant-safety car seats in

1951, I got to hold our one-month old baby for the whole trip. Looking back, knowing what I know now of automobile safety, the image is frightening. At the same time, I think about a picture that hung on the kitchen wall in my childhood home showing a beautiful angel with outstretched arms and unfolded wings following close behind two children walking on a dangerous bridge crossing. I loved that picture. And I know we unwittingly enjoyed that same, sweet protection as we innocently traveled along the route from Orlando to Dayton.

That days-long trip was a short stretch of travel compared to the many days it would take to drive from Ohio to California. Ernie's caring and thoughtful parents decided it would be too tedious and too difficult for me and their first grandchild to make that trip by car. So, they arranged for Ernie and his fifteen-year-old brother, Paul, to drive our little maroon Chevy and pull the small trailer packed full with our belongings and bought me an airline ticket to fly from Dayton to Los Angeles.

A Bumpy Beginning

It would be my first flying experience and, at the time, I sincerely hoped it would be my last. Airplane comfort and smooth flyways had not yet been developed, and I had a miserable experience. The plane had to land twice to refuel between Dayton and Los Angeles, and I grew miserably airsick at each takeoff and landing. While trying to care for Ernie Jr., I had to keep grabbing for one and then another airsickness bag. It seemed like an endless trip. I found no joy or glamour in traveling by airplane and determined never to do it again—never imagining that Ernie and I would one day rack up a near endless supply of frequent flier miles.

The miserable trip finally did end, and Ernie and Paul were eagerly waiting for my plane to land at the Los Angeles airport. Ernie was so looking forward to welcoming his wife and baby to the land of our future prospects. He wanted to show me the wonders awaiting us. I was so sick that all I wanted to do was hand him our baby and quietly rest and recover. However, I didn't want to disappoint him, so I made a great effort to take in this newness and see things through his eyes. But as we drove along the highway toward

Upland I was completely unprepared for what seemed like alien territory. I was shocked by the brown California foothills that all looked strangely barren. I wanted to be shown streams of water and ponds or green fields. Where were the familiar maple trees and vining hedge rows?

My Ernie tried to understand my disappointment and treated me with loving patience. He was indifferent to the brown, barren hills; instead, as we neared the small town of Upland, he pointed out the splendor of snowcapped Mount Baldy and the manicured citrus groves neatly planted in perfect rows. He had already accepted this land, with all of its unique differences, as a welcoming place. He now had a chance to plan for graduate school while also taking advantage of the opportunity of an Upland College position that would allow him to earn a salary for his little family. He felt secure and confident to be connected to a college that was supported by the church that was a part of his family's heritage: the Brethren in Christ Church.

Ernie and Paul had arrived in Upland a week or more ahead of me because Ernie wanted to have enough time to find a place for us to live and to have everything well prepared for my arrival with Ernie Jr. Some very dear classmates from Messiah College were now on the faculty at Upland College since Messiah and Upland were "sister colleges" of the Brethren in Christ Church. These friends and members from the Upland Brethren in Christ Church congregation helped Ernie find an apartment and some used basic pieces of furniture. How pleased he was to show me our home with the throw rugs and other pieces he had unpacked from our trailer already carefully placed in the apartment to help me feel the warm touches of home. He was most proud to show me the baby crib that someone loaned to us. I remember how deeply touched, impressed, and amazed I was by all his efforts to please me. I caught his happy spirit, and together we determined to make our new location in Upland, California, a blessing that would open us to whatever plans God had for us.

Little House, Big Life Changes

Looking back now on all the various houses where we lived, I know this one was by far the smallest. It was truly the most minuscule of all our "mansions."

The house included three small rooms and a bathroom, and the bedroom was so tiny there was barely enough room to walk between our three pieces of furniture—a bed, a crib, and a dresser.

When Ernie Jr. was about nine months old, he discovered he could pull himself up to a standing position and reach the top of the dresser. One day after his nap he did just that, grabbing a new container of deodorant and somehow figuring out how to get the top off of his new toy. As his parents, we were pleased with his quick intelligence but really worried when we found him happily licking the last of the contents of the jar. We called the doctor and rushed Ernie Jr. to the hospital emergency room. Our doctor, Jim Alderfer, called a pharmacist who reported back that the ingredients in the deodorant were not poisonous so we would not need to go through the trauma of having his tiny stomach pumped. He did warn us, however, that Ernie Jr. might be especially happy for a while, because of some of the ingredients in the deodorant.

We paid $40 a month to our landlords, who were very kind church members. Some months they would tell us to pay only half the amount, and they often offered us food. The church members were keenly aware that the college wages were extremely low and would show their kind hearts and also give us donations. I know it sounds unbelievable, but our monthly salary that first year was $80. Even in the year 1951, that was extremely low.

Our Miniscule Mansion was one half of a one-story duplex with a welcoming front door entrance at 723 Vernon Drive. A friendly young policeman and his shy wife and young child lived in the other half of this tiny house. I loved to carry Ernie Jr. out the back door and stroll among the sweet-smelling orange trees that blossomed in a grove close to the duplex. We lived on a quiet side street with few houses that was just far enough away from San Antonio Avenue to give me a little sense of rural country pleasure. Our baby and I would often walk to the nearby campus looking for flowers and green bushes that grew in the small patches of irrigated land. I would pick some blooms to bring back to freshen up our tiny home, and we would meet Ernie as he was finishing his day's work. We had to catch those very special family moments whenever we could. Life here was very different from just a few short months earlier when Ernie and I had worked side by side from the Honeymoon Mansion in Orlando.

At that time, Upland College included a secondary school, where Paul enrolled as a high school junior—a move he had agreed to when he set out as Ernie's travel companion on the long trip from Dayton. For a little while, he had to sleep on our living room couch until he moved from our tight quarters into the men's dormitory. Even after he moved, I still made his lunches, and Ernie's parents paid us for any services to Paul to help us with our finances.

We had a used washing machine set up in the kitchen, the only room with enough space for it. It was the old-fashioned kind with a wringer, and I used it to wash diapers, all of our laundry, and laundry for Paul and several other students.

During the winter months, Upland sometimes had touches of frost that could seriously damage the orange crop. Students would sign up for the job of working all night in the orange groves to keep fires burning in smudge pots to help protect the oranges. It was extremely dirty work as the smudge pots burned kerosene that gave off thick black smoke. Paul and some friends often tended the smudge pots, and I would wash their black, smoky clothes in my relic of a washing machine that I had to fill and drain by hand.

In a short time, we realized I should apply for a part-time nursing position even though I had done no nursing since graduating as a registered nurse (R.N.) the month before we were married. The hospital interviewer at the Upland San Antonio Hospital said they had a job opening for a nurse in the labor and delivery, obstetrical, and newborn nursery areas. It was arranged for me to work weekends so that Ernie could be home to take care of Ernie Jr., who we now often called Ernie Lee. How could I know that first-time position in obstetrics would direct my area of interest and love for many years to come?

On the Road to the Future

It also was here, while living in this Minuscule Mansion in 1951, that Ernie started on the road toward a whole new career that would in many ways define his future. Our life was very different here in California than it had been in Florida. Although Ernie was sometimes called on to preach at the Upland church and also at Brethren in Christ churches in Pasadena and Chino, he was not preparing sermons on a regular basis.

But he continued to be involved with the church and was solicited by the General Church Conference to be a member of the Commission on Youth. In that role, he wrote a regular column for the church paper; the column was called "Let's Face It!" and was directed to young people. Young people would write letters about their problems to Ernie, and his answers to their problems were printed in the next issue. He enjoyed analyzing those problems, but I thought it was a big assignment on top of his other duties. I don't remember how long he kept answering those letters, but I do know that he was very mindful about giving careful, biblical answers.

The first semester after we arrived at Upland College, Ernie was given the position of fund-raiser for the college among church members. It was his least favorite of any job he ever had. Ernie was uncomfortable discussing with people their ability to give a substantial donation to the college, and he did not like to have to leave his little family to travel to Kansas and Oklahoma, where churches were expected to support the college.

This was a period of huge adjustment for Ernie and for me. Instead of having the opportunity to work together every day, he now went off to work at a tiny office space at the college, or he had to leave home for periods of time to travel while soliciting funds. I did not know it then, but that was just the beginning of a future where we would often be separated due to his work. We never fully adjusted to that difficult reality.

Fortunately, by the second term, he started to teach. He taught speech, debate, and homiletics and maybe other courses that I can no longer recall. Speech and debate stand out in my mind because I sometimes got to go and listen to the debates. The debate teams traveled to various campuses to participate in intercollegiate tournaments, and their outstanding performances were heralded in the Upland newspaper and in the college newspaper, "The Spartan Spotlight."

One account states, "The Upland College debate squad competed in the first debate tournament of the season at Los Angeles City College. Out of a total of sixteen debates, the Upland debaters defeated teams from Cal Tech, Palomar, San Diego, Pasadena City College, and Long Beach City College. One Upland team was undefeated in four rounds and received "superior" certificates and "undefeated" medals."

There were an equal number of men and women who participated with much success in both debate and also in speech tournaments sponsored by Pi Kappa Delta, the national forensic society where the Upland College students were ranked highest in their division. Ernie always explained that the high success rate was because of the very unusually high capability of the students. But I also like what one of those high-rated students wrote me, "Ernie was an excellent coach; showing us how to go about researching our topic, preparing the body and the rebuttals. He was always positive and encouraging and although he wanted us to win our events he never made us feel stupid or inadequate for losing." The debate topics were very demanding, requiring much study time to prepare affirmative and negative sides of a proposition. For example, the topic one year was "Whether tariff protection or free trade is better for the U.S. economy, and whether the U.S should join the General Agreement on Tariffs and Trade." In 1955 teams debated the question of whether the United States should recognize China.

The successes continued into the following years. Ernie was pleased to be able to arrange for his students to have a wide range of opportunities, which was quite unusual for a very small, conservative, Christian, and unaccredited college.

We settled into our new lifestyle and began to fully enjoy the academic environment. However, we felt that the Minuscule Mansion was too small and too restrictive, so we started looking for a house with more living space and asking friends and colleagues if they knew of any possibilities.

CHAPTER 3

HOUSE 3

The Growing Nest Mansion

Upland, California
1952

"It isn't the place or the furniture that make it home, but the love and peace that's in it."

—**Irving Bachellor**

We left the Minuscule Mansion not only because it was too small to invite friends and students into our home, but also because we knew more space was now urgently needed given our exciting family news. We were going to have a new baby in October!

We used the summer months of 1952 to move from the Minuscule Mansion to a college-owned house. The best name to give this house is "The Growing Nest Mansion." There would soon be two little ones in our family nest, instead of one.

This house was on the edge of the Upland College campus and, like other structures on the campus, was showing its age. However, we were happy that it was available because the rent was cheaper than what we had been paying and—although there were still only three rooms—the rooms were quite a bit larger than those in the Miniscule Mansion. Best of all, there was an alcove off of the living room. We happily installed a heavy drapery across the opening, creating a second bedroom that could be entered through the living room. This additional space was important because of the planned arrival of our second child.

Although we lived in the Growing Nest Mansion for barely a year, it was a home of great celebration because this is where we lived when our precious daughter, Beverly, was born on October 19, 1952. We brought her home from the Upland San Antonio Hospital to this Growing Nest Mansion.

Ernie was an eager participant in the joy of the birth of our second child. Because I was an obstetrical nurse in this small community hospital and had good relations with the medical doctors and nurses, I was able to ask for the special favor of having my husband nearby during the birth.

My doctor, James "Jim" Alderfer, was a church member and a dear friend to both of us, so it was easy for Ernie to ask Jim if he could stay with me during my labor and go with me right into the delivery room for the birth. Even in that friendly setting, it was a radical request to make of a doctor in 1952. A father's participation and observation of the birth of his child was not allowed in hospitals until ten or twenty years later.

Everything worked in our favor. I arrived at the hospital at 1 a.m. and was ready to deliver by 3 a.m. No other patients had been admitted, and it felt so natural and easy for Ernie and me not to be separated. It was a blessing for Ernie to be right there to welcome our baby girl, Beverly Kay, and he was thrilled beyond words. Being from a family of three boys, he had dreamed of a sister for Ernie Jr., and we joyfully celebrated Beverly's birth as an amazing blessing from heaven.

A Surprising Arrival

Ernie had planned a big surprise for me, secretly arranging to have my mother fly from Pennsylvania to California to stay with us for several weeks to help us manage the care of our newborn and Ernie Jr., who was then sixteen months old. The day after Beverly's birth, Ernie drove from Upland to the Los Angeles airport to pick up my mother. The trip, which was approximately fifty miles each way, was tedious and slow in the era before freeways, and he drove the whole way to the airport while holding his toddler son. He told me that he managed to prop a bottle of milk while still holding Ernie and driving. Again, thankfully, their guardian angel protected them.

I can never forget the heartwarming relief I felt when I heard the sound of familiar footsteps coming down the hospital maternity hallway—my husband and my mother, who was carrying Ernie Jr. Visiting hours were almost over, and I had been frantically waiting all afternoon for Ernie's visit, knowing nothing about his secret plan for my mother's travel.

At one point I had grown so worried that I asked one of my nurse friends to use the phone in the nurse's station to call my best friend, Frances Harmon. This was long before the advent of cell phones, and I had no way to call anyone or to try to locate Ernie. Thankfully, Frances, who knew of Ernie's secret plan, came immediately, bringing pretty, hand-crocheted pink booties for our baby girl. She thoughtfully asked the nurse to allow me to hold my baby to distract me from worrying about Ernie.

Finally, I heard those footsteps, and the three of them—Ernie, my mother, and my toddler—came bustling into my room with great triumph. Their arrival set off a most special celebration that we could be together with our new baby girl, along with my dearest mother. This was truly a special moment of praise and thankfulness for God's amazing blessings of happiness and peace.

Asking Hard Questions

By now we felt very established within the college community and had formed many dear and permanent friendships. We all were poor in material things, but we were wealthy in things that money cannot buy, and the atmosphere of love and kindness warmed our hearts.

We wives did many creative things together, and the whole group frequently shared meals, watched each other's children, and touched each other's lives with small acts of kindness. We loved entertaining among the faculty families and felt bonded to everyone's children. For Ernie and me, it was a period of spiritual and social growth; I learned so much from these Christian wives of Ernie's colleagues.

Ernie's favorite recreation was being involved in deep discussions with his many colleagues. Many years down the road, when Ernie and I would look back at our lives and reminisce, we would agree that these were our favorite years and our most fond relationships. The bonds we built were strong because we were all in the same boat and all committed to keeping our lives centered on our commitment to Christian education.

Remarkably, there was absolute loyalty and dedication to the success of Upland College. The college was experiencing a renewal because of the newly hired, young, gifted, and energetic faculty. Ernie, like most of the faculty members, was diligently pursuing a doctoral degree while also teaching at the college. He was strongly motivated to complete his degree and regularly drove the long trek from Upland to the University of Southern California (USC) in Los Angeles. There is no denying that all the teaching, debate coaching, and studying for his degree—along with the care of the family—created stress. We felt the pressure, but were determined to help make things work out as we were hoping.

Ernie was also becoming interested in the development of the curriculum and was formulating his own educational philosophy. Being a member of the college curriculum committee ignited his thinking and passion. To me the ideas about college curriculum seemed like something vague and obscure, but I did become interested and was amazed at Ernie's ideas. At dinner he would tell me about meetings of the curriculum committee, such as a discussion they had about requirements for general education and about how to best educate the students. Given his passion, I started to understand his fascination with the subject and recognize the importance of the work he was doing on this committee; in many ways, he would continue to do this work over the course of his life.

In particular, Ernie said he asked committee members why they would seek to duplicate the curriculum being offered at nearby Pomona College rather than talking about the needs and interests of the Upland College students. He asked, "Where did Pomona get their standards for general education?" and was told "From Harvard." But Ernie did not feel that Harvard's standards were necessarily right for every college and thought they probably were not right for Upland College. Ernie's question led to a very long committee meeting, causing him to get home late. Although he felt the curriculum questions were important, he also felt bad when the meetings went on too long, because then he missed out on helping to get Ernie Jr. and baby Beverly settled for the night.

Discussions about curriculum and other university issues often continued when faculty families hired Upland College students as baby-sitters and met in each other's homes for potluck meals, which was a favorite activity. The men enjoyed continuing these deep discussions in an informal environment. Of course, curricular issues were not the favorite conversation among the wives, who would soon retreat to our own corner of conversation to talk about our children, recipes, and housekeeping woes and joys.

Later I would get a report from Ernie about the husbands' points of view on educational issues and the unsettling questions Ernie would ask his colleagues like, "Why do all students need to go through the same bureaucratic hoops that are based more on tradition than tests of excellence?" These ideas were getting twisted up in my mind as I was getting a new kind of education from sharing in my husband's world of new education ideas.

As Ernie was becoming more interested in and occupied by educational issues, I think we both knew his passion was gradually more clearly defining his future. These small-college experiences at the age of twenty-four marked the beginning of a philosophy that would define his future writing and influence.

Nightmare Prevented; Dream Realized

Our little family thrived in this Growing Nest Mansion, conveniently located on the edge of the campus with its various student activities and educational events. But we narrowly avoided a disaster when a floor heater ignited the drapery that separated the living room from the makeshift bedroom. Thankfully Ernie's parents were visiting, and his father moved very quickly to smother the fire before it caused any damage. But that frightening experience convinced his parents, Ernie, and me that we needed to move to more satisfactory housing with a safer heating system.

At the same time, we learned about a little house that was for sale. When Ernie and I walked through the house we kept exclaiming that the house seemed to be built just for our family. It would be a financial stretch to buy a house rather than rent, but it would also be a big dream come true to have a home that we could call our own. Ernie's parents encouraged us, agreed to co-sign for the loan, and helped Ernie work out a loan arrangement through a church member who was a real estate agent.

Clearly, we were taking on a big responsibility that seemed somewhat terrifying. But we had already encountered situations that caused uneasiness and stress, and we knew that with prayer and faith we could depend on God. We also knew we had to take action on our part to make our dream a reality. So Ernie increased his college responsibilities, and I began working more evening hours at the hospital. The purchase contract was signed, and we bought our first house. By that point, the moving boxes had been filled and were ready to be moved out of the Growing Nest Mansion to our own home, "The Dream House Mansion."

CHAPTER 4

HOUSE 4

The Dream House Mansion

Upland, California
1952–1954

"A happy home is a home for which every young woman dreams and hopes; it is a home for which every young male toils and saves."

—Unknown

If my heart could speak, then perhaps I could truly and clearly explain the precious joy that the Dream House Mansion brought to Ernie and me. Even now, almost sixty years later, I can draw a detailed floor plan and enthusiastically elaborate on how all the spaces were used.

This house caught our eye when we realized we needed to move from the Upland College-owned home due to safety issues. It seemed to us that it would be a dream come true for our family to be able to own and move in to what we thought was the perfect house.

By many standards it was a simple and small house, but after we carefully planned and prayed, we made the house ours. We could now make plans to be as creative as possible on our limited budget. It was a fine and solidly built stone house, and we instinctively knew that this Dream House

Mansion required a certain dignified touch. We were sensitive to the quite sophisticated, older couple next door and the way they carefully cared for their yard and house.

Even before we moved in with our household possessions, the house interior felt luxurious to us because of the nicely carpeted floors in the bedrooms and in the living-dining areas. Up to that point, we had only lived in houses with linoleum floor covering. We could already imagine how nice that soft carpet would feel between our toes when we got up in the middle of the night to care for a crying child.

There were two bedrooms that were conveniently connected and a small room designed as a sun room that we used as a study and a guest room since it could be closed off as a private space. It was a perfect guest room when Ernie's parents or my mother came to visit and a perfect study for Ernie, who needed private space to prepare for his Upland classes and his ongoing PhD studies at USC.

The kitchen was roomy and bright with lots of storage and cupboards built around the sink and counter. The cheerful kitchen was delightful to me as it was way beyond anything my mind could have fancied in any of our earlier mansions. We especially loved the roominess that offered plenty of space for a table big enough for our family meal times.

We never thought twice that having only one bathroom was a problem. We did not have any friends with more than one bathroom; no one in our circle was that upscale.

A big attraction and bonus was the large living room, and we worked hard to make this room attractive to our eyes and the eyes of our guests. Ernie (probably with his brother's help) painted it and even papered one wall, and he used his homemade book shelves to divide the long room, giving us a section for living room furniture on one side and leaving plenty of space for a dining room area on the other side, next to the kitchen. The front door opened into this room, and we hoped to create a lovely, welcoming space. We even bought a modern style luxurious couch, and I made draperies for all the windows. I confess that to us it seemed elegant and harmonious. In truth, it was probably quite ordinary.

The Joy of Home and Family

Ernie had created friendships with colleagues in his graduate program at USC, and we enjoyed welcoming them, along with our many friends from Upland College, into our own home. We could fit quite a few around our dining room table, and Ernie always had lots of people on his mind that he wanted to invite. I loved entertaining and took the food preparation for company very seriously. I was excessively particular about the food and the details that added the fancy touches. I'd work late into the night making radish roses, carrot curls, and lavish desserts. I fully enjoyed cooking creatively for company. But Ernie would try to help me to take a more relaxed, casual attitude, reminding me that the goal of entertaining was friendship—not a display. Truth be told, I'm quite sure he enjoyed the results of my fuss almost as much as I did.

Along with caring for our two small children and keeping the house—which included preparing and hosting these dinners—I continued my work as an obstetrical nurse at the small community hospital. I enjoyed my work but preferred to stay home with the family. But working the evening shift on weekends when Ernie would not have classes and could care for the children, helped pay some of the bills that came with owning a home.

The house address was 404 Ninth Avenue, on a shaded street almost adjacent to the hospital. Being this close to the hospital was very advantageous because it meant that if I walked very fast, I could be home in five minutes to eat dinner with my precious family, using a casserole I had prepared before I left work that Ernie could heat in the oven. I only had a thirty-minute dinner break, but I loved walking in the door to my family's happy cheers. Ernie would already have Ernie Lee and Beverly sitting in their child seats at the table and the hot casserole ready to dish out as soon as we had offered our prayer of thanks for our food. Ernie Lee would sweetly say, "Thank you for this food, Amen," while Beverly folded her little hands. Of course, the work schedule and the rush of time made those times less than perfect, but we were finding a way to maintain our family lifestyle and our special routine.

Ernie was masterful at caring for the children—at keeping them happy, entertained, and clean. He never shirked from changing diapers or giving baths. But Ernie and I both struggled for a while when Ernie Lee, who was not yet three years old, nightly demanded to see God before he would go to sleep. Perhaps at this early age he was beginning his own search for God's presence in his young life. Ernie Sr., with gentleness and quiet patience, would tell him, "We know God is here because God gives us love and gives us all the lovely things around us, and He can even live in our hearts—but we don't need to see Him with our eyes." After many repeated reassuring words, Ernie Lee would finally fall asleep, only to repeat the same plea the next night and the night after that. Ernie and I knew it was our duty to help our children clearly see God's nature of unconditional love, and we did everything we could to make that possible.

Occasionally I was asked to work the weekend day shift, and Ernie would stick with our Sunday morning routine of Sunday school and regular church service. He'd dress Ernie Lee and Beverly in their Sunday finery that I would lay out. I don't remember whether he kept both of the children with him during the Sunday school hour or if Ernie Lee got to go to a class for two- and three-year-olds, but he managed to care for both of them, without me. Many onlookers were utterly amazed. A friend who was also a young mother at the time recently told me that Ernie was the only father who used the room designated as the "mother and baby room" to change a diaper. I recall him telling me he felt uncomfortable having to use that room, but it was the only place available for this parenting chore. How I missed worshipping with them as a complete family, but that is how we managed during that period of our lives.

A Property Filled with Family

It was helpful that our house purchase included two rental properties located behind our home. One was a small, one-bedroom house with its own small lawn and parking area. In 1953, shortly after we had bought the property, Ernie's older brother, William (Bill) and his wife, Esther, my older sister, moved from Greenville, Illinois, to Upland where Bill joined the Upland College faculty as a physics teacher. They moved into our rental house.

Their daughter, Carla, who was exactly halfway between the ages of Ernie Lee and Beverly, became the prize cousin playmate for our children, and they happily spent most of their play hours together. I can still clearly visualize them in their dress-up clothes playing house on our front lawn. Ernie Lee and Carla, with tiny Beverly standing on the back of Carla's tricycle, would whizz up and down the sidewalk in front of the Dream House Mansion, pretending they were going to the store or to church.

At the same time, Ernie's younger brother, Paul, returned to Upland College for his college freshman and sophomore years before transferring to Harvard University. For his first year, he lived in our second rental, a mid-sized room that was attached to the garage. Esther and I took turns giving him breakfast, and he used our bathroom.

We marveled that so much of our family had ended up together, yet each with our own space. We had been separated for some years, and now were thrilled we could share and help each other on a daily basis. It was such a special happiness for the two families, and especially for the three brothers—Bill, Ernie, and Paul—and the two sisters—Esther and myself.

Learning to Let Go

We regularly attended the Upland Brethren in Christ Church, and it was there that we dedicated Beverly. The pastor held our baby and offered a prayer of blessing on her life. Ernie and I also prayed for that blessing as we together dedicated Beverly to God for His loving care and for His service.

Because of his overload of responsibilities at Upland and USC, Ernie cut back on the number of preaching assignments he would accept. However, he joined a group of his dearest friends and donated his time to chair a committee that developed a very successful radio program called "Gems of Grace." Important to the success of the endeavor was the producer, writer, and announcer, David Carlson. The program included an excellent chorus of highly talented singers under the direction of Royce Saltzman. Ernie was a speaker along with Owen Alderfer, the religion teacher at Upland: Bill was the business manager.

As I look back I try to decide why this group of Upland College professionals, who were already devoting many, many hours to their teaching positions and graduate studies, created another challenging and time-consuming responsibility. Clearly, they enjoyed being together and found stimulation using their creative energy together. But the prime reason they took on this program was because they were responding to the Holy Spirit that urged them to send out the Christian message.

As pleasant as it was to be an integral part of this caring college campus community, our future goal remained paramount. To complete his graduate degree, Ernie was driving from Upland to Los Angeles several times a week, a ninety-minute trip through slow traffic and heavy car exhaust fumes. This was before the time of freeways and improved car emissions, and the difficult situation caused increasing stress. Ernie eventually developed a throat irritation and a persistent cough.

Dear friends of Ernie's parents, Marie and Harvey McCullough, lived in the Los Angeles area, and they arranged for Ernie to stay with them several nights a week. This did relieve some of the stress, but we all hated to be separated on the nights he stayed at the McCullough's home.

We now faced a real dilemma. We had to choose between equally undesirable alternatives: Ernie could give up on his goal to earn a PhD; he could continue to drive the long distance through polluted traffic; or we could enact a difficult, radical plan, one that we found very hard to face although in our hearts we knew what we needed to do.

That very painful, radical plan was to move close to USC. But how could we sell our cherished Dream House Mansion? Our hearts were all wrapped up in that house, and I cannot describe how sad we felt as the realtor put up the "For Sale" sign at the end of about two years.

Leaving the Dream House Mansion was a major lesson and a life principle that we had to learn: "Do not cling to precious possessions and favorite places." It was a necessary rule Ernie and I had to learn to follow in order to keep focused on our overall goal. Given what was to come in our lives, this was a principle we would have to apply many times in the future.

Adding to this difficulty was the heartache we felt upon leaving the Upland College community and our dedicated group of Christian friends. Here were all of our dear friends with whom we felt such a close bond. Our move would also mean that we would not be living close to the church of our valued heritage for the first time.

Reading Deuteronomy 31:6 gave us the courage to move forward: "The Lord your God goes with you, He will never leave you or forsake you." We knew it was the right thing to do and so made the move without any misgivings. I completely understood and valued Ernie's determination to complete his PhD and was eager to do everything I could to help him fulfill that important dream and help the children share in it too.

CHAPTER 5

HOUSE 5
The Interlude Mansion

Los Angeles, California
1954–1956

"Home is where your heart resides. . . .
Wherever life takes you.
Home can be as close as your heart."

—Joni Eareckson Tada

We knew this Interlude Mansion was a temporary place. We also knew that we wanted to make it into a warm and welcoming home. However, it was difficult to imagine how we could foster feelings of welcoming warmth in this unfamiliar location after we sold our Dream House Mansion and moved to Los Angeles.

The Interlude Mansion was a first-floor apartment in a large Victorian style house that had been divided into four rather large apartments. At one time, it must have been a house of grandeur on West Adams Gardens Street.

As the wealthy people left the area, their large houses were converted into affordable apartments for graduate students and others. Our apartment was on a wide dead-end street with no through traffic. This wide open space had probably been a beautiful garden area long ago, and it was now important to us because it gave the children a safe place to play. This location was good for our little family, and close enough to the USC campus for Ernie to walk to class.

Our apartment was old but striking with fine-quality hardwood floors in the large living and dining areas. There was an outdated but workable kitchen and two good-sized bedrooms. All the rooms had high ceilings with elaborate molding and bordered edges. Clearly, the house had been a place of elegant beauty in its prime, and we could still appreciate the remaining artistic workmanship. Even with its many years of wear and tear, we were determined to transform it into a warm, welcoming home.

The apartment above ours was a copy of our apartment, and the family living there had two children who were about the same ages as ours. The husband was an army captain who had been sent to USC to get his master's degree, and his wife, Dede, was my age, very friendly, and full of ideas. She said that even though she was an army wife and had to move often, she always fixed up each of their residences as if she were going to live there permanently. She painted, wallpapered, and tiled her kitchen and was eager to help me do the same to our apartment; but I was content with our modest surroundings and did not want anything to interfere with Ernie's goal to move steadily ahead. I simply made fresh curtains, and Ernie hung our familiar wall pieces. With both of us adding our touches we felt we were indeed creating a welcoming home without even using Dede's redecorating ideas. But I did appreciate her offer to help and sometimes conferred with her.

Although I was content making simple decorating changes, I knew the house needed some deep cleaning efforts. For the first time in my life, I was going to be fighting the many cockroaches that scampered everywhere. Housekeeping here was going to be very different from any place I had lived.

A New Teaching Position

I felt confident about meeting whatever housekeeping challenges awaited me and also about managing our household and many of the family affairs. I was determined to free up as much time as possible for Ernie so he could complete his PhD at USC in record time.

Ernie Lee and Beverly weren't in school yet, so the move was not too difficult for them, although they keenly missed their fun playmate cousin, Carla. However, our little family was together more, which was why we had made the radical decision to sell our Dream House Mansion and move close to USC. The children's grandparents bought them a big swing set to help them adjust to the new neighborhood; the swing set, in turn, attracted neighbor children and resulted in several good playmates.

Soon after our move, we were enormously blessed when Ernie was offered a full-time position at nearby Loyola Marymount University as an assistant professor and director of forensics. The university kindly arranged for him to teach all of his classes on Tuesdays and Thursdays so he could have the rest of the week for his intense graduate program demands.

This new job, with a salary that was more than double his Upland College salary, completely overwhelmed us. For the first time, I could walk along grocery store aisles and pick out the items on my list without writing down the cost of each item, tallying the total cost as I went so I would not exceed the amount of cash I had in my purse for that week's groceries.

I hardly knew how to think about what seemed like too much money. Would it somehow have a negative effect or cause us to become self-centered or materialistic or lead us to make wrong decisions? I guess I was thinking about 1 Timothy 6:10, "The love of money is a root of all kinds of evil." In actuality, it was only an assistant professor salary, but it was a big change for us. I clearly remember Ernie and I talking about it; I told him it would be best if he never increased his salary because of the enormous responsibility to handle the money wisely. Through the years Ernie was generous and selfless.

Wisdom Required

We were deeply purposeful about not delaying Ernie's completion of his degree. I'm afraid I went overboard with my reminders to the children to not be too noisy and not to demand too much of their Daddy's study time. He did much of his work for USC in a corner of the bedroom that was set up for his study area. One day I fastened a wide cord across the bedroom door and gave Ernie Lee and Beverly orders not to go beyond the cord and disturb him.

When Ernie later opened the door he was surprised to find the door blocked. When I explained, he immediately took down the barrier and told me never to restrict them from coming to him whenever they wished, saying family needs and wishes were far more important to him than his study efforts.

As parents, we discussed our child-rearing philosophy and discipline principles and agreed that when we told the children to do something, we as parents would not relent. It was an important agreement, but one time it did not work for me.

A friend, Marie, invited us to bring the children to her house to watch *Peter Pan* on her television. She was one of our few friends in Los Angeles who owned a television. That afternoon I told the children they had to take their naps to be able to go. Beverly went right to sleep, but Ernie Lee did not. The movie was only showing that one night, and I knew it would be a very special treat, but our little four-year-old was so excited he could not relax enough to fall asleep. I was frustrated that he would not sleep because I knew it would be a late night for our young children. I sang him soft lullabies and kept telling him that his eyes were getting heavy, but he did not go to sleep. I felt I had to stick to our parenting philosophy, which meant he would not be able to watch the movie since he did not take his nap.

When Ernie came home to a most unhappy household, he soothed everyone and wisely decided that we would make an exception this time. We dressed the children in their pajamas, wrapped them in blankets, and enjoyed an enchanted evening watching the *Peter Pan* movie together at Marie's house. Afterward, we carried our satisfied and happy children from the car to their beds. For weeks after seeing the movie, the children entertained themselves by enacting the *Peter Pan* story. Ernie Lee determined to never grow up but to stay in "Never Land." As I watched them in their happy play, I was glad I had relented. Reassessing the events of the day, Ernie and I and decided there would be many more circumstances that would call for special wisdom and flexibility.

Birth of a Blessing

We enjoyed much happy living in our Los Angeles Interlude House Mansion, such as a birthday party when Beverly turned three. I recall Dede tossing a homemade corsage out of her upstairs apartment window and telling Beverly to catch it. Dede then came down and pinned it on Beverly's new pink outfit. All of our Upland family came, and even my mother came from Pennsylvania. It seemed so right for "Grandma Tyson" to come that distance to celebrate the birthday of the grandchild she had cared for in her first weeks of life.

Ernie had colleagues from his department at Loyola Marymount who had families similar to ours. We had enough in common to enjoy casual family times together, and we even took a camping vacation to Yosemite National Park with one family. I made friends with the wife of another of Ernie's friends; she and I shared a lot because her husband had also been a minister who was now working on his PhD, and she gave me a lovely baby shower when we were looking forward to the birth of our third child.

During the nine-month pregnancy of our third child, we traveled to Upland for all my prenatal doctor visits. As the time to give birth neared, Ernie and I were concerned that I could have our third baby in the car while making the long, slow trip from Los Angeles to the same small Upland Community Hospital. So I prepared a birthing supply kit and felt ready for any emergency. But it turned out not to be needed because we went to Upland a few days early and stayed with Esther and Bill, who still lived in Upland, where he continued as a physics professor at Upland College.

On June 8, 1955, our precious baby boy, Craig Allen Boyer, was born. Again, our doctor friend, James Alderfer, arranged for Ernie to be with me for the labor and delivery. Craig's birth was a momentous and joyous experience for us, and we were very eager to have Ernie Lee and Beverly meet their baby brother. We had been preparing them by reading sweet stories about growing families. Now the big moment had arrived; the waiting was over, and they could finally peer at him in amazement and hold him in their little arms.

In days to come, when I sometimes would lay Craig on the couch, Ernie Lee and Beverly would kneel on the floor in front of him and make their cute child word sounds to try to make him smile. Craig was a gift from God to our family circle. We were delighted by this blessing that added joy and contentment within our cozy nest in the Interlude Mansion.

While we were away from our own denominational church, we attended the First Presbyterian church in the Los Angeles area where Louis H. Evans was the pastor. The large, beautiful sanctuary was always packed as Evans was an outstanding preacher who later went on to lead the congregation at the National Presbyterian Church in Washington DC.

Ernie, being a professor of forensics and speech at Loyola Marymount University, was very intrigued with Evans's preaching style and the unusual clarity and significance of his profoundly moving messages. We felt blessed and challenged each Sunday to keep growing in our commitment to be of service for God's kingdom.

Adding to our joy was the remarkable and creative teaching in the children's program at First Presbyterian. The first Sunday we attended, as we walked in the front door holding the hands of Ernie Lee and Beverly, a friendly lady met us and said she would introduce them to the children's program. Ernie Lee clung to his daddy's hand, but Beverly, showing us her more open personality, took her brother's hand and nudged him to go with her. After the church service, we found him close beside his sister, not crying, but smiling. It seemed almost miraculous. Members in the church nursery sweetly cared for Craig, so Ernie and I got to sit together for the whole service. We returned every Sunday while we lived in Los Angeles, and Ernie Lee and Beverly were happy to go off to their own Sunday school program to hear Bible stories and sweet lessons.

We returned to our home church in Upland for particular occasions, such as on a Sunday in September 1955. Ernie had made arrangements with the pastor, Eber Dourte, to have baby Craig dedicated to God in that church. As with the dedications of Ernie Lee and Beverly, Craig's dedication proved to be a heart-warming and loving experience for Ernie and me. That Sunday at the Upland Brethren in Christ Church, the two of us stood in front of the large congregation. Ernie was holding our baby, and at the indicated moment, he handed Craig to Pastor Dourte. Craig did not cry but watched bright-eyed when the pastor placed his hand on his head and prayed that God would take Craig's life and use it for His service. Together Ernie and I pledged to give Craig to God to direct his life and solemnly promised to give him scriptural guidance.

Interlude in Dayton

At this point, we had a four-year-old, a two-and-a-half-year old, and a newborn, which made for a very busy household. However, Ernie was nearing the end of his doctoral program and definitely needed some months to concentrate fully to finish writing his dissertation. In October of that year, 1955, I decided the only way he would be able to give his full attention to his writing would be if the three children and I were out of the house. His parents, Grandma and Grandpa Boyer, understood my concern and invited me and our three little children to stay at their home in Dayton.

Ernie's parents owned a store and a wholesale mail order business for Christian greeting cards and supplies. Their store, which was some blocks from the center of Dayton, fronted Main Street, and the living section of the house was connected to the rear of the business area.

Ernie's father and mother were truly remarkable during the four months we lived with them. They lived their Christian testimony every day—being completely selfless and giving. We felt their sweet love as they showed us their compassion and helped me with the children.

During that time, we all went to the Dayton Mission Church that had been started by Ernie's grandfather, William H. Boyer. The children and I were so welcomed, especially by Ernie's Grandfather and Grandmother Boyer, who lived in the mission house next door. Ernie adored his grandparents and told me many times that he wanted to model his life after his Grandfather Boyer. This mission church was where he had heard his grandfather preach three times on Sundays. Grandfather Boyer's faith was so deep that he would break down in tears as he spoke and prayed for those who had turned away from God. Now the children and I had this special opportunity to attend and hear Grandfather preach and pray.

For those months, we looked forward to attending the mission church and going to Angeline's Sunday school class each Sunday. Angeline had served as Ernie's own Sunday school teacher, and she now also captured our children with her love as she now taught their Sunday school class.

At the end of each church service, eighty-five year old Grandfather Boyer would stand at the door to give each one his warm personal attention and make everyone feel very special. It did not matter if he or she was a homeless person who wandered in off the streets of Dayton or a great grandchild; all felt the love of Jesus shine through Grandfather Boyer and the way he cared for them. As I held Craig in my arms and Ernie Lee and Beverly stood close beside me, Grandfather would get down on his knee and fuss over how much they were growing up and tell them how much he loved them. Those were very precious moments for our children.

Ernie Lee would help his grandmother, my mother-in-law, fill the mail orders, and Grandma French, my husband's maternal grandmother who lived there as part of the family, would sing and play simple games with Beverly. Craig, at five months, was a contented baby. The children and I were doing fine—except I had a very difficult time being away from Ernie. Only through my determination and my trust that God would give me daily courage did I manage being separated from Ernie for those months.

Ernie was even lonelier than I was as he lived in that empty Los Angeles apartment. At least I was surrounded by lots of activity and by Ernie's most loving family. All he had was the Interlude Mansion that was empty of his family's warmth. He was consoled knowing his little family was happy in Grandma and Grandpa's big house that was filled with love.

Before I left, I had prepared as many individual meals that the refrigerator's small freezer would hold. Those meals would soon be finished, and I was concerned about Ernie eating his own kind of food—one shredded wheat biscuit with milk for breakfast, two biscuits with milk for lunch, and two biscuits with hot milk and melted butter for his dinner. Occasionally, he would accept an invitation to eat at a friend's house and get a nutritious meal. But he was too deeply focused on finishing his dissertation to accept many invitations. He was determined to complete his writing so he could feel relaxed when he came to Dayton to spend Christmas with his waiting family.

He met that Christmas deadline, and what a grand celebration we had when he arrived at Grandpa and Grandma's the day before Christmas. The children's grandma, a happy shopper, had a supply of children's gifts for Ernie and me to sneak off and wrap to help make this one of our happiest Christmas days, with the complete family together.

A Gold Cup Celebration

Thankfully, our loneliness and separation was all in the past and we were in the mood for jubilation. In our minds, we were already celebrating his upcoming June 1956 PhD graduation from USC. I love recalling the feelings of triumphant joy we felt when the extended family shared our celebration at the famous Clifton's Cafeteria in Los Angeles with its tropical gardens and waterfalls. We sat under a thatched roof where periodically "rain" would fall to add to the atmosphere. I was so proud and thrilled that my husband now had a PhD. Growing up as a farm girl, I had never dreamed of anything like this; in fact, I'm not sure I had ever heard of a PhD. Ernie wanted to correct my prideful thinking and said anyone could earn a doctorate if they just have enough persistence.

Four-year-old Ernie Lee may not have fully understood about persistence, but he clearly understood that his daddy completed something important and that the large family gathering was a celebration dinner for his Daddy. The day before the family gathered at the restaurant, I explained the reason for the celebration to Ernie Lee, who surprised me when he said he wanted to give his Daddy something for what he did. Then he got busy gathering some paper and a box of crayons and spent a long time drawing and very carefully coloring his creation: a gold cup. Then Ernie Lee cut out his gold cup as best he could with his child's scissors. I helped him to carefully put it into a large envelope that he proudly and secretly carried to the restaurant and protected from raindrops dripping from the thatched roof overhead.

It was hard for him to wait until his Daddy finished helping everyone get seated. Finally, after Grandpa's long prayer of thanks, he slid off of his chair and stood close to his Daddy with a big smile. Taking his prize out of the envelope, Ernie Lee gave his precious gift to his Daddy. Ernie gave his ingenious four-year-old son big hugs and held him on his lap as they ate dinner together. That gold champion cup proved to be Ernie's favorite graduation gift, and he kept it for the rest of his life. After Ernie was gone, I put the cup in a special place, then returned it to its creator a few years ago.

Where to Go Next?

The mission of the Interlude House Mansion was now fulfilled, and we were ready to move into the world beyond USC and West Adams Gardens. All of our efforts to ensure Ernie could earn his PhD were behind us, and we were relieved, thrilled, and eager to move on.

At this very time, Ernie was notified that he had been selected to chair the speech department at Long Beach State University. The offer was a surprise since he had not even applied for the position. Ernie said it was a very attractive position in his exact field of study, but we were not sure of God's direction. Perhaps it would have been wise to wait instead of accepting the offer, but Ernie gave his acceptance.

In addition, we thought this would be a good change for our children. Ernie checked on the school system, since Ernie Lee would soon be ready for kindergarten. When we found a charming house just one block from a beautiful beach, we put down a rent payment. It was all pretty exciting for the family.

At the same time, however, a serious conflict was developing. John Martin, the president of Upland College, was making repeated trips to our apartment at West Adams Gardens to try to persuade Ernie to return to Upland College as the academic dean. Ernie felt he should stay in the field of his doctoral study and repeatedly declined the persistent invitations. But President Martin did not give up, as he believed Upland was where God wanted Ernie. (President Martin later told me that he made eleven visits to Ernie to try to convince him to move back to Upland College). It was a frustrating and difficult situation for us. We thought our friend John would give up, only to find him again ringing our doorbell.

Finally, Ernie told President Martin that he would consider the offer if the Upland College Board of Trustees could assure him he would have the freedom to earnestly pursue a plan for regional accreditation for Upland. He knew that the contacts he had made at USC, especially with Dr. Earl Pullias, chair of the Department of Education, might make accreditation possible. Very quickly Ernie received that confirmation from the Upland College Board of Trustees.

Ernie then made the most difficult decision to withdraw his acceptance as chair of the Speech Department at Long Beach State University. We wondered then if we had made a great mistake by accepting the offer when we had not been sure that it was God's plan for our lives. Of course, there was anguish about going back on his word.

President Martin and Ernie went to the appropriate administrator of Long Beach State University to present the situation and ask for Ernie's release from the position. Things were settled with kindly consideration.

We then had to explain to the children that we would not be moving into the special beach house that so excited them. But when they learned they would be moving back to Upland where they could again play with their dear cousin, Carla, they quickly forgot about the house near the beach.

Once the decision was made, we were assured that it fit into God's plan for our lives. More than five decades later, my heart still confirms that it was the right decision. We felt extra joyful about moving back to our dear friends, and Ernie, thriving on challenges, looked forward to the new possibilities for Upland College.

The time we spent packing for the move to Upland gave us time for giving our good-byes. It also gave us time to reflect on how well this Interlude House Mansion had fulfilled our hopes for a warm and welcoming home.

The summer was slipping by, and we still needed to find a house to rent in Upland. At this point, we were very sorry that we had sold our Upland Dream House Mansion, as our realtor friend said there was nothing very appealing available. Nevertheless, our good-byes were over, and as we headed with our loaded rental truck toward the one house we found in Upland, we prayed for God's blessing on our move.

CHAPTER 6

HOUSE 6

The Wild Flowers House Mansion

Upland, California
1956–1957

"In the cottage there is joy,
All the earth's a garden sweet when there's love at home."

—J. D. Brunk

Moving back to Upland with the confidence we were meant to be there helped us to peacefully settle into the rental house we found at the edge of town, one block from the busy Arrow Highway on Drake Avenue. Since we did not have much time to find a place to live, and there was not much choice in Upland, we had to trust that this house at 367 Drake Avenue would prove to be a sweet and blessed home.

This home was like a cottage, and the smaller rooms were an adjustment after the large and high ceiling rooms in our Los Angeles apartment. But we liked the short, quiet, rural Drake Avenue and its few cars. The house was halfway down the street toward the train tracks, and wild flowers grew in a field behind the house.

The flowers in that beautiful field were mostly wild poppies, which blossomed frequently in the warm California sun, to our great delight. Ernie Lee was enchanted with the poppies and their deep black centers and showy red-orange colorful petals. However, they had to be enjoyed from afar because the field was also infested with prickly thistle plants. A casual stroll through this wild flower field was perilous for the children, who often ran barefoot. Those field briers were so prickly and painful for our young children that they quickly learned to play in the smaller, safer, side lawn—and to enjoy the poppies from afar.

It seemed natural to pick up with our many dear friends exactly where we had left off three years earlier when we moved from Upland to Los Angeles. We were again part of the faculty group that met to share dinners and socialize in our homes.

Ernie and I took our turn, inviting everyone to our Wild Flowers House Mansion. The hosts of these events were expected to plan a time of fun, and for one evening in 1957 Ernie came up with the idea of the game of charades, and I remember being impressed by the faculty members and their bright and creative minds.

Our hearts were also warmed to immerse ourselves again into the familiar church program, where Ernie was again asked to teach the Sunday class. It clearly felt good to be back, and we felt as if we had made the right move. Was the Upland College president correct when he told Ernie, "Upland was the place where God wanted him"? We certainly believed so.

We arrived in late summer, in time for or Ernie to fix up his own office in the administration building before the beginning of the academic year at Upland College. This was a first-time experience because in previous years he had always shared a small space in a tiny office. Now he was planning for his brand new job as academic dean in a more distinguished environment. I don't recall if he had apprehensions, but there must have been some anxiety about what lay ahead. Given he had no formal training for college administration, he was always very conscientious about doing quality work.

However, we were focusing most of our apprehension on our first child going off to school. In June we had celebrated Ernie Lee's fifth birthday, and now he was about to leave the security of his home to begin kindergarten. Ernie and I were anxious for him because we knew that it was not easy for Ernie Lee to do new things on his own. We tried to prepare him, but even so he was still frightened to go without his sister, Beverly, who was younger but much braver at that time about facing new experiences. She was his encourager, but she could not be there with him on that first day of school.

On the first Monday of Ernie's school, there was an air of tension hanging over the whole household, although we attempted to hide it. We decided it was best for Ernie to drive Ernie Lee, while Beverly, toddler Craig, and I said goodbye from home. Ernie later told me how much it crushed his heart to leave his clinging, crying little boy when the teacher asked him to go because she said she would be able to help Ernie Lee better on her own. Miss Schmidt turned out to be a masterful teacher, and after a short time Ernie Lee went off to school without so much anxiety. I wish I could say the same for me and for Ernie.

No Tent Poles, No Tent

Ernie had to drive to his job at the college, where he was also required to put in longer work hours. Because we only had one car, I now had to find new ways to fend for myself and again manage more of the needs of the children and the household. I felt far from the center of things and isolated from the campus activities, the faculty wives, and my sister. Drake Avenue was just too far from it all.

But the children and I took on creative projects, making gifts for family "back East." And I discovered an old trail along the busy Arrow Highway where we could safely walk. We all valued the family dinners and evening fun time when we shared the story time, bedtime routines, and prayer time.

Still, there were times when my efforts to do things on my own turned out to be total failures. For example, as academic dean, Ernie was expected to preside at the graduation commencement ceremony. While he was doing that, I was at home frantically trying to prepare and pack the camp food and all our camping supplies, including the various tent pieces. We were heading off immediately after commencement for a week's vacation at Yosemite National Park, where we would meet Bill and Esther's family that evening.

I finished packing by the time Ernie got home, and we were happily on our way. All of us were very excited to be off on a holiday for a special family time where we would have Ernie's full attention. By the time we arrived, Bill and Esther had a nice camp site reserved, and they helped us set up our camp equipment in the dark—only to discover that we had no tent poles, which I fear I had not packed. No tent poles, no tent.

We slept in the open air, under the amazing heavenly stars. In the middle of the night, we were frightened to wake and find a big bear tramping over us and sniffing around our precious food supply. I can't even remember how we saved ourselves or our food, but I remember how terrible I felt for not packing the tent poles. Ernie consoled me by taking the responsibility for not being there to help me with the packing.

In the morning, with Bill help, we improvised poles, and our tent was set up that night. For the rest of the week we slept under cover, protected from wandering bears. So the story does have a happy ending, and it has provided a narrative that has been repeated and joked about in our family over the years. No tent poles, no tent.

Thistles among the Blooms

My sisters and I had learned to sew from our mother's subtle teaching when we were very young. I always wore homemade dresses, and I naturally learned to sew. I continued to sew, and now was making Beverly's dresses too. When Ernie Lee began his second school year, Beverly was ready for school as well. She was excited to begin kindergarten and to get to wear one of the new school dresses I made for her. The beginning of that school year was much easier for Ernie Lee, and Ernie did not dread taking them that first day. Also, by now he was looking forward to his second academic year at Upland College.

Craig was now two and a half years old, and he had to learn to play alone while his brother and sister were in school. One day, he came to me while I was sitting at the sewing machine making Beverly another school dress, asking for Beverly. He knew it was about time for her to be coming home from school. I tried to assure him that the school bus would soon bring her home, and he stayed next to me hugging his teddy bear that was almost as big as he was.

I shifted my attention back to a sewing detail, and when I looked up, Craig was nowhere in sight. In great fright I began calling and searching for him. A neighbor lady, who spoke no English, pointed toward the train track. Sure enough, I saw Craig walking along that train track, dragging his teddy bear. With my heart pounding, I ran and grabbed him up. With tears of relief and thanks to God for sending his precious guardian angel, I cradled Craig and carried him home. A little later, I shivered as I heard a train whistle as a train went by at full speed.

Craig gave me another traumatic scare one day when I discovered him on our roof! A large grape arbor that reached to the top of the back porch roof made a very convenient climbing place for Craig, who was a skilled little climber. When I spotted him on the roof, I told him to stay right where he was and I would come up to get him. He was delighted to be on the rooftop, but I was franticly worried he would fall and get hurt. I managed to bring him down safely, but these two experiences contributed to my negative feelings about living in this house, and Ernie was equally anxious and distressed.

In addition, both Beverly and Craig developed skin problems that did not respond to treatment. I told Ernie that there seemed to be something toxic in the paint on the inside walls of the house causing their problem. As we became more and more troubled about the many negative characteristics of the house and the location, we agreed we should find a safer family home. We had no sadness about planning to leave, and our retired neighbor was probably happy to see us go; he was easily irritated by the children's normal play and had never warmed to our efforts to be friendly. Even the title "Wild Flowers House Mansion" had turned out to be a bit of a betrayal since the area was overrun by wicked thistle plants. It was a cottage we had filled with our own joy and love, but it lacked the "earth's garden sweetness."

There are some positive memories, of course, with one of the best coming right before we moved. A woman I barely knew, who lived at the end of the street, stopped by to say she had a friend who had a two-year-old dog that needed a good home. She thought it would be a perfect pet for the children.

Ernie had a beloved dog, Sandy, when he was a boy in Dayton, and he had been thinking a dog would make a great family pet. Since I had grown up on a farm where our dogs lived in the barn or an outdoor dog house, I wasn't sure about a little house dog. But I easily picked up on the rest of the family's enthusiasm, especially after we all became very attached to Chico, who arrived in time to join us in the move. He was a very sweet, loving addition to our family for twelve years, and we were grateful that the blessing of an unusually fine dog provided us very good feelings about The Wild Flowers House Mansion.

CHAPTER 7

HOUSE 7

The Family and Guest House Mansion

Upland, California

1957–1959

"Although we normally associate the word home with a place that's built of bricks and mortar—or studs and siding—home is much more than that."

—Sarah Susanka

Moving our family of five only a year and a half after arriving at the Drake Avenue home loomed as a big undertaking. We were embarrassed to again ask our friends to help load the heavy appliances and furniture onto a rental truck. Plus, we were just plain weary of packing and once again going through the unsettled feelings that always accompany moving. At the same time, we were relieved to move from the house that we had thought would be a pleasant Wild Flower House Mansion but had turned out to be a disappointment.

This time we were determined to find the right home, and we considered our choices carefully. We all agreed on three requirements for the new house.

First, it had to be located in the same Baldy View School District where Ernie Lee and Beverly were halfway through the school year. Second, it had to have a fenced-in backyard that would be adequate as a safe play area and a place to let our new dog, Chico, run freely. Third, we needed three bedrooms and plenty of space for entertaining the out-of-town guests Ernie was now bringing to the campus and often to our home.

Since we were limiting ourselves to the school district, we felt pleased to find what we were looking for at 367 W. 7th Street, a house that was near the elementary school and the Upland College campus. The house fit our other specifications as well. There were three bedrooms and a kitchen that opened out into a sizable living and dining room area. Our two white leather couches fit in perfectly! And the fenced-in yard out back was an exciting play area for the children.

By this point in 1958, Ernie's efforts toward accreditation for the college were moving ahead, and generating much excitement. Many new steps were in process, and one critical requirement was that a certain percentage of the faculty needed to hold doctoral degrees. Ernie was thrilled when he got word that two such candidates, Alden Voth and Elias Wlebe, had accepted offers to head two departments. These were fine faculty appointments who would add to the college's academic standing.

Imaginary Treasures and Real-Life Blessings

As important as Dr. Wiebe was to the college, his appointment turned out to be even more important to the happiness of our children. The good news was that the Wiebes had a son, Danny. The news got better when the Weibe family rented the house right next to our own. There was some happy jumping up and down when our children learned Danny would be our next-door neighbor, as they assumed he would be a willing playmate.

Danny was between the ages of Ernie Lee and Beverly and proved to be a perfect playmate. He had been raised with the same Christian principles and teachings as our own children, and they usually played together with agreeable understandings. They liked playing the same games, and all agreed to include younger Craig into the imaginary worlds they worked to create.

Ernie built a large tree house for the children in a big shade tree in our back yard. For a time, it was turned into a Viking ship in Ernie Lee's six-year-old, make-believe world. He tried to turn his playmates—Danny, Beverly, and Craig—into Viking pirates.

Later, we began reading *The Boxcar Children* by Gertrude Chandler Warner before bedtime. Our children got so caught up in the story of the four children who were orphans who had to survive on their own and did so by living in an old boxcar that they turned the space between our two houses into a make-believe boxcar, and for much of the summer our children imagined they had to survive on their own. They scoured the vacant lots across the street for discarded spoons, cups, and dishes as did the kids in the storybook. I'm amazed that decades later Craig was able to describe in detail the spoon he found as the treasure he needed to help him survive as a boxcar child.

Ernie and I delighted in their neighborly and joyful play. Teaching our children and passing on God's truth to their young minds and hearts was our greatest priority. We made many decisions with their interests at heart, but we were fallible parents and occasionally made mistakes and were not always sure our choices were the wisest. We sometimes questioned what activities were wholesome for our children and whether our church was also nurturing them. We wanted what was best for them and what would prepare them to lead lives pleasing to God.

Inaugurating January Term

Ernie applied to the Ford Foundation in New York City for funding to implement an idea that he described as the "January Term." This was the first time he had written a proposal requesting funds from a foundation for academic benefit, and it paid off for Upland College and, in many ways, higher education as whole.

There was much rejoicing when the proposed idea was approved and the college received the Ford Foundation grant money. I do not remember the amount, but at the time it seemed like a remarkably large grant. It was also a positive newspaper story for the small Christian college.

Ernie's idea was for all regular classes to be suspended during one January term so that every student could become an active participant in an all-college, comprehensive study of Russia. It was a timely subject, and well-known authorities who were scholars versed in all areas of Russian society were invited to the college to lecture and meet with groups of students. In the evenings, community members were also invited. Students were required to attend all events and do assignments, such as writing research papers, on aspects of the all-campus study theme.

Robert M. Hutchins, the president of the University of Chicago, and Royce Pitkin, the president of Goddard College, then arrived as January-term speakers and dinner guests in our home. I was self-conscious when preparing dinner and serving these kinds of widely known educators and scholars, and I always breathed a sigh of relief when those evenings were done. But Ernie always helped me so much and made me feel satisfied with my participation. I learned to relax so I could appreciate the privilege of learning from these outstanding minds.

The Ford Foundation took a surprising interest in this new approach of a short mid-year term. Dr. Mike Giles, a foundation officer, made trips from New York City to Upland College and provided very positive evaluations of the program. Ernie was invited to go to New York City to confer with Elizabeth McCormick, the foundation director, and her team who were interested in publicizing the idea beyond the small Upland College campus. Since that time, many universities and colleges in America and overseas have adopted some form of a mid-year term for their students.

"One in a Million"

The high standards for transforming Upland into an accredited college demanded an enormous amount of diligent effort and painstaking planning. Ernie and all of the administrators and department chairs who worked with him were putting their whole hearts into the effort and working long hours.

Appropriate professional contacts and friendships were proving to be crucial. For example, Ernie came to deeply appreciate his friendship with Earl Pullias, a former dean of Pepperdine College who at this time was a professor at the University of Southern California and also president of the Los Angeles County Board of Education. Out of that friendship, Dr. Pullias kindly took on the challenge to help Ernie make other important contacts and critical decisions. With his help, many mistakes were avoided, and the completion of the accreditation requirements moved closer.

Ralph Tyler, another outstanding American educator and scholar, who was widely regarded for his work in education assessment and evaluation, came to the Upland campus as a most valuable consultant and friend. In 1991, Ernie wrote, "Ralph Tyler, more than any person, reinforced his understanding that goals, curriculum, and evaluation are the essential issues every educator must confront."

My mind flashes back to the time at Los Angeles International Airport when Dr. Tyler and I were waiting for Ernie to return with the parked car so we could drive together to Upland for Dr. Tyler's campus visit. We were making conversation about the exciting things happening at the college when he asked me if I knew that my husband was "one in a million." When I later told Ernie about the remark, he did not take it seriously but casually concluded that God made everybody "one in a million."

There were benefits that came along with the hard work of administration. One included the opportunity to meet a wide variety of outstanding creative thinkers and scholars, and Ernie thrived in this environment. For instance, he and I were invited to a conference in Michigan for academic deans and their wives. These kinds of invitations were precious gift vacations for us—times to be refreshed and inspired and to enjoy the wonder of being together. We were able to turn these trips into a special treat for the children, too, because Ernie's devoted parents often took time off from their work to care for them. On this occasion, they rented a cabin on a lake near our conference site and pampered our happy children for the duration. Their grandpa even went swimming with them in the lake.

The main speaker and teacher at the deans' conference we attended was Benjamin Mays, president of Morehouse College in Atlanta. He proved to be one of the most profoundly moving speakers we had ever heard. I can clearly remember how Ernie and I and many of the conference attendees gathered around him late into the night, pressing him to continue to teach us from his forgiving heart and marveling at his lack of hatred or any desire for revenge for the many times he had been treated with cruelty because of the color of his skin.

In particular, he told us about the trip from Atlanta to Michigan to attend the conference, and how he and his wife were often turned away from motels, hotels, and restaurants. Service personnel in establishments who turned them away gave him no respect for being a godly minister and highly regarded educator who had advanced degrees from distinguished institutions such as Bates College and the University of Chicago. During a late-night discussion, Ernie urged Dr. Mays to share more examples of how to lead a college with an emphasis on values and how to educate students about love and integrity.

Other meetings that Ernie attended also influenced his ideas that higher education could help form students who would be uncompromising individuals with moral and ethical principles to go along with their intellect. At one of these meetings, he met Dr. Samuel Gould, president of Antioch College, who would turn out to be an important influence on Ernie's thinking about education, which affected his future direction.

After years of work and intense preparations for accreditation, it was finally time for a visit from the regional accreditation team. When the team returned a positive report, the whole campus celebrated. It was, indeed, a very commendable achievement for this small Christian college. Ernie had fulfilled his purpose in returning to Upland College as academic dean.

Opting for a New Adventure

During the three years Ernie had been dean of Upland College, he had left behind his own professional field. There was a big and lingering question in his mind about how and when he could return to his doctoral field of language development and pathologies of speech. He thus decided that a good way to answer that lingering question would be to apply for a nine-month, postdoctoral research fellowship at the University of Iowa and the University Hospital in Iowa City. In order to do so, he asked for a nine-month leave of absence from his position at Upland College.

The University of Iowa was widely recognized for its research in Ernie's area of doctoral study, and he wanted to move ahead with his own research. This was clearly a fine opportunity for him to pursue his original goal. However, we had a great deal of concern about how such a drastic change would affect our family. It was a very difficult decision to make because we wanted to be sure the move was what we were to do at that time in our lives. After all, we were very happy in our Family and Guest House Mansion. Everyone was enjoying our daily routine and Ernie's now fairly predictable schedule.

Ernie and I enjoyed entertaining dinner and overnight guests. Some came to the college as guest lecturers, and others Ernie invited when he was seeking support and guidance on accreditation procedures. Many would become our lifelong friends.

Furthermore, Ernie continued to teach the adult Sunday school class every week. It was a large class, and he welcomed open discussions as he taught from Scripture about a life of faith and a commitment to discipleship as a follower of Jesus. I was content and joyful with the many faculty wives' activities, our Christian group fellowship, and with service in the church women's ministries.

Ernie Lee and Beverly were happy in their school and with their friends. Craig, who was now four years old, had a safe play area in the backyard, and the sidewalk along W. 7th Street where he could pedal his big farm tractor for long periods of time in his own adventures. Other times, he cheerfully worked beside me, helping me plant and tend the flower gardens.

This was the first house where I had become interested in planting and maintaining flower gardens, but I only knew about what would grow in the Pennsylvania soil of my childhood. How blessed we were to have a retired minister and his wife as neighbors who had a picture-perfect backyard lined with beautiful flowers. They gave me many tips on growing flowers in Southern California. On Saturdays Ernie loved to help me keep the flower beds neatly edged and weeded, and he enjoyed mowing and trimming the lawn.

I do not mean to make it all sound so perfectly idyllic because we were just a simple and normal family who tried our best to protect what was good and to deal with the hardships. I am just trying to convey that as a family we had absolutely no driving reason to leave 367 West 7th Street, where life was pleasant and agreeable. However, I was fully committed to support Ernie in his desire to follow the research interests he had developed while in graduate school at USC. We had an equal understanding of one another's needs and wishes, and thus it appeared right for us to make this change.

So we tried to make this interruption in our pleasant way of life, especially for our children, an exciting adventure. The good part was we could explain to the children that we would only be gone for nine months and would move back into the same house. We described Iowa as a place for new adventures and new friends—friends that could just be added to their Upland friends.

We were also able to sublet the Family and Guest House Mansion and avoid the big task of packing everything because we were going to a furnished house and our renters needed a furnished house. Things fell into place, and we were soon prepared—at least partially—for a very different experience.

We headed off to house Number 8 in Iowa City, Iowa!

CHAPTER 8

HOUSES 8, 9, & 10

The Unexpected Mansions

Iowa City, Iowa

1959–1960

"We can be at home in any dwelling, for our safe keeping lies not in the place where we live, but in God Himself."

—David Roper

All three houses, numbers 8, 9, and 10, need to be grouped together because they are all a part of a short nine-month adventure that had a very unexpected ending. It had been difficult for Ernie to decide to take a leave of absence from his administrative position at Upland College and leave the warmth of Southern California in January for snow and freezing temperatures in Iowa City. It was even more difficult to find housing for a family of five in the middle of winter.

With the help of some contacts, Ernie learned about an elderly gentleman, Mr. Wilson, who was planning to go to Florida for six months and was willing to rent his house to our family. Unfortunately, Mr. Wilson's plans to go to Florida did not work out, but because he had promised to rent us his house, he was fully committed to honor that promise.

Mr. Wilson had a strong friendship with the Allen family, his remarkable neighbors across the street, and they invited him to move in with them for six months before they would be moving. We all became friends, and when Mr. Wilson's daughter came to visit him from Florida, we invited him, his daughter, and the Allen family all for dinner—in his own dining room! His kindness seemed quite unusual to us. We who arrived as total strangers now lived comfortably in his beloved homestead while he could only look at his home from across the street. Such kindness made a lasting imprint on our family.

I probably liked this house, Unexpected Mansion # 8, more than the rest of the family did because it reminded me of my dearest grandparents' farmhouse in Silverdale, Pennsylvania. The kitchen had an old-fashioned sink with a wooden drainboard and a very old-style stove and refrigerator that still worked, surprisingly. The rooms were small with low ceilings, and most of the furniture pieces were creaky antiques. However, it was well heated for the long, cold winter and had a kind of assuring coziness.

Outside, snow banks piled up so high that the children could climb on the snow to the top of the garage roof and slide down. This surely was a new kind of fun for children who had only experienced the playtimes of sunny California. The street was residential, with the sidewalk close to our front porch, so that we could see children walking to the school, which was only about two blocks away.

The curriculum at the school was at least a half year more advanced than what they had experienced in their school back in Upland. This gap created a problem for Ernie Lee, who was in the third grade; his Iowa classmates were practicing long division, but he had not been introduced to any division in his California classroom. In addition, Ernie Lee was shocked to find that the boys in this new school all wore trousers with a pressed crease and regular shoes—not jeans and sneakers, as he had been accustomed to wearing in California. And there was a whole new order of social expectations, which were probably even more challenging than the academic adjustments for our third-grader. Fortunately, the differences were not as significant for Beverly in the second grade.

Ernie and I felt responsible for finding ways to help the whole family adapt and to learn lessons on how to deal with different and difficult situations. These were challenging issues, and Ernie used much enterprising energy to make this Iowa experience pleasant and exciting for the family. We took advantage of whatever the university had to offer and became frequent visitors to the planetarium, marveling at the heavens displayed by the device that simulated the skies and learning fascinating details about the planets and constellation formations. We also enjoyed other museums and science shows that were available in a university city.

As the snow melted and the days warmed, we made sight-seeing trips around Iowa, including an evening spent with a Mennonite family at their large farm a distance from the city. We hoped that all these activities and good times together would be enriching and good for the children.

With no Brethren in Christ church in town, we had hoped to find a Mennonite Church that was within easy driving distance. The Brethren in Christ and the Mennonites were sister churches, but we were disappointed to find that there was not even a Mennonite church for us to attend. While searching for a place to attend Sunday worship, we studied the works of some of the original Quakers like George Fox, who said, "I live in the virtue of that life and power that takes away the occasion of all wars." We decided to visit the local Quaker meeting (as they are called) and found unusually kind and friendly people. A family with children about the same age as ours invited us to their house after the service for a wonderful Sunday dinner. The father was a university professor, and the mother shared with me about her full-time role as a mother that was so similar to my own.

We continued to attend the welcoming Quaker meeting and discovered that we shared many beliefs and found the services inspiring. This was the second time that we had been away from our denominational church, and we realized what mattered was not the name, but the true teaching of God's word. Of course, we very much missed the dear fellowship of our own church friends; however, the children even had their own classes now, and we grew in our faith as individuals and as a family while in Iowa City.

Groundbreaking Research and Day-to-Day Adjustments

The year was 1960, and the University of Iowa Hospital's department of otolaryngology was known at that time for the work of Wendell Johnson, a professor and surgeon who specialized in inner ear injuries and impaired hearing. He was doing groundbreaking research and perfecting new surgical techniques. Day after day, through the long, cold winter winds and the springtime rains, Ernie walked across the Iowa River bridge to the University Hospital to work alongside Dr. Johnson. Ernie would perform hearing tests before, during, and after the very delicate surgical procedures for middle ear deafness.

Ernie and Dr. Johnson wrote and published their research findings together, and the article in a professional journal was one reward for some of the work Ernie did during his nine-month fellowship. He also taught classes at the University of Iowa's Department of Speech and Hearing and worked in a clinic with children who were linguistically disadvantaged.

During this postdoctoral fellowship, Ernie was completely immersed in his professional field, which is what he had prepared for during those years of intensely pursuing his PhD. Now, with his professional degree and the resources of the University of Iowa, he was determined to make a success of the goal he had envisioned.

It took some time, but with the new activities and our extra efforts to provide stimulating experiences, the family made a successful adjustment. The lone exception was Ernie Lee's school situation, which was only partially solved. The bottom line—he just never adjusted to having to wear his "Sunday pants and shoes" to school.

I made friends with some faculty wives and accepted invitations for daytime visits. Craig was by my side, always gentle and obedient. He would quickly fall asleep for his afternoon nap, because he knew when he woke up, I would pull him on the sled though the snow. At the top of the hill, I'd let him sit on the sled and give him a push so he could whiz down the hill.

In the springtime, the whole family found new and exciting outdoor adventures that helped us experience the spring awakening. This change of seasons amazed us; despite its pleasant climate, Southern California lacked seasons, and we had missed these types of dramatic transformation.

Unexpected Mansion #9 and an Unexpected Offer

Before our six-month rental agreement ended, we had a party for Craig's fifth birthday and invited Mr. Wilson and the whole family across the street to come help us celebrate while we were far away from our extended family. Clearly, Ernie felt blessed that his family had been cared for during those six months, thanks to Mr. Wilson. But there were three more months left in his nine-month sabbatical, and we needed to find another place to live.

Ernie had learned about an English professor at the university who was taking a summer teaching assignment overseas, leaving his large, fully furnished family home available. The rent was very reasonable because we agreed to care for the family's large bulldog, Duchess, and mow the lawn. It proved to be a happy arrangement, and this house was a real gift for the three remaining months.

This house, # 9 to be exact, was as up-to-date modern as Mr. Wilson's house was old- fashioned. It was roomy and felt luxurious with thick carpeting and many rooms with big windows. There were extra bathrooms, and the children each had their own bedroom. The fully equipped, contemporary kitchen overwhelmed me because I had never before had so many modern conveniences. The lawn upkeep was no problem for Ernie as he had always found it to be relaxing work, and the children enjoyed playing croquet in the backyard and with Duchess, their newfound friend.

This might have been an ideal situation, but Ernie's mind was suddenly forced into turmoil because he had to make a decision of great consequence when the University of Iowa offered him an important administrative position in his professional field. Accepting the position would mean dropping all his work in the field of education and leadership at Upland College to move into a career in the field of his doctoral degree—language development and the pathologies of speech. Ernie had felt very satisfied with his successes during the fellowship, but the plan had been for him to return to Upland and to his position as academic dean.

This was a momentous decision that would carry lifelong consequences. I encouraged Ernie to accept the University of Iowa's outstanding offer because I still carried the vision of his career goal vividly in my mind. Even so, I was aware of the many difficult changes such a decision would bring. After a time of considerable evaluation of the pros and cons, Ernie decided the University of Iowa offer gave him a special opportunity to step right into the career he thought he wanted all along. He thus accepted the offer to be a full professor with administrative responsibilities at the University of Iowa.

Unexpected Mansion #10; Unexpected Outcome

Since our new plan was to settle down and make Iowa City our hometown, the reasonable next step was to buy house #10. We found a house for sale just two blocks from house #9, where we had lived for three months, that fit the needs of our family perfectly. We made the purchase and spent most of our summer evenings getting it ready for the move. We even hired a contractor to remodel the kitchen and family room. Ernie painted all the rooms, and I made curtains for every window in the house while the children delighted in playing in the empty rooms and exploring the large lawn with tall trees and hiding places.

As the summer came to an end, we were making plans to return to California to finalize Ernie's termination from Upland College and pack our household items for the big move to Iowa. Suddenly, Ernie was flung into another spinning whirlwind of uncertainty, one more intense than any other.

The whirlwind was created by a call from Mitchell Briggs of the Western College Association, who asked Ernie to become the director of the Joint Commission to Improve the Education of Teachers in California. The Commission was sponsored by the Western College Association and the California Council on Teacher Education, supported by the Ford Foundation, and chaired by William Brownell, who served on the faculty at the University of California, Berkeley. Ernie was being asked to direct a new enterprise, and he could also remain involved at Upland College as dean.

I confess that although I was dedicated to Ernie's ambitions and successes, I was totally against him accepting this offer. He had already made up his mind to make his career in language and speech pathology. Why should he be asked to change his mind again? It was irritating to live in the whirlwind of these seemingly unending decisions that were being forced on

Ernie—decisions that affected our whole family. We had already made our choice, and I did not think we should change plans again.

I also confess that I was thinking of the home we had just bought and how lovely it was since we had devoted the summer to make it into our own sweet, charming place. I imagined the children becoming happy Midwesterners, and I reasoned that if Ernie took this new job in California as director of the new commission he would be forever turning his back on his chosen career path.

Ernie knew what I was saying, and he said my objections all made real sense. However, he told me that for some reason he could not feel at peace about the idea of rejecting this new position in education. He seemed to be sensing that his experience in the field of education had showed him he belonged there.

After a time of deep soul searching, he felt firm in his decision to accept the invitation to be director of the Joint Commission to Improve the Education of Teachers in California and to turn down the offer at the University of Iowa. He told me he felt clear in his mind and was at peace, believing this was God's plan for him. I was then convinced that the plan was right and good and that everything would work out for the best.

Along with Ernie, my heart was now ready to give up on the cherished house that we just bought, remodeled, and decorated as our second dream house. We put it on the market and found our hard work had made the sale a profitable endeavor.

Although we had found ways to be happy and fulfilled in Iowa, there was a sense of unease, generated perhaps by the sweet remembrance of our warm circle of friends in California. They were the people who shared our past and our religious beliefs, and they were thus the friends with whom we were most comfortable. We had tried hard to make the new location successful, but we now all rejoiced at the thought of moving back to the place where we had family, our church, and many friends waiting. Ernie Lee and Beverly could also happily return to their familiar school; Ernie Lee was especially happy that he would no longer have to wear trousers with a pressed crease and could go back to wearing jeans and sneakers to school.

Ernie's nine-month postdoctoral fellowship experience at University of Iowa had lasting value throughout his life. He wrote and spoke frequently about the "centrality of language" and the power of human communication. He and I always looked back to that time as important and significant in our life journey.

The house on 7th Street in Upland was vacated by the renters in time for us to move back in as if we had never been gone. We had missed our sweet dog, Chico, who we had left with the renters. What a happy, grand reunion we all had with him, and we all welcomed our return with peace. Moving back into our familiar setting felt just right.

Again, we had that feeling of things being more permanent and decided that it would be wise to consider buying our own family home in Upland.

CHAPTER 9

HOUSE 11

The Orange Grove Mansion

Upland, California

1960–1962

"A home is more than a place to live in. It is a place of beauty to the eyes and heart."

—Unknown

There was general agreement the house we were looking to buy had to surpass and even outshine the house we reluctantly gave up in Iowa. The pain of giving up the thrill of moving into the house where we had put so much of our love and creative energy was still very fresh in our minds. We needed to find a house that would help us to forget that loss and give us a sense of where we would begin the next chapter in our lives as a family.

The possibility of actually finding such a house was hard to imagine. But believe it or not, the house we were hoping to find was just one street beyond our current house, the Family and Guest House Mansion on 7th Street. The Orange Grove Mansion was right there on 8th Street, and it even exceeded our hopes.

Besides being a well-built, two-story stone house, it had a front yard with two palm trees and a kumquat tree. This tree produced an abundance of small citrus fruit with a sweet rind and an acidic pulp that the children loved to pick and eat on the spot. I proudly learned to make kumquat jelly.

The property also had avocado trees that produced more than we could use, allowing us to share lots of avocadoes with our friends. Acres of beautiful orange groves bordered the lawn and extended off into the distance. Much to my chagrin, this would be the closest we would ever come to feeling like farmers. Growing up as a Pennsylvania farm girl, I had always assumed I'd be a farmer's wife. Now, in 1960, I had a sense my girlhood dream at last might come true.

Ernie was proud to be at least partially fulfilling my girlhood dream by trying his hand at farming—albeit California-style. We all enjoyed the excitement of managing the irrigation system, allowing water to rush through deep ditches to soak the ground around the orange trees. The ditches had to be kept open to let the water flow. It was real work, but everyone liked to help, including the cousins and Ernie's brother Bill.

My dear friend, Frances Harmon, went with me to find a large dining room table and matching chairs at a second-hand furniture warehouse. It seemed important to make this purchase because this house included our first separate and more formal dining room. Another favorite feature of the house was the large and bright open space for the kitchen and family room, which included a carefully built stone fireplace. We envisioned this would be the perfect space for student discussion gatherings and potluck dinners with faculty and staff.

The children's bedrooms were upstairs. Ernie painted Beverly's room purple, and I made matching purple drapes, bedspread, and pillows. But Beverly soon discovered she was more comfortable climbing out her window into a nearby tree than lounging in her designer bedroom. Being at home in the California sunshine, she never found playing in her room nearly as exciting as sitting high in the tree branches to read. Or she would join her brothers in the new tree house Ernie had helped them build in the other side of the same big tree. When her girlfriends came, she would teach them too how to climb out her window onto the tree. Neither Ernie nor I worried about Beverly's safety, but we had to caution her about trying to teach some of her less adventuresome friends to make that climb.

We gave the boys the biggest bedroom, and Ernie built a small partition so each would have his own space. Ernie Lee was an avid reader and needed space for shelves for what eventually grew to be a sizable library.

Both boys wanted BB guns, and Ernie decided that would be all right if we enforced some restrictions. He built them a target practice area, and we forbade them to shoot birds. If they shot any of the oranges hanging heavy on the nearby trees, it was never reported at the dinner table. Their most exciting adventures came while exploring the orange groves with cousins and friends. Craig started kindergarten rather reluctantly, as he much preferred running free in the big outdoors to his new classroom, which initially seemed too confining.

Asking Questions about Shaping Lives

The demands of Ernie's two positions as a director and dean called for my loyal understanding and presence. There were many functions at Upland College I wanted to attend with him as his wife, and there were many new people from the commission and the Western College Association who Ernie wanted to entertain in our home.

Life here was very different from what it would have been in Iowa City, but we felt completely satisfied and fulfilled with our life in Upland. It clearly seemed we had made the right choice.

The biggest change for our family was that Ernie had to be away from home periodically for a night or two when he led the commission meetings in Fresno, California, the location of the Western College Association. There, he worked with commission members who were professors from fourteen outstanding universities and colleges in California, some of whom he knew from the Upland College accreditation process or education conferences. Without them, the goals of the new California education commission would never be accomplished.

His ongoing position as academic dean of Upland College held its own fascination for Ernie. He used these years and this position to further develop his educational philosophy, one that focused on students and the college's responsibility to provide an education that would shape their lives.

Ernie had many questions about teaching and learning, such as, "Could learning be put into a larger context and be guided by values and affirmed beliefs?" He was asking himself if there was a core of learning appropriate for all students and what environment was appropriate for that learning. Students and faculty gathered around the fireplace in our family room often engaged in deep discussions about these kinds of thoughts and questions. I was grateful we had an excellent space for these gatherings and tried to serve some healthy hors d'oeuvres and treats to help to make everyone feel comfortable and welcome.

The Beginning of a New Calling

Although the two positions put increased demands on Ernie and me, our family enjoyed our lives in the Orange Grove Mansion, and we were not searching for any big changes. But Ernie was mindful that his two-year assignment with the Commission to Improve the Education of Teachers in California was nearly complete.

During these two years, Ernie had realized that he was most interested in educating students about how to live with values and affirmed beliefs. He did not miss his own professional field and had no regrets about leaving it and the position at the University of Iowa behind. During these years, he had continued to teach the adult Sunday school class at the Upland Brethren in Christ Church and sometimes even gave sermons for special occasions.

He chose to attend national education conferences and went to other education meetings, such as the Independent Colleges Association meetings, where he had now first met Samuel Gould years earlier. Dr. Gould, who had become the president of the University of California, Santa Barbara (UCSB), was aware that Ernie was completing his work at the joint commission of the Western College Association and the California Council on Teacher Education. So Gould asked Ernie to move his family to Santa Barbara and establish at UCSB a Center for Coordinated Education.

In a news interview, Ernie stated, "The Ford Foundation is underwriting this operation because it realizes the great potential the program has for the improvement of educational standards throughout the nation." I remember thinking that our life was being bombarded by the outside world, forcing us to face frequent decisions that required our family to move. However, I do not recall we felt stressed while considering this offer. In fact, it was the beginning of what Ernie later declared was his calling to serve public education.

Ernie had a magic touch that allowed him to make the move to Santa Barbara seem like a very desirable thing for the family. After all, he told us, Santa Barbara is an extraordinarily beautiful, seaside community with perfect weather almost year round. Although we couldn't deny the draw of Santa Barbara, we again prepared ourselves to say many sad farewells in Upland, California.

I expect we somehow knew that this move would be our final good-bye to Upland, where we would leave behind six houses that had become part of our deep roots. It was especially difficult to end those years with Upland College and to separate from our very dearest friends and close family members.

In 1962, we reminded ourselves that we were not losing friends but that we would be adding new friends when we settled in Santa Barbara. By now, even the children had learned to believe that line. House #12 was to be in Santa Barbara, California.

CHAPTER 10

HOUSE 12

The Hilltop Mansion

Santa Barbara, California

1962–1963

"Just as a beautiful sequence of a place leads to the door of another, so the preparation can delight you."

—Unknown

We put our beloved Orange Grove Mansion up for sale while we looked for a suitable house to rent in Santa Barbara. Before we left Upland, Ernie talked with his friend, Roger Voskuyl, the president of Westmont College, a Christian liberal arts college similar to Upland College although it was much larger. President Voskuyl told Ernie about a professor and family who would be away for part of the summer and would be willing to sublet their house to us. The temporary move would give us the time we needed to find the right house in the best school district.

The house was a small bungalow that was congested and disorganized, but we were grateful to have it for the short time we needed it. By arranging our own living spaces and freshening things up, we had a pleasant five-week home. We knew that grandeur was clearly not a prerequisite for a happy and contented family.

But little did we know that this strange house and this short time would turn out to provide an entrée into a wonderful three years of joyful experiences for the whole family. In earlier years, this house had been part of an exclusive, private boys' school situated on a 100-acre campus that had been closed for many years. The gentleman responsible for all of this estate was Mr. Reynolds. He and his wife were now rather elderly and lived in a grand, older house at the entrance of this large property. The whole hundred acres was called Oakleigh, and we soon learned that Mr. Reynolds was the very visible, kind, and thoughtful master of the estate.

Even with their most proper manners, Mr. and Mrs. Reynolds created an air of acceptance and warmth for the many children who lived within Oakleigh. There were four rented houses in the community, but it was the outstanding Shennum family that was the attraction for our children. Arlene Shennum was the registrar at Westmont College and a saintly mother I immediately admired. She had six children, and two of her boys, Jody and Jerry, matched in age with our children.

Ernie Jr. (now 11 and no longer wanting to be called Ernie Lee), Beverly (9), and Craig (7), were amazed to find they had landed in their own paradise. During the first week, I would walk the acreage trying to track down the children. Mr. Reynolds would hear me calling to them but told me they were very safe and I must let them be free to have fun on their own since the estate was free of danger. Ernie and I found the whole situation a wonderful delight.

The polite and kind Shennum children were guided by their Christian mother and demonstrated high principles. We relaxed our minds and gave thanks to God for this delightful blessing of friends who shared our values. Our children were young, and their lives were being shaped as they formed assumptions about life. In that process, the Shennum children were a good influence.

During these weeks, Ernie was also concentrating on his new responsibilities at UCSB. Thankfully, before the summer ended, and with the help of Westmont College officials, who shared their listing of houses for rent, a charming hilltop house became available that was within a very short walking distance from Oakleigh and the Shennum "clan." It seemed like it was a gift of happiness to find this house at 590 Barker Pass Road.

Set on the hillside with a steep driveway that led to a carport and the back door, the Hilltop Mansion was well-planned and fit our needs perfectly. There were four bedrooms, an extra workroom off the kitchen, and a bright breakfast nook with a built-in table and benches. Ernie Jr. spent much of his time with Jody building model airplanes in that workroom, hanging dozens from the ceiling in his bedroom. From the porch with the tall pillars, we could look down and see cars on the narrow road below. This steep hill was planted with a succulent ground cover, which the children and their friends used as a long slide, like a sledding hill of snow. However, in Southern California they didn't need snow—just flattened cardboard boxes because the plants became very slippery. Some of the kids didn't even need the cardboard boxes; they just took big jumps and slid down on their feet.

The main play area was still Oakleigh because what could be more exciting than having all the raw materials of nature to build forts and fortresses, hiding places, and outdoor houses? That's what Oakleigh offered, and the children lived in a state of complete happiness with their own creations.

There was an understanding that when the children heard my powerful Tarzan yell, which I developed with practice, they were to come home without delay. When they heard my yell drift from the Hilltop Mansion, someone would answer with a more polished and more powerful Tarzan yell. Soon they would appear huffing and puffing up the hill in time to sit down to dinner.

Beverly's precious kitten, Frannie Baby, moved with us when we left the Orange Grove Mansion in Upland, but poor Frannie Baby got confused when she was moved to the Oakleigh Hilltop Mansion. After several days, she escaped the house to explore the area and got herself lost. Beverly's heart was so very sad, and we all grieved with her. But even her Daddy, who could always take care of everything for her, could not find her dear cat. Amazingly, three months later, while Beverly was trick-or-treating in a nearby neighborhood, she saw Frannie Baby crouched under a parked car. Overjoyed, Beverly was able to woo the cat out from under the car and lovingly carried her home, tucked safely in her trick-or-treat bag. She made sure her dear lost cat was secure in her bedroom, and Frannie Baby never got lost again. She stayed close, finding sweet security on Beverly's bed.

Special Opportunities for Growth and Adventure

Ernie viewed our move to Santa Barbara to establish and direct a center for coordinated education as a special opportunity. Only thirty-four, he had already formed the conviction that education could build bridges of understanding at all levels. He believed collaboration could improve teaching and research, and he felt the center opened doors to pursue other goals in higher education.

In a news release, he noted, "Elementary and secondary schools, private and public colleges, and universities and technical institutions all tend to function independently and operate in isolation one from another." He stated that the Santa Barbara project would seek to find ways to close this educational gap between the elementary and secondary years of education and that the work of higher education was to build a coordinated program. Santa Barbara County was to serve as laboratory for this pilot study.

The fact that the family was able to quickly feel settled helped Ernie feel free to concentrate on efforts to start up the new center. He had a suite of rooms and hired a staff and an assistant. Before long, the work of organizing the activities was completed, and the center was in full operation.

The setting, located on the Santa Barbara oceanfront, seemed idyllic. Sometimes I would pack a picnic, and we'd all go with Ernie to his office and enjoy the beach. Ernie would take an hour or two for a picnic lunch with us, which was a real treat as he typically was fully focused on his work duties.

The children did not complain about Ernie's developing career that was moving us to different places, and in fact were able to enjoy and absorb the positive experiences and opportunities that came with those changes. Ernie and I felt responsible to make sure the circumstances would prove to be constructive. As Christian parents, this was always a priority in our minds and in our planning, as I stated many times.

We went as a family to the Friends (Quaker) meeting. The clerk of the meeting, Charles Cooper, was an exemplary Christian. He always opened the meeting by welcoming everyone and then giving a Bible reading and a short exhortation on that passage of Scripture. Then he would explain that everyone should quietly meditate on that passage and, if the Spirit moved, should share their thoughts. Ernie often spoke, using words that could be understood by everyone, including the children.

A Widespread Scare

In October 1962 there was a major Cold War scare—the Cuban Missile Crisis, a very tense episode in the ongoing confrontation between the United States, Cuba, and the Soviet Union. Ernie watched TV and followed the news closely, but he tried to protect the children from the fear that was widely felt. Reports on the evening news made it seem like the world was just a heartbeat away from annihilation. The children heard frightening rumors at school that the world was coming to an end, and the school conducted safety drills in which the children were instructed to hide under their desks for protection from atomic bombs.

The fathers in the Oakleigh neighborhood dug a deep hole in the ground where they could hide for protection. Ernie did not help with the digging because his approach was more philosophical, but he did not discourage the children from helping their friends dig. In a way it was like playtime for them, even if it was hard work. But they told each other that they were digging for an important purpose.

I remember the children's fear and their questions. Ernie reminded them that God gave us His protective love. At one point, we were all riding in the car when someone asked about the scary news. Seven-year-old Craig said, "At least we'll all go to heaven together." Ernie agreed with Craig, and we drove along the highway feeling assured and protected. Decades later, I still treasure that endearing exchange.

During an interview at a later date, Ernie was asked to look back and reflect on the missile crisis. He initially answered in question form:

> What is the moral equivalent to the atomic bomb? I mean if that's an example of intelligence used for destruction, where are the centers of inquiry in which we would pursue human safety and peace with equal urgency? Where's the Manhattan Project for Peace? Where are the centers where the best minds are brought together to inquire around the infinitely more difficult, but in the end the ultimately more important question of the uses of knowledge toward human advancement? And one would think if we turn our imagination to that, there would be exciting breakthroughs, but we seem frozen within the traditions of nationalism, within the traditions of self-centeredness, and even, if I might say, within the traditions of confrontations, where it is unsafe, and even almost unseemly to stretch our imagination there, while on the other side we allow entrepreneurial interest and imagination to run unlimited in figuring out Star Wars arrangements around the tensions and conflict.

Mental Health Efforts

There were fascinating endeavors that were of great interest to Ernie even though they were unrelated to his field of education. For example, in January 1963, he joined the board of directors of the Mennonite Mental Health Services (MMHS), a program of the Mennonite Central Committee (MCC). During World War II, a number of our friends had chosen to refuse to serve in the armed forces. They were referred to as "conscientious objectors." As pacifists because of their Christian heritage, they took a stand against armed conflict and went into "Alternative Service" which was a government-approved program.

Some of these conscientious objectors were assigned to work at state mental hospitals where they found the conditions and lack of treatment and care very disheartening. Our friends would tell us unbelievable and even brutal stories.

The sad reports from the men working in these psychiatric institutions were not ignored by Mennonite Church leaders. In reading a report that was written in 1965, I found the following statement in a magazine published by the MMHS:

> Two decades ago when Mennonites first began thinking seriously of going into the field of mental health, it was clear that a great need existed in this area. The state hospital systems were on the whole merely warehouses in which the unfortunate were stored and where most often they were not even labeled before they were forgotten. In cases where it was absolutely essential, coercion was used in an attempt to restrain behavior although no serious prospect remained that people could really be helped. It was clear that under such conditions tender loving care and the involvement of the church in the field of mental health needed little defense.

I do not recall who asked Ernie to join the board of directors of MMHS, but he became a hardworking, loyal board member and was nominated as chairman. His service began while we were living in Santa Barbara, and he seldom missed a meeting because he so strongly believed in the Christian mission being provided for those who had been mistreated and neglected. After each meeting, he would talk about his profound respect for the people who served on the board, for their high intellect, their commitment, their persistence in providing the highest quality of services, and their full devotion to God. He always came home wholly inspired and committed to serve.

There were five hospitals that were providing comprehensive mental health services, and he would travel to their locations for meetings. Two were located in California—Kings View Hospital in Fresno and Kern View Hospital in Bakersfield. The other three were Prairie View Hospital in North Newton, Kansas; Oaklawn Psychiatric Center in Elkhart, Indiana; and Brook Lane Farm Hospital in northwest Maryland.

Wish Comes True

We were comfortable in the Hilltop Mansion, but adjacent to Oakleigh and facing Westmont College was a lovely home. Ernie and I had privately said to one another, "That's the house that we wish had been for rent before we moved to Parker Pass Road." The front door of that house faced the new, modern-looking, large Westmont College men's dormitory, and there was only a short walk between.

Remarkably, the house became available for rent at the same time I was asked to take the position of director of student health services at Westmont College. The office, clinic, and infirmary unit were in the men's dormitory. I knew that I would enjoy the work and that I would especially enjoy being involved with the Westmont students. Ernie strongly encouraged me to accept the position; the children were twelve, ten, and eight years old by then, and each felt quite self-sufficient. Nevertheless, it was a big important decision we had to make. Prayerfully, we decided it would not interfere with the family routine since I'd be working only steps from the house and because my work hours were scheduled when the children were in school and Ernie was at his work. I began the job in September 1963.

We were still young and energetic, so, with everyone helping, the move down the hillside from the Hilltop Mansion seemed to be just part of the work we had to do to keep life moving forward in the smoothest fashion. We had lots of help and even had fun. So it was that during our second summer in Santa Barbara we moved to Cold Spring Road—back to Oakleigh—the very place where all of us felt happiest and most welcome.

CHAPTER 11

HOUSE 13

The Oakleigh Neighborhood Mansion

SANTA BARBARA, CALIFORNIA

1963–1965

"Love begins at home by sharing love through thoughtfulness, by kindness, by sharing joy, by sharing a smile. . . . Love begins at home through the little things."

—Mother Teresa

This house at 885 Cold Spring Road, which was just a short walk from the Westmont College campus, was very unlike any other home in which we had lived. Large sliding glass doors in the kitchen, family room, dining area, living room, and master bedroom all opened onto a patio area and swimming pool, which were enclosed by a high wooden fence. The house had less space, with one less bedroom than the Hilltop Mansion, which disappointed the children, who had loved having their own rooms. But the thrill of again living right at Oakleigh and the fun of sharing the pool more than compensated.

We established a list of safety rules and then declared the pool open to the Oakleigh neighborhood. It became a favorite spot for food and fun;

the children devised many pool games that included everyone, and they all became just as comfortable in the water as a school of fish.

The ideal Santa Barbara weather made having a pool as part of our living space a special gift not only for our children and the neighborhood, but also for Ernie. He was a strong swimmer and found the water relaxing therapy after the demands of his workday and a delightful way to have fun with the family. I sometimes joined in, but since I was not a good swimmer, I concentrated on cheering the teams and putting out the food.

Problems at School and in the Country

By the time we moved to the Oakleigh community, Craig was in the second grade, and Beverly was in the fifth grade. The two of them walked together to Cold Spring, the small public elementary school just down the road. Both had excellent teachers, and Beverly did well in school while Craig tended to daydream of running around outside with his Oakleigh friends.

Ernie Jr. had to take the bus to the Santa Barbara Junior High School, which turned into a difficult experience when other kids on the bus began bullying him after they discovered he would not fight back. The problems escalated until Ernie Jr. dreaded getting on the bus and going to the big inner-city school. Ernie Sr. was very much a problem solver, but he could not find a real solution to this troubling problem. His efforts with the Junior High School never brought the results that we all hoped. Through it all, we took special time to listen and talk with Ernie Jr., trying to relate to the ways he was insulted and his hurt feelings, and trying always to affirm him. This unsettling experience undoubtedly influenced Ernie Sr.'s later work and writings, such as *The Basic School: A Community for Learning.*

Although Ernie had limited success with Santa Barbara Junior High, at the Center for Coordinated Education, he was successfully developing many contacts and connections while bringing together leaders from the various levels of education. Some of the contacts happened in unexpected ways. Although he had never seriously played golf, Ernie accepted invitations to join groups of educators on the golf course, discovering it provided time for friendly talk and a chance to promote his plans. But he also found these games intimidating because most of his companions were experienced and committed players who would show up wearing sporty country club outfits and carrying classy golf clubs and bags. Ernie had none of this kind of golf regalia and only wanted to focus on his goals for the Center for Coordinated Education. Years later he would describe this period of his career with much humor. Although he never became a serious golfer, Ernie did get better at the game and once even made a hole in one! From then on he was no longer intimidated by his second-rate equipment.

Just when everyone in our family was living comfortably in the routine of each day, the tragic news of the assassination of President John F. Kennedy on November 22, 1963, sent us and the whole nation into a terrible tailspin. Our household was deeply saddened, and for days we closely followed all the events on TV. It seemed like things stopped functioning while everyone grieved, no matter their political differences. Ernie was concerned about world conditions and knew the wounds would take a long time to heal.

An Extraordinary Birth

In the midst of national grief, we were about to experience another extraordinary event in our lifetime of wonderful events. During one dinner hour, late in November 1963, I answered the telephone and heard that my pregnancy test was positive. It was an on-the-spot announcement for all the family to hear, and a big whoop of wonder and excitement filled the air. Ernie and I had continued to hope for a fourth child even after the sadness of a miscarriage I had suffered about four years earlier.

I had been working at my nursing job at Westmont College for only three months, and was not sure how this pregnancy would affect that. But I was able to finish the assignment with no problems, working to the end of the school year in June.

The anticipation mounted in July as I neared my due date. The Lamaze method of preparing an expectant mother for natural childbirth was just being introduced into obstetrical practice at that time. Ernie and I studied it and practiced on our own, and at each prenatal visit, I would remind Dr. Paul, the head of the obstetrical unit at Cottage Hospital-Santa Barbara, that

Ernie and I were prepared to use the Lamaze method, that we were planning to stay together for the whole experience, and that I would use no pain-killers. This plan required Ernie to join me in the delivery room, which was still a revolutionary request in 1964. Dr. Paul agreed, but I sensed that he felt pretty certain we would not be able to really carry out our plans.

Ernie was eager to help me, and because we worked together, everything went exactly as planned. On August 5, 1964, our baby boy, Stephen Paul, was born with great fanfare and much celebration. Many hospital professionals crowded into the room to witness a father in the delivery room and a labor and delivery with no medication or medical technology involved.

Beverly, who was almost twelve, had said she wanted a sister but never once said she was disappointed to have a third brother after Stephen Paul arrived. Thirteen-year-old Ernie Jr. and nine-year-old Craig were so proud to have another brother. What a sweet and grand addition to our family! There were many eager hands among the siblings and from the Oakleigh neighborhood to hold Stephen Paul and help in many ways. The whole community participated in our joy. Even the sophisticated Mrs. Reynolds, the wife of the Oakleigh property owner, came and brought her friend to watch our baby splash and enjoy his bath. Our children's neighborhood playmates often did the same.

During this time, we attended the Montecito Covenant Church along with Oakleigh and Westmont College friends. Imprinted on my memory is the Sunday morning when we arrived at church in our overloaded station wagon. Upland cousins and Oakleigh friends vied for the privilege of carrying baby Stephen into the church and holding him during the service. Neither Ernie nor I were given a turn. Baby Stephen rewarded his admirers with delightful smiles and cooing sounds.

When Stephen Paul was about five months old, we returned to Upland to have our baby dedicated at the Upland Church where we were still members. Ernie had arranged for this service with Eber Dourte. As with our other children, we believed this dedication was our response to Jesus, who said, "Let the little children come to me" as He held and blessed the children in His life. In the same way, Pastor Dourte held Stephen Paul and spoke a prayer of blessing on his life. The service was also a time for friends and family to share in our joy and marvel about the gift of our new family member.

Long-Blooming Lessons from Oakleigh

Now, so many years later, I realize the unique benefits the Oakleigh community experience brought to our family. There were so many ways of sharing and being together. The neighborhood children would frequently raid our refrigerator and cupboard for supplies so they could prepare their own food in their fort or elaborately built outdoor houses. Some of their concoctions, such as roasted oranges, did not sound very appetizing to Ernie or me, but the children were proud of their creativity and independence.

In addition to enjoying playtime adventures, the children also worked as a team to help Mr. Reynolds keep his large, lovely rose garden and vegetable gardens free of weeds. Ernie Jr. and Jody got paid twenty-five cents an hour because they were the oldest, while the younger ones got ten cents an hour. But their real pay was getting to enjoy heated sweet rolls and cold milk on Mr. Reynolds's back porch after their work hours.

Working or playing, the neighborhood children spent much time together and devised all sorts of group games and activities. Some evenings Ernie and I would join the Oakleigh gang on our side lawn where we lay on blankets, watching the heavens and counting the falling stars and naming the constellations.

Through it all, each individual was aware of his or her importance to the community and each felt strong support from the whole. Many valuable lessons in interpersonal behavior were learned in this tight group of good friends.

It is fascinating for me to speculate about how some of those Oakleigh lessons were taking root in Ernie's mind and would bloom into full expression years later in his professional writings. By this point in our lives, we had been blessed with many situations where strong community clearly sustained and enriched us. Certainly, the years in Upland and the entire family's experience in the Oakleigh neighborhood were examples of the benefits of community. Ernie and I considered those experiences tremendous blessings from God.

Traveling Joys

Every year that we lived in California, Ernie would start planning months in advance to travel back East for a portion of each summer to visit with grandparents and family. I would sometimes complain and suggest that we might not need to go every summer. I loved our daily routine and selfishly wanted to keep on my usual schedule without the interference of all the packing, closing the house, and tending to all the details required by an extended time away. However, I would eventually give in to the family enthusiasm surrounding me, and join into the spirit of traveling, seeing new places, and, in particular, seeing precious family and friends. Ernie tended to be more spontaneous than I was, but we were both strongly loyal to family and felt sad to have taken our family far away from grandparents and other close relatives.

One time we traveled across the country by train, which was a fun family adventure heightened by the "Indian chief "and his "warriors," who jumped on and pretended to take over the train like in a Wild West movie. But the long trips by car were the most special because Ernie always mapped out new places to see along the way, providing geography lessons to the children, such as taking them to the spot where they could easily step into the four states of Utah, Colorado, Arizona, and New Mexico.

In between those summertime trips to our Eastern relatives, we relished shorter vacations and learning California history. We became very familiar with the Spanish missions because we frequently took many of our visitors to tour the Santa Barbara Mission, and we traveled south to the famous San Juan Capistrano Mission where an annual parade marks the time when the swallows return to build their mud nests.

Fleeing a Fire

Our most frightening experience in California came when a horrible wildfire spread with uncontrolled speed over the Montecito mountain range right toward the Westmont College campus and our house. It all happened so fast; suddenly there was a vehicle driving by our house repeating an almost incomprehensible command through a scary-sounding loud speaker: "Evacuate, you have fifteen minutes to be out of your house!"

Personal Photo of the Boyer Family

Ernie and I outside the Honeymoon Cottage Magical Mansion in Orlando, FL.

Personal Photo of the Boyer Family

Children gathering in the front of the Brethren in Christ Church in Orlando, FL to sing for the congregation.

Personal Photo of the Boyer Family

Ernie preaching from the pulpit in the Brethren in Christ Church in Orlando, FL.

Personal Photo of the Boyer Family

Exterior of the Brethren in Christ Church in Orlando, FL.

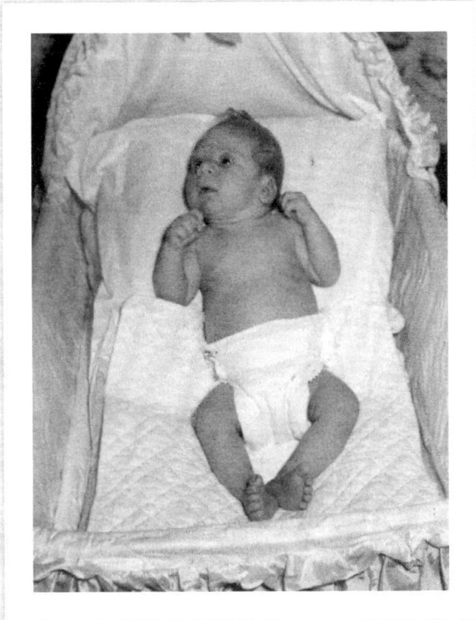

Personal Photo of the Boyer Family

Ernie, Jr. shortly after he was born.

Personal Photo of the Boyer Family

Ernie, Jr. and Beverly played for hours on their play set that Grandma and Grandpa Boyer bought for them.

Personal Photo of the Boyer Family

Ernie and I with Beverly shortly after she was born.

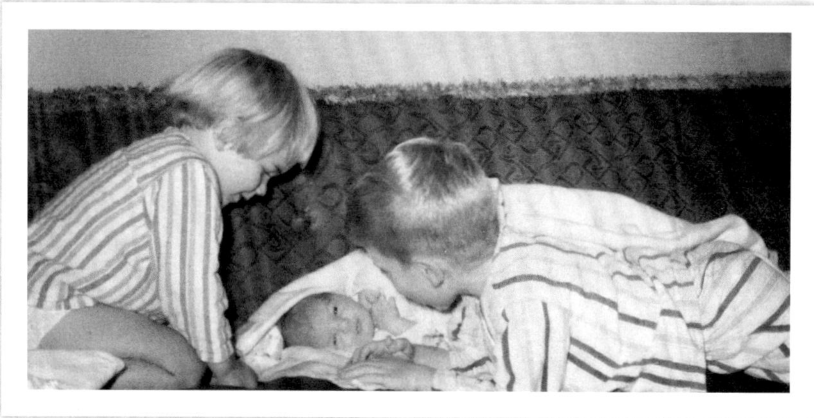

Personal Photo of the Boyer Family

Ernie, Jr. and Beverly trying to get Craig to smile shortly after he was born.

Personal Photo of the Boyer Family

Craig, Ernie, Jr., and Beverly on Easter Sunday outside of the Brethren in Christ Church in Upland, CA.

Personal Photo of the Boyer Family

My mother, Katie Tyson, with Craig outside of the Interlude Mansion in Los Angeles, CA.

Personal Photo of the Boyer Family

Craig, Beverly, and Ernie, Jr. with the family dog, Chico.

Personal Photo of the Boyer Family

Me with Stephen (Paul) as an infant.

Personal Photo of the Boyer Family

The Orange Grove Mansion in Upland, CA.

Personal Photo of the Boyer Family

The Oakleigh Neighborhood Mansion on the edge of the Westmont College campus in Santa Barbara, CA.

Personal Photo of the Boyer Family

Our family station wagon—complete with a U-Haul cargo carrier on the roof—packed and off to Albany, NY.

Personal Photo of the Boyer Family

Taking a break on our way from Santa Barbara, CA to Albany, NY—Stephen (Paul), Beverly, Craig, and their best friend, Jerry, who joined us for the trip.

Photo Used with Permission of the Ernest L. Boyer Center Archives, Messiah College

Ernie with New York Governor Nelson Rockefeller during Ernie's inauguration as Chancellor of the SUNY System.

Photo Used with Permission of the Ernest L. Boyer Center Archives, Messiah College

Ernie negotiating with Ralph Kurland (President, College Student Association), Scott Flynn (Vice President), Tyrone Trammel (student), and Amos Johnson (student) at the State University College at Buffalo.

Personal Photo of the Boyer Family

The back porch of the Round Lake Cabin Mansion in Berlin, NY.

Personal Photo of the Boyer Family

Ernie with his beloved mother, Ethel Boyer.

Personal Photo of the Boyer Family

Ernie and I with Grandfather (William) Boyer who founded the Brethren in Christ Mission in Dayton, OH. In many ways, Ernie modeled his life after his grandfather.

Personal Photo of the Boyer Family

Craig bought this home in upstate New York for $4,500 and lived there for three years. He came to know Christ in large part through the witness of a Mennonite community not far from this house.

Personal Photo of the Boyer Family

Ernie and I on our 25th wedding anniversary.

Personal Photo of the Boyer Family

Ernie and I singing "Somewhere over the Rainbow" at the Aspen Institute in Aspen, CO.

With frantic beating of our hearts, Ernie and I tried to appear in control as we instructed the children to take their pillow covers and quickly fill them with clothes. Ernie Jr. filled his with books and then very intently ran to the outside shelter, putting his prize pet guinea pigs into two cages that he pushed into the back of our station wagon. Beverly grabbed an overnight suitcase from her closet and filled it with some clothes and the Bible that she treasured from her Grandpa. Then she franticly ran to corral her cat, Frannie Baby.

I don't remember what Craig brought with us, but I remember he did not bring shoes and so was barefoot for the whole time we were evacuated. Ernie got the family documents and photographs; I yelled for him to get my portable sewing machine while I tried to think of everything I'd need for three-month-old Stephen.

We jumped into our jam-packed station wagon and joined a line of cars trying to flee the fire. There was some nervous screaming as we watched burning embers blowing toward us at high speed while we waited. We were all together, but would we be safe? It was a time of greatest anxiety and prayer, and I kept saying to myself that we should no longer live in this beautiful city or in Oakleigh. We were hard-wired with the need to feel safe and to provide protection for the family, and at that moment, this neighborhood no longer felt like a safe place to live.

We had dear friends, a young couple who lived near the university, which was far from the fire and close to the Pacific Ocean shoreline, who allowed us to stay with them. He was a colleague of Ernie's; she was a schoolteacher, and both had very caring and understanding hearts. I marvel that they took us in with our four children and all of our odd paraphernalia for the three days and nights when we had no place to live. They agonized with us over the fact that Beverly never found Frannie Baby and we had been forced to drive away without her.

I think we stayed up most of the first night listening to the news. In the morning, Ernie called a friend from Westmont College to see if he could learn any news about our house and the college. To our great surprise and wonder, Ernie was told that some Westmont students had battled the fire in the burning timbers all around our house during the whole night and actually saved our house from any destruction. How we thanked God for all the protection and favor! However, even as we rejoiced because our house was safe, we were grieved to learn of serious damage to some of the buildings on the Westmont campus.

It was three days before we were permitted to return to the fire-scarred area, and we worried greatly during those days about our cat, Frannie Baby. When we returned, we rejoiced at seeing our beloved house but were grieved to see so much had been destroyed around us. Beverly immediately began searching for her cat, calling and calling for her. After a while, she heard a weird, sad, crying sound, and followed it into an overgrown bushy area, where she spied her kitty cat, looking wide-eyed but moving through the briers toward the sound of Beverly's gentle voice. Dear Frannie Baby had used another of her nine lives, surviving the terrible wildfire.

Headed East

The Center for Coordinated Education project was funded for a three-year period and, as Ernie approached that deadline, he felt pleased to have fulfilled his goals. He had also been successful in having articles published in educational journals that described how collaboration between educational institutions could improve teaching and research and provide a way to share common concerns.

Dr. Samuel Gould, the president of UCSB who had recruited Ernie, had closely followed his progress and was keenly interested in the accomplishments of coordinated education. One day, Dr. Gould invited Ernie to his office and said he had been asked to accept the position of chancellor of the State University of New York (SUNY). He then asked Ernie to join him—as vice chancellor and executive dean.

The invitation and all it involved seemed very overwhelming. If Ernie accepted the role, we would have to move to Albany, New York, the location of the SUNY headquarters for the system's sixty-four campuses. Plus, the position would be another big step away from his doctoral training in medical audiology and speech pathology. Furthermore, it would mean leaving behind the joys of Oakleigh and learning to adjust to long, freezing winters with snow and ice, a big change after years enjoying the perfection of the Santa Barbara climate. All this would be hard to explain to the children and also to friends and relatives.

But truthfully, Ernie and I welcomed the offer; in fact, we were overjoyed! Only a few months earlier, we had suffered the trauma of almost losing all of our belongings in the wildfire. Lately, Ernie had been having some misgivings about what he would do when his work at the center was completed. Upland College was expecting him to return after the three-year leave, but this offer to work in Albany seemed right and promised to be the kind of challenge Ernie found exciting. To us, the offer was like a gift from God, presented with His perfect timing.

We took a flight to Albany to look for a house to buy that would please every family member. We agreed on the perfect choice at 29 Westover Road in Slingerlands, a ten-mile commute from Ernie's new office.

Even though we were excited, this parting from our dear California cousins, Ernie's brother Bill, my sister Esther, all our Oakleigh friends, and our Oakleigh lifestyle was the most difficult good-bye in all the good-byes we had made over the years. Ernie came up with the plan that we should bring a part of Oakleigh with us to lessen the painful parting and to ease the transition for the children. So we invited Jerry Shennum, everyone's favorite, to come with us to our Slingerlands home for the remaining summer months.

The big moving van with our worldly belongings pulled away in the summer of 1965. Our Upland family came to help with the final clean-up and to participate in the final sad send-off. After tears and prolonged lingering, we sadly pulled away.

Our station wagon was filled with the seven of us, plus our sweet dog Chico, and a cage holding Craig's pet squirrel. Ernie extended the middle seat by filling the floorboards with suitcases and placing a board across them and the seat to make a steady bed and play area for eleven-month-old Stephen Paul. (Even for our fourth baby, car seats were not yet on the market.) I sat on the seat next to the improvised baby bed, and Chico was very content to sit at my feet.

Ernie devised a seat-rotation strategy and planned sight-seeing excursions, and we played car games and always stopped early at motels with a swimming pool, making our cross-country car trip into a week of fun and adventure. We happily survived that memorable trip from Santa Barbara, California to Slingerlands, New York, arriving safe and sound on a perfect summer day.

Unfortunately, our arrival was marred somewhat when the cage door slipped open as Craig was lifting his pet squirrel out of the station wagon. The squirrel ran for freedom, and we never saw him again. Although the loss saddened us, we were all so completely taken by this big, empty house, the lawn, flowers, field, wooded area and a creek to be explored, that nothing could spoil our enthusiasm for long. We decided the squirrel was just as happy with his grand new home, as we were with ours—House #14, the Homestead Mansion. We felt life was a gracious gift, and we wanted to live it with joy in this beautiful setting.

CHAPTER 12

HOUSE 14

The Homestead Mansion

Slingerlands, New York

1965–1971

"Home ain't a place that gold can buy or get up in a minute; Afore it's a home, there's got to be a heap of living in it."

—Edgar Guest

In June 1965, we were about to begin a "heap of living" at 29 Westover Road in Slingerlands, New York, what we planned to be our family homestead. For Ernie and me, it felt like we were moving in the right direction—toward home. Albany was still a long day's drive from my Pennsylvania family, and Ernie's Dayton home was a two-day drive. Even so, it felt good to be within driving distance of lots of family.

Ernie and I had always thought of California as a temporary place to live, although we ended up living in California much longer than we had originally planned. We had no regrets; those years had been very happy and fulfilled ones, but Ernie felt that living east of the Mississippi River was more permanent and satisfying. I too felt a deep comfort in our move to the East.

This Homestead Mansion, located near Albany, appeared to have been built just to satisfy the exact needs of our family and our four children. The two-story, stone and wood frame house had six bedrooms upstairs, which gave us a room for each child, a master bedroom, and a guest room, along with three bathrooms.

I wish I could remember how our family decided on dividing up the rooms. My guess is that everyone agreed Ernie Jr. should have the largest room because he needed many bookshelves to hold his hundreds of books. His room also had a door that opened onto the attic staircase, which was an interesting place for his burgeoning model airplane display.

Beverly chose the sweet gem of a room with an interesting ceiling line and private bathroom. Craig, who was seldom in his room and didn't want to bother with many clothes or other possessions, was perfectly happy with a smaller room. We placed one-year-old Stephen Paul in the room adjacent to the master bedroom, which left a nice-sized guest room next to a bathroom.

I loved the cedar-wood closet in the upstairs hall, feeling like this was a special gift since I now had to care for wool clothing. Our California houses, not surprisingly, never included cedar closets.

Downstairs, a double arch led from a large living room with a fireplace to the music room with a piano and a door that opened onto the screened porch. Beyond the main entrance and the open stairway was the cheery dining room with a large picture window where we could enjoy views of my backyard flower gardens in the summer and piles of snow during Albany's long winters. My favorite spot was the kitchen because it was a gathering place with an eating area and a view of the outdoors. There was also a library-study room, and beyond that another staircase going upstairs and a staircase going down to the basement, which included a game room and lounge area.

In a separate basement room, I set up a pottery wheel and craft area. I had taken pottery classes at the Santa Barbara Community College, and Ernie bought me a pottery wheel for my birthday. I enjoyed pottery as a fun and useful hobby, making many Christmas gifts such as bowls, vases, and mugs. In the room with my pottery wheel, Ernie built a sandbox for Stephen Paul, and we set up a little art area for him. On winter days, he could be happily exercising his creativity while I was attempting to be creative—but with less success than young Stephen. In this workroom, I would busy myself with clay pottery projects on the nights when Ernie was gone for overnight campus visits. This late-night busyness also helped me to feel less lonely when he was away.

The Homestead Mansion was situated on a short half-circle street with little traffic outside of our neighbors in this friendly, unpretentious neighborhood. We had plenty of grass to mow on the two acres of our property, and Ernie made a path through a thicket hill that led to the creek and a wooded area that little Stephen loved as he grew older. On warmer days, Stephen would beg whoever was around to join him there for a picnic lunch, even persuading his Grandma Boyer, who was afraid of insects, to eat with him along the creek. When no one else was around, Stephen and I would picnic on our own. I enjoyed it as much as he did because of our discoveries in nature. Every spring we would look for the elderberry bushes that were a little hidden on that trail, gathering enough berries for me to make elderberry jam and an elderberry pie for a special treat.

Adjusting to a New Home

Before leaving Santa Barbara, we had arranged for the veterinarian to take care of Beverly's dear cat, Frannie Baby, while we were en route to our new home. The day after we arrived we got word that she would be put on an airplane in Santa Barbara the next day to fly to Albany. With great expectation, Ernie and the children went to the airport to meet Frannie Baby and bring her to our new home.

But when Beverly eagerly took Frannie Baby out of the travel cage, we immediately knew something was wrong. Poor Frannie Baby fell on her side when she tried to walk. All that night, Beverly sat and held her cat, putting little drops of milk from a medicine dropper into her dry mouth. Beverly's kitty cat lived through the night, but we knew she was terribly sick. The new veterinarian didn't give much hope, but Beverly did not give up and continued to care for Frannie Baby with a sweet, loving touch. By the second evening, the sick cat actually managed to take a few steps but could only walk sideways. Thanks to Beverly, Frannie Baby kept getting better and lived a total of nineteen years, although she always walked a bit sideways. Over the years, we've tried to figure out how many lives Frannie Baby lived in her long and adventurous life; we're pretty sure she lived all of her nine and then some.

It was great to have the children's good friend, Jerry Shennum, come with us for that first summer to help our children adjust away from our cherished Oakleigh neighborhood. Jerry was so friendly and likable that he helped our three older children make friends on our street and in the area near the school—much to Ernie's and my relief.

One girl, Debbie, told Beverly about a nearby swimming hole that was about seven feet deep and included a rope tied to a branch where you could swing out over the water. On many summer days, everyone would hop on their bikes and ride the four miles to the wonderful swimming hole, which turned out to be even more fun than our Oakleigh house swimming pool, especially with Jerry joining all of the others. We also enrolled the children in a two-week day camp, hoping they would make friends who could make their first school days easier. The children's adjustment to the cross-country move and lifestyle changes prompted by Ernie's new job was our major concern.

We were hoping the change of schools would be advantageous after Ernie Jr. and Beverly's uninspiring and sometimes scary experiences at Santa Barbara Junior High School, and the Voorheesville School proved small, safe, and low-key. It was a good and important change, especially for Ernie Jr., who was now a high school freshman. Beverly, who was an eighth grader, immediately felt welcomed and developed strong friendships. Ernie Jr. found it harder to adjust to leaving his Oakleigh friends so he settled in his room reading advanced literature. Craig made lots of friends in our neighborhood and soon made friends in his fifth-grade class who would go bicycling and exploring with him.

Welcoming New Challenges

We arrived at our new home in early June and had that month to work together to unpack the boxes and get the house settled. Ernie had a designer's sense about the best way to arrange furniture, and he knew what colors would enhance our home atmosphere. We were very grateful to have the month to settle in before he began his new job on July 1, 1965.

Ernie was thirty-six years old and was welcoming the new challenge. I was feeling his excitement and very eager to support him in every way possible. Together we felt contented and peaceful while looking forward to the new opportunities. We loved this larger Homestead House, which offered more possibilities to invite family and friends for overnight stays or even a reunion with our extended family.

Ernie would go to work at the State University of New York headquarters in Albany as vice chancellor for university-wide programs. The new chancellor, Samuel B. Gould, was hired with the mandate to build a distinguished university system, and he had recruited Ernie with the idea that they would re-create the State University of New York, which had begun a decade or two before, as what Ernie described as a "holding company for ten teachers' colleges and a handful of specialized institutes."

Ernie and Dr. Gould decided to strive for a great institution with many points of excellence, and the two of them spent long hours in conversation. Ernie was concerned about how to create a sense of unity while managing a diverse and sprawling university system. That was his function and focus as leader of university-wide programs.

The children and I had to find creative ways to adjust to his longer workdays and absences from the family when he traveled to campuses across the state, seeking top administrators and working to help develop programs at each campus. I have a copy of Ernie's calendar from 1966, the first full year in this position, and in its pages, I see clearly how Ernie took care to reserve regular times to ensure he would still be a vital part of our world back in Slingerlands.

He never tried to impress the children with the work he was doing; he only wanted to be closely connected to their world. His world and my world were always closely connected, no matter where he was. He would call me at least once each day; in these times long before cell phones it was sometimes very difficult to find a phone, but Ernie always managed. The best time to talk was at the end of the day, so that we could share details about our day and also help each other prepare for any challenges we anticipated for the next day.

Ernie fretted because he had always helped me with the children and the duties around the house, but now that his job was more demanding and we had four children and a bigger house, he felt that I was working too hard. Through a contact in the Mennonite Mental Health Board, where he continued even with his new SUNY role, Ernie learned about a Mennonite (MCC) Trainee Program that sounded like it could be the answer to his concern. This program selected young Mennonite women from European countries and brought them to the United States to live with a Christian family as a helper.

I liked the prospect of having some help, hoping someone from the Mennonite program could help us ward off some of the stress in our active household, and I was touched by Ernie's thoughtfulness. We were very fortunate when Christina Rueb, from the Netherlands, was assigned to our family. She was an excellent helper and delighted all of us with her energy, her many charming skills, her creativity, and her guitar playing and singing. In addition, she taught us so many things about her culture. For example, at Christmas she made gifts for everyone in the family and wrote original poems attached to each gift that were then placed at each bedroom door on Christmas morning. The charming and handmade surprises were a wonderful addition to our own Christmas traditions. We also took trips and did special things to teach her about the United States. She turned out to be everything Ernie had hoped for, becoming a friend for the whole family and an excellent helper for me.

Again we had to decide where we would worship on Sundays. There were no churches of our denomination in our area, but we were happy to find a Quaker meeting in downtown Albany. It was an active meeting, and we felt drawn to the worship, where each Sunday there was an earnest spirit of seeking and inspiration. I taught a children's class, and Ernie spoke often at the adult meeting.

Despite all the outside pressures and extra responsibilities, Ernie and I stayed strong and unshaken in our Christian beliefs and commitments, and even while being involved with the Quaker spirit-filled meeting, we remained loyal to the Brethren in Christ Church. Ernie's calendar even shows that he was a speaker at the Brethren General Conference in July 1966, and even chaired some youth sessions.

Success Brings More Responsibilities

Ernie held the position of vice chancellor for university-wide activities for three years, from 1965 to 1968. During those years, the university system was rapidly developing and gaining visibility, recruiting the best faculty in an effort to build a great network of sixty-four campuses. For example, Ernie found some of the campuses were particularly strong in the fine arts, with exceptional music and well-established art galleries. Those campuses then worked together to create a university-wide faculty committee on the arts that sponsored concerts, festivals, and worked with professional companies in theater and dance. This program, plus many other university-wide activities, blossomed and created positive outcomes, including gaining support from New York Governor Nelson Rockefeller.

In August of 1968, the university board of trustees appointed Ernie to the position of vice chancellor of the state university system. This position came with enormous responsibilities and demands, giving him executive authority in academic areas and the power to act in full command in Chancellor Gould's absence.

Ernie then focused on bringing the best people to the university, including strong presidents to lead each one of the campuses. He created a perpetuating faculty senate and met with them regularly and set up other groups to help direct important academic areas. Looking at his daily calendars for that period, I see his days were filled with activities in a wide scope of areas, such as budget hearings, development meetings on Equal Employment Opportunity programs, board of trustee meetings, faculty senate retreats, staff meetings, meetings with state legislators, and many speaking engagements.

Outside of his SUNY responsibilities, there was also travel to trustee meetings at several private colleges, such as Messiah College, where he served as a board of trustee member for twenty-seven years, six of them as chairman. A handwritten note on Ernie's 1968 calendar shows he cleared time to travel to Philadelphia to meet with the leadership of Temple University and discuss plans for a partner relationship with Messiah College. In essence, the plan called for Messiah College to acquire a group of row homes across from Temple University where some Messiah students and faculty would live. The Messiah faculty would also teach a couple of courses. Otherwise, the Messiah students would be enrolled in Temple programs, such as social work. Over the years the plan developed into a uniquely outstanding program that has benefited hundreds of Messiah College students.

Even with Ernie's increased responsibilities, there was always a way to make time for relaxation with the whole family. We enjoyed music and the arts together and we found great benefit from Ernie being a member of the board of directors of the Saratoga Arts Center in Saratoga Springs, New York, attending many concerts and performances with family and friends. It was the summer home of the Philadelphia Philharmonic Orchestra and the New York City Ballet Company, and each summer Ernie would arrange for all the university campus presidents and their spouses to enjoy an evening at a Saratoga Springs concert or ballet performance.

Family First, Always

Ernie made a great effort to have his meetings scheduled in Albany rather than some distant campus because he and I agreed that our family dinner time together was essential. Granted, it was not unusual for me and the children to have to wait for his arrival. When he would call and say he'd be home in half an hour, we would prepare ourselves for an hour. When he got home, his heart would be filled with eagerness to hear about all our activities and how each of us fared during the day and whether anyone had any new ideas that we would love to discuss over dinner. Ernie and I also looked forward to the later evening when we could be alone and share in great detail about our day's joys and hardships. This was our time for encouraging each other and for praying together.

Ernie tried to cultivate some interest in playing golf and hoped to get the boys interested. Ernie Jr. did not enjoy it very much, but Craig tried it with some success. Our Slingerlands neighbors, the Ardman family, had a boy, Michael, the same age as Stephen. As preschoolers and beyond to about second grade, Michael and Stephen spent a considerable amount of time together in delightful, childhood play. One warm, spring day when the tulips and daffodils were in full bloom and the kitchen window was open wide, I watched as they ran with swinging arms, yelling repeatedly, "God is everywhere!" They followed each other to every open lily flower, peering down into the open petal spaces, believing in simple faith that God was in each beautiful flower they discovered.

In the winter we all went ice skating at the neighborhood pond, and the children went on ski trips organized by the school. Ernie also loved to ski with the children. He teased them that they were not allowed to rush down the hill past him, but before long their skills far exceeded his. I was more comfortable on the short slopes of the golf course where Stephen and I skied in the afternoons after his school dismissed.

We loved the summer months in particular, when Ernie had a month of vacation. Through one of his campus friends he learned of a house that we could rent at Tully Lake, just east of the New York Finger Lakes. The next summer, when we rented the same house, I took a concentrated summer science course at nearby Utica College. Ernie strongly encouraged me and took charge of the family all on his own. With his creative mind and efficiency, it turned out to be a great vacation for them at the lake, and I had my own different kind of a vacation doing something I also loved doing.

The three older children had now adjusted to living in New York. Nevertheless, they still had ties to their Santa Barbara friends and we invited Jeanine, one of Beverly's friends, to come for the summer of 1966. She joined us on our July vacation to a national park in Maine, when we pulled the Boyer family pop-up trailer that could sleep all of us. We camped in a beautiful spot surrounded by nature's glory although I remember less about the location and more about campfires, roasting marshmallows and making s'mores—and cooking for our growing and seemingly always hungry children.

Through Ernie's friends at the Mennonite Mental Health Board, he learned about a bicycle trip in Indiana for Mennonite youth. Ernie talked it up to fourteen-year-old Craig, who was interested. He flew from our Maine vacation spot to Indiana to ride with this well-organized bicycling group.

Craig was quite confident in his abilities and excited about this adventure. I must admit Ernie and I were a little nervous to send him, but very pleased with the special opportunity for Craig to be with Christian youth.

Ernie's parents sold their business and retired, moving into a smaller house, still in Dayton. After several years his father, Clarence Boyer, started to have a constant low-grade fever that was a great concern because there seemed to be no clear diagnosis. Ernie consulted with a physician friend, Dr. Powers, who attended the Albany Quaker meeting. He suggested Ernie's father travel from Dayton to Albany so he could examine him. Thankfully, Dr. Powers did find the problem, but the treatment required a series of four surgeries, and the recovery took several years. The healing required Grandpa Boyer to completely rest his digestive track, so for a year he could not eat food and was permitted to drink only the same preparation developed to nourish astronauts in space. Craig was old enough to drive by this time, and every day he drove to the drugstore to get his grandpa's daily fresh supply of nurturing drink.

Grandpa was very sick and weak for a long period, but he was always in bright spirits and so interested in everyone's activities. He was gentle, never complained, and we all joyfully gave him care. It was clear that Grandpa and Grandma Boyer could not return to their home in Ohio, so we prepared a room for them as their own space and warmly welcomed them as part of our household.

I remember the time when Grandpa was too sick to stand or walk and had lost so much weight that we did not even expect him to live. It was an emergency, and with urgency Ernie lifted him from the bed and carried him to our station wagon and transported him to the hospital. Remarkably, Ernie's father recovered and lived another twenty years. However, this period of his illness was a difficult time for Ernie's mother. With her sensitive heart, she felt that they were causing hardship for our family. She was unforgettably loving and caring and was a precious friend to me, helping in many more ways than she knew. Our children dearly loved their saintly grandparents and were richly blessed by their close relationship.

The Age of Student Activism

The story of this period, 1968 to 1970, would not be complete without mention of the student activism that caused considerable disruptions and even violence on many campuses across the U.S., including those of the SUNY system. Some campuses had only very minor interruptions, but Ernie needed to go to others to mediate any agitation.

By this time, Ernie Jr. and Beverly were students at Earlham College in Richmond, Indiana, and Craig was in high school and later at the State University of New York at Potsdam College. Like most students, our children were affected by what was going on around them. Craig took on a "hippie" look, with long hair and rather unconventional clothes. His high school art teacher painted yellow flowers on the shoes that Craig had painted red.

At Earlham, Ernie Jr. and Beverly took part in the social activism going on there. Beverly became a confirmed vegetarian when the college added that option in the cafeteria. Ernie and I kept an open, loving, and accepting manner, and, in the end, good prevailed within our children.

The student protests and demonstrations were primarily against the war in Vietnam, the draft, and racial injustice. Furthermore, those in leadership lost credibility simply for being a part of what the students perceived as the "establishment." Ernie's position as vice chancellor made students suspicious of him, but he told me that when he talked to the agitated students and looked in their eyes, he felt love for them. They were the same age as our own children. He wanted to listen and reason together and make sure each student was protected and respected.

Adding to his concern with the students and his efforts to help the struggling campus presidents was a conflicting attitude within the board of trustees. Several of the older, influential members insisted that Ernie should direct all the university campuses to take a firm-handed approach during student demonstrations, even to the point of utilizing the National Guard to protect the campuses.

Ernie and I shared prayerful times before he met each of these board members individually at scheduled lunches, attempting to use his reasoning and persuasive skills to convince them that the university's responsibility was to respect and wisely educate the students—without military force. His mind was firmly made up on this issue. In the end there were no serious incidents on any SUNY campuses, in contrast to the tragedy at Kent State University in Ohio where the National Guard was called to campus and several students were killed.

A Difficult Position, an Even More Difficult Move

About this time, in late 1969, Chancellor Gould resigned, which was greatly disturbing to the university system and to Ernie. Things seemed to happen rather quickly after that. There was a search for Dr. Gould's replacement; Ernie was asked to stand as a nominee. He did not apply, feeling that the vice chancellor position was difficult enough. Nevertheless, in late 1970, Ernie was notified that he and I were to meet with the board of trustees. We were escorted to the room adjoining the large board meeting room, where we waited with very strong emotions.

Ernie paced back and forth anxiously across the length of the room. He feared that the board was voting on the nominees and feared that he might be chosen, saying it was an impossible job that he did not want. I replied that it was not too late and urged him to signal the chair, Elizabeth Luce Moore, that he absolutely wanted his name withdrawn as a nominee. Together we walked to the door; just as Ernie reached for the door, it was flung wide open, and a large number of trustees were standing, clapping, and yelling, "Congratulations!"

Ernie was speechless, and I was dumbfounded. We must have been in shock as our minds flashed to what it would mean for our family for Ernie to serve as chancellor of the State University of New York, the largest university system in the nation.

Events escalated from there, with a large reception, media interviews, and many demands on where we needed to be and what was required. Ernie's greatest concern was to protect the children from changes and to protect my time that I wished to save for the family. My mind was swimming with respect and pride for Ernie. At the same time I was fearful of what it would all mean for him and the family.

On April 6, 1971, Ernie, at the age of forty-two, was formally inaugurated as chancellor of the State University of New York at a ceremony at the University Center on the Albany Campus. He made it clear to the planners that he did not want an ostentatious affair and asked for the least amount of money possible to be spent on the ceremony. He chose a hall at the University Center, in part, because it had only 500 seats. He had been to many inaugurations with thousands of people attending and wanted to avoid such an expense and fuss. Part of his rationale was his own humility and discomfort with such events. Part of it also had to do with the considerable public scrutiny universities were facing at that time.

Governor Nelson Rockefeller spoke at the ceremony and said:

> We find ourselves at a critical moment in the University's life and Dr. Boyer is the kind of creative administrator these times demand. In our young Chancellor we have a perceptive bridge between the generations. The students know this. They are constantly in his office. They are constantly in his home. They are very much in his life.

I was not as experienced at hand shaking as "Happy" Rockefeller, the governor's wife, who was standing next to me in the reception line after the beautiful ceremony. Many of our family members were there, including Ernie's parents and my mother. Few young people in this the era wore dress-up clothes, but our children did so for this very special event, honoring their father. All 500 of the guests came through the line to greet the new chancellor, his wife, Governor and Mrs. Rockefeller, members of the board of trustees, and other dignitaries. No one else in the line seemed to find it as exhausting as I did. Ernie was holding up well, but I do not ever remember being so exhausted. It must have been just too emotionally draining for me.

Ernie and I were just beginning to learn about dealing with the stress this new position would cause in our family's lifestyle. His first request to the board of trustees was permission to remain in our cherished Homestead Mansion, and they easily granted it. The family was very grateful because it meant we did not have to move into the state-owned Chancellor House at 40 Marion Avenue in Albany. Along with the board's kindness in agreeing that we could stay in our own home, they also provided a housekeeper who came to our Slingerlands' home. They wished to free my time so that I could be available to help Ernie offer hospitality during the many activities that would be scheduled at Chancellor House.

It was then decided that the state-owned Chancellor House would be used regularly for meetings such as those of the faculty senate, the council of campus presidents, the student association leaders, and retreats for the staff—all with my hosting, menu planning, and making catering arrangements for the various group lunches and dinners. It seemed like an excellent use of this large house, which was meant for the chancellor's use. Having the house available for these group meetings was especially important for Ernie's style of leadership, which was characterized by collaborative discussions and hospitality. Even better, Ernie and I were thrilled that there would be minimal changes and interruptions in our cherished family home.

However, that all changed radically about six months later when Chancellor House was pictured on the front page of the Albany newspaper with the headline, "New Chancellor Boyer Refuses to Live in State-Owned Home." The articles continued day after day, filled with angry words about how the university was wasting state money but no mention of the regular, ongoing use of the house for the benefit of moving the work of the university forward. The daily newspaper stories stirred up public reactions. Because of occasional turmoil on some of the campuses, there was already mistrust between the university and the community, and Ernie felt that we were caught in the middle.

We learned that both the newspaper editor and publisher were family men, and we felt they certainly would not want to be forced from their homes. Ernie made appointments to meet with each of them, but there was no reasoning with them. Ernie, with a most disappointed heart, told them they won and that he gave up. Against our wishes, we would live in Chancellor House.

We had faced conflicts before, but this seemed the most serious because it involved every aspect of our family life. We were most concerned about Stephen and Craig's school situations. Furthermore, we were deeply connected to every aspect of our Homestead Mansion home—more so than any of our other numerous homes.

Ernie Jr. and Beverly would not have their familiar rooms, which by now were extensions of their personalities, when they came home from college for the summers and holidays. None of us were attracted to the twenty-two-room Chancellor House. The children called it "the fortress" and said they would be ashamed to bring their friends there. To them it seemed to be representative of the "establishment," which the young adults especially abhorred. Ernie and I shared in their frustrations.

Ernie's mind churned over and over as he looked for solutions; together with the children and his parents, we discussed some possibilities and came up with a plan. Ernie's father was recovering slowly but steadily. All his surgeries were finished, and he was now on a liquid nourishment diet and could take care of himself. Since Craig did not want to move into Chancellor House, Grandma and Grandpa liked the idea of Craig staying in our Homestead House to help them and to be a grandson companion. He could do their errands, keep them company, and continue with his schooling at Voorheesville High School. I would drive Stephen from Chancellor House each morning to his same school and spend some time most days caring for our own house and any of Grandma and Grandpa Boyer's needs.

For the sake of the news reporters, Ernie and I and Stephen were living at the Chancellor House. In reality, we were living in both houses as we slowly looked for ways to live comfortably in a place we would never have chosen as home.

It was difficult for Ernie, who said he could not find any warm, cozy, intimate spaces in Chancellor House. It was more difficult for Stephen, a seven-year-old who was used to wide-open outdoor spaces and a next-door playmate. In contrast, this house, on an upscale street with almost no play area and certainly no children in sight, was the most distressing place we lived. We got Stephen a pet rabbit and a new dog, but they could not replace what he lost.

However, there are answers and peace for life's hard places that are given to us if we have faith and trust. Ernie learned there was a cabin for sale on the shore of Round Lake in the Berlin Mountains—a mere thirty-five-minute drive from Chancellor House. This would be the place for Stephen to have a reprieve from the repression of Chancellor House and a hideout for all the family.

We did a "heap of living" in the place that we had planned as our homestead. But, we had hoped for much more living there, and the lake cabin was our substitute to fill in for our loss. We bought the cabin property in June 1971, and it became Round Lake Cabin Mansion, House #15.

CHAPTER 13

HOUSE 15

The Round Lake Cabin Mansion

Berlin, New York

1971–1976

"There is beauty all around, there is joy in every sound, when there's love at home."

—J. D. Brunk

The lake cabin in the Berlin Mountains became our place of celebration. We were initially concerned about owning a second property, even a simple cabin-style place, and considered its extra cost and upkeep carefully. But we felt it would be a good thing to do for Stephen and good for all of us to have an informal place to go. It would also be a positive way of managing the trauma of having to move from our beloved Slingerlands home to a strangely cold and formal house. The simple informality of the cabin, where we could spend much of our time in the summer months, was a gift to ourselves for which we would be very thankful.

We purchased the lake cabin in June 1971, about the same time we officially moved to Chancellor House. That summer, and several subsequent summers, we retreated there, enjoying the peaceful haven. Grandma and Grandpa Boyer and the rest of the family would come and stay for several weeks at a time. On Sundays, we would gather in the living room, and Ernie would conduct our own little worship service. Sometimes he'd ask Grandpa to explain the Scripture while he sat and listened.

Ernie drove back and forth from the cabin to his university office in downtown Albany. He liked spending long evenings and Saturdays fixing up the outdoor area or rearranging the indoor furniture placement. We worked together to add our personal touches. Amazingly, the purchase price included all the furnishings which were durable and clean.

It was a log cabin, which we found to be rustic and cozy, with two bedrooms and a bathroom upstairs off a balcony overlooking the living room. This large living area stretched the width of the house and included a big stone fireplace, several couches, antique tables, and lounge chairs. Behind the living room was a hallway with a larger bedroom and bathroom at one end and an old-fashioned kitchen and an eating area at the other.

Two summers after we first purchased the cabin, we were wanting more entertaining space and a place to have cookouts during the frequent visits from extended family and friends. So, we had our young nephew Jeffery come from California to build a big front deck.

Standing on the deck and looking out over the lake provided an inspiring view. Remarkably, no motorboats were allowed on the lake, and that simple rule provided for us the tranquility of watching small sailboats, canoes, and rowboats peacefully gliding across the clean, clear water of the lake.

Ernie had no training in carpentry, but he could make the repairs that were needed around the cabin, and after some careful planning and calculations, he took on a big project he had been contemplating as a challenge, building a strong dock that extended out into the lake for launching small boats. The dock also became a place to sit and relax with a book or dangle our feet in the water while enjoying the view across the lake, contemplating the beauty of God's creation.

While Ernie sawed and hammered as he was building the dock, his most fascinated observer, our eight-year-old, Stephen, was by his side from morning to evening. One evening, as they gathered up the tools and started the short uphill walk to the cabin, Stephen said, "Dad, I wish you were a carpenter, instead of . . . you know what."

When Ernie told of that incident, he said he regretted that his intense daily work at the State University of New York seemed to show no results, concluding that his job was meaningless to his son, who thought he was merely carrying around a briefcase overflowing with papers. Ernie freely admitted that it was very satisfying to slosh around in the lake water, making something that visibly had a clear purpose. He still kept his "paper carrying" job, but he always had great respect for those who worked with their hands.

The three older children worked summer jobs, but they came to the cabin as often as they could. All three were strong swimmers, and their favorite sport was to challenge each other in a race swimming across the lake. It was a comparatively small lake—about a quarter-mile wide and a half-mile long. With no motor boats to interfere, they would safely race across the lake to the far shore. I was always uneasy when I could not see them, off in the distance. Then they would have to swim all the way back. Ernie could swim the distance across, but he preferred to do it by gently swimming side by side with the children.

At the farm where I grew up, surrounded by hay fields and cow pastures, and with only a knee-deep creek nearby, I had missed the opportunity to become a strong swimmer at an early age as our children did, and I could not comprehend their strong confidence in water. I contented myself by swimming to the big dock built by the lake association, which was only about thirty yards from the sandy, manmade beach.

Come Sail Away

In this relaxing, easy atmosphere, many fun things happened. When my brother visited, he quickly noticed that Stephen busied himself putting together things that could float and hopefully would be strong enough to hold him up in the water. Their two creative minds started to work together. They found some scrap wood in the crawl space under the cabin and worked energetically to hammer together these odd scraps into a raft that could float and hold Stephen in a sitting or lying down position. They improvised a sail to catch the wind, and Stephen was euphoric with their big success. It was a bit scary for me and Ernie to realize our eight-year-old, a would-be sailor, could go sailing off across the lake. So his Dad tied a rope to the crude floating contraption and attached the rope to our new dock. Now he could sail—as far as the rope would allow—and all was well.

Clearly, no one in our family was a real sailor, but we all wanted to support Stephen's efforts, so we did something rather silly and, some might say, a bit shameful. One of us saw an advertisement and a coupon in a magazine from Kool cigarettes for a free Styrofoam sailboat. Thinking of Stephen's crude efforts to sail, I decided to send off the coupon. We were amazed when a boat actually arrived in the mail. The boat needed to be assembled, but we were ashamed of the large advertisement for Kool cigarettes boldly printed across the sail. Certainly, we did not want our young son promoting cigarettes, so Ernie painted over the advertisement with dark paint.

Fortunately, the dark paint worked, and our son could now sail about the lake without becoming a floating cigarette advertisement. Surprisingly, it turned out to be a well-designed boat that sailed like magic. It was just the right size for two people to manipulate the sail and move across the lake—feeling like true sailors. That unique little sailboat was the beginning of many sailing adventures for Stephen and his son Avery. In 2011, at age eighteen, Avery saved enough money to purchase a fine sailboat that he sails in the waters near Ithaca, New York, where his family lives.

For the five years that we lived in Chancellor House Mansion, we spent as much time as possible at the Round Lake Cabin Mansion each summer. Here we could enjoy our normal lifestyle, and it was no hardship for Ernie to make the thirty-five minute drive from the cabin to his office. After evenings and weekends at the cabin, he would be refreshed and ready to put his whole energy into his work.

But when school started each September, we sadly closed down everything, already looking forward to the next happy summer season. We were very grateful for what seemed like a gift bestowed by God as our hearts were replenished from the time we spent at our Round Lake Cabin Mansion.

CHAPTER 14

HOUSE 16

The Chancellor House Mansion

Albany, New York
1971–1976

Part I: House and Family

"The more a house experiences the passions of its inhabitants, the more at home those inhabitants will feel."

—Sarah Susanka

Although the state-owned Chancellor House, with its stately and dignified exterior and twenty-room interior splendor, was the only house we ever lived in that might rightfully be called a "mansion," it did not feel like our kind of mansion. All of our other houses were grand residences in our hearts' view. In reality, many were small, old, and of lower grade, but they were mansions in terms of the ways they nurtured our family and cultivated memories that would last a lifetime.

The Chancellor House, on the other hand, was truly grand in the eyes of many, but it was difficult for us, initially at least, to see it as a nurturing place. In fact, this mansion at 40 Marion Avenue in Albany was a very strange house for our family. The second floor had only two bedrooms as the rest of the upstairs space was taken over by a large hall and living room area that was accessible either by a grand staircase or an elevator. The downstairs was dominated by a large dining room with its elegant chandelier and an oversized kitchen, pantry, and service rooms. The dining room and service area were connected by a foot buzzer used to summon the kitchen help.

The rest of the downstairs was chopped up into a guest waiting room and doors leading to rooms of different sizes that seemed to be for unknown purposes. What a strange arrangement—would Ernie and I ever get used to this place? How could we ever turn it into a home?

Every room was decorated with top-of-the-line, formal-style furnishings. We kept looking for a cozy corner or two, but I fear, in the end, we could not find one. Our spirits sagged as we ambled about the mansion in search of something that resembled the warmth and glow of our former "mansions." We decided there had to be a solution and resolved to figure out a way to turn Chancellor House into our hearts' view of a mansion, thereby assuring that The State University of New York would benefit from the investment it made in selecting Ernest L. Boyer as its second chancellor.

After much discussion, Ernie came up with the idea of moving our family quarters into the modest space above the three-car garage, where we could be tucked away from the public eye. The area probably was meant to be living space for the house service staff; it had a small kitchen, a bathroom, a small bedroom, and a long, narrow main room that stretched the length of the three garages. Truthfully, it was not very appealing, but Ernie was determined to turn it into a cozy spot for the family. He was able to envision a more livable and intimate family place disconnected from the main house, which would give us a sense of privacy and feel like a hidden apartment.

Together we found ways to make this area feel more like a family space, except for a serious flaw that made us deeply question if we could actually fit into this one-bedroom apartment arrangement. We needed two bedrooms—one for Stephen and one for Ernie and me. The only other space was a tiny room in a short hallway with one small window and three steps down. Ernie and I hoped to fit in a regular-size bed for us, but the room was only big enough for a twin-size bed, a tiny dresser, and a small desk. In the end, it was the only place for Stephen's room, but we so much regretted he did not have his own proper space after having to give up so much in this Chancellor House move.

There were regrets for Ernie Jr., Beverly, and Craig, too. When they came home from college for holidays and summertime, they had no space to call their own—like their own treasured spaces in our Slingerlands' homestead. Here our only choice was the third floor in the main house. It was just a big open area that was reached by a long narrow stairway entered through a hidden wooden door in the second-floor hallway. All we could do was divide this open area into three makeshift rooms, which were much too hot in the summer and too cold in the winter.

Not a Normal Move

Aside from all of that, moving into Chancellor House was not a casual event. Ernie was perceptive about the ways some crafty members of the media watched for a chance to tell a story. Using caution, he had staff from the central office of the university go through every room, nook, and cranny to itemize and photograph every piece of furniture, wall hanging, kitchen equipment, silver, china, crystal, and any other little item that could be found. Clearly, there would be a time when we would leave this house, and he wanted us to be protected by being able to check off the inventory list to be sure that everyone knew what belonged to the state-owned house and what was ours.

Here I am feeling a little sorry about providing so much negative narrative about the Chancellor House. It is important for me to say that in spite of so many negative factors, we quickly settled into our own version of a cozy apartment space. I can remember that we moved in praying to be equipped to face the challenge with enthusiastic energy. We did not bemoan these times of change but looked at them as new opportunities and new adventures that would be a blessing. We had the heart and determination to move joyfully through even these frustrating moments.

We did not move many of our own possessions to Chancellor House. We wanted our "Homestead Mansion" to remain undisturbed for Grandma, Grandpa, Craig, and our niece Carla, who were all living there.

After Stephen's school started that September, we closed down the lake cabin, and the three of us settled into the tiny apartment, working out a family routine and schedule. Ernie's university responsibilities kept rolling in, with each challenge appearing to be more urgent than the last. Ernie's schedule looked overwhelming to me. The secretary gave me his weekly calendars and then his daily schedule so I could clearly see when I needed to be present with him at events. Thankfully, we had learned how to support each other long before these days, and knew that, above all, we needed to constantly ask God to stand by us.

Our life here was destined to be very different than what we had experienced up to that point. We would be living in a public, state-owned house where people would frequently come in and out—some with their own keys. We loved a simple, private, family lifestyle, but here everything was much more complicated, more open. The demands and expectations of Ernie's leadership role were intensified beyond anything we had experienced.

I had always delighted in cooking and caring for the house and flower gardens, like a normal housewife and mother. Now I was surrounded by a staff of two housekeepers, three gardeners, and maintenance staff. They did all of the cleaning, laundry, and starching and ironing of Ernie's shirts, family clothes, and sheets. They made up the beds each day, answered the doorbell, and received guests. They had been trained to perform their duties well and had no plans to change their routine just because new Chancellor House residents had arrived. Everyone was polite and friendly as they tried to figure us out.

The lead housekeeper took her job seriously and seemed not to welcome any help from me. In fact, she made it clear the kitchen was her territory and was off limits to me except for weekends when she was off duty. Fortunately, I could cook our family meals in the apartment. I tried very hard to put myself in the housekeeper's shoes, but I must confess her rigidity was disheartening to me.

Ernie had always found that working outside was relaxing, but here he did not have a minute to think about it and so was glad to leave the mowing, trimming, and care of the swimming pool to the staff.

Offering Hospitality at Working Dinners

From our earliest days in Chancellor House, we felt it was important to reach out with warmth and hospitality to many groups. Ernie wanted to focus his leadership on students, so our first big event at Chancellor House was a large reception for student-body presidents, members of student senates, and student editors from all of the sixty-four SUNY campuses. A little later, we gave a reception to show friendship to the people living on our street, and then to a large group of members of the news media. Ernie and I shook hands with everyone and then moved among the guests to show friendship.

The main function of the house was as a gathering place for the daylong meetings, special lunches, and formal dinners. These could involve groups of the campus presidents, administrators, faculty leaders, student representatives, Ernie's central administrative staff, and others. The goal was to create a warm, friendly, home-like atmosphere that would make it easy to create personal connections. Ernie and I both made considerable efforts to remember each person's name at every event. This was all part of his leadership style, and I enjoyed working in partnership with him. I planned the menus and directed events, which gave me wonderful opportunities to meet many outstanding students, faculty members, and administrators.

Much food was prepared and catered for the house activities, and my schedule was full so that I had to keep organized by making lots of lists, recording all the menus and names of guests at each event. I never wanted to serve the same menu to any group twice.

I planned regular meetings with the campus presidents' spouses, all women given the male-dominated governance structure of higher education in the 1970s. We exchanged management ideas because all the wives were performing similar tasks on the individual campuses, which frustrated some who wanted to have more of their own time or wanted to be paid for their services. I made an effort to get salary support for the presidents' wives, but because

New York was in an economic recession, I fear I was not successful. Most of us worked beside our husbands without pay, very willingly and with pleasure.

One of Ernie's major roles was to deal with the state legislature, always seeking to insure sufficient funds for all sixty-four campuses. An effective way to maintain friendly, open relationships with the top-level senators and representatives responsible for funding the university system was to invite them, along with Ernie's legislative staff, to the Chancellor House for dinners. They would discuss hard issues but found being face-to-face over a delicious meal was always helpful.

These dinners were never completely relaxing for me as I served as hostess at one end of the table, while Ernie hosted the other end. It was during these kinds of events that I became comfortable with that fancy floor buzzer to signal the servers when it was time to clear for the next course. Prior to each event, Ernie always gave me a thorough briefing on who would be attending and what issues would be discussed. These dinner meetings were friendly in tone, often long, sometimes quite tedious—but always very interesting. Warm, cordial good-byes were Ernie's signal that his goals for the university had been met that evening.

The dinners for media members called for a special kind of caution. Some of them liked to corner me and ask questions about Ernie's plans or for details about family affairs. I learned to show friendship and say very little, preferring to let Ernie give all the answers.

Not all events were tense. In my journal I wrote of a formal dinner for campus university presidents—Emmett Fields (Albany), Cliff Clark (Binghamton), Bob Ketter (Buffalo), and Alec Pond (Stony Brook), along with their spouses. They were our good friends, and Ernie liked to bring them together as working colleagues. It was an evening of socializing and friendly campus comparisons, and Ernie was complimentary about their attitude of willingness to share and support each other.

Making Chancellor House a Home

A couple of years after we had moved into Chancellor House Mansion, Craig was ready to leave the local high school and begin a year of studies at the

State University of New York, Potsdam. Miraculously, Grandpa Boyer had recovered by this time and was strong enough to function normally and even to drive. It was now possible for him and Grandma to live on their own, and we were thrilled to find a lovely little house that was perfectly suited for them just three blocks from Chancellor House.

Stephen could easily walk there and use it as a second home when it was necessary for me to be occupied with the house functions or traveling with Ernie. The joy was all ours to have Ernie's parents so accessible, and they loved the comfort of being close to family and being able to be helpful. Still, it was a big heartbreak when it was clear that we no longer would use the house that was the dearest of all our houses. Sadly, it was time to sell the Homestead Mansion; it sold quickly but felt like a loss for a very long time.

Having lost our family home, we made every effort to make Chancellor House feel more like our home, but we never asked the university to spend money to make house renovations. Still, Ernie found a way to conveniently use a section of two adjoining rooms downstairs for a family living room as well as small meetings and luncheons. We moved some of our own furniture into the house, and again, with work we established a very cozy living area. Ernie and I laughed when we looked around our newly created warm and cozy area, remembering our frustration when we first walked through all the rooms trying to find just one corner that felt like home.

Over time, we migrated more and more from the isolation of the apartment above the garage to this more comfortable living space. Our niece, Carla, was a student in Albany, and we decided to completely move from that upstairs apartment and turn it over to her. Stephen was happy to move from the closet-sized room to a bright bedroom where he even had space for a housebroken pet rabbit named Thumper. Ernie and I moved into the main bedroom across the hall. We now had no guest rooms, but Grandma and Grandpa helped us out by sharing their guest room. Some of our most pleasant memories of Chancellor House are the many family events in this downstairs space, including the day that our first grandchild, Nathan, delighted us with his first early steps.

New Cultures, New Adventures

In the midst of the constant bustle of energetic activity, we were thrilled to see our older children branching out into activities of their own, even though we missed being with them full-time. By the mid-1970s, Ernie Jr. and Beverly were both students at Earlham College, and they both went to study abroad in Tokyo at Waseda University during the 1973–74 school year.

Craig was then a student at the State University of New York, Potsdam but was not happy living in the college dormitory. He had saved several thousand dollars, and with that he bought ten acres of land with a tumble-down house and an old-fashioned barn in a very depressed area of upstate New York. There were vacated and deteriorating farms all around him. But he felt it was the perfect place to set up housekeeping with a vegetable garden, chickens, and a few animals.

Ernie and I felt that the 1973 Christmas holiday provided the opportune time for the four of us to fly to Japan and gather the whole family for two grand weeks together. Ernie Jr. and Beverly wanted to share so much with us about their life in Japan. All six of us embraced this time together in Japanese style, trying the public bath houses and eating food with chopsticks at a low table while sitting on the floor. We thrilled at the speed of the bullet train that took us from Tokyo to Kyoto to see the famous and spectacular moss gardens. My heart could not take in all the beauty; it was as if angels had planted those garden formations on purpose to give us overflowing joy.

Ernie Jr. and Beverly's host families—along with everyone else we met—extended the warmest of hospitality, and we were sad when it was time to leave our children and this relaxing time we enjoyed together. As we were saying good-bye, the father of the home where Ernie Jr. was living struggled to tell us something about our son, but his limited English made it hard for him to find the right words to express his sentiments. Then his expression lightened as he smiled and said in English, "You breed well." It was a happy send-off.

A Frightening Trip

There were other adventures for the family, which we remember most dearly. One exciting and unusual experience turned out to be too risky for me to ever try again. This was a vacation for Stephen, Ernie, and me as the older children were too occupied with their own pursuits to join us. The three of us traveled to Utah to take a long river-rafting trip on the Snake River, sleeping out at night under the stars.

The river was high, and on our last day we hit some serious rapids with drops of eight or more feet. We hung on to the raft for dear life as we went down one fall after another, completely immersed into the water. Suddenly, Stephen, who was sitting in the front of the raft, was washed overboard. I saw him go over, and I screamed to God to save him. Stephen's life jacket brought him back to the surface where he was able to grab onto the raft. Ernie, like a flash, grabbed hold of Stephen's wrist and hoisted him back in the raft. What a scare and what immediate help!

Stephen was not all that frightened and even thought it was a fun adventure. However, Ernie and I had a different response. This trip had not been my choice for a vacation; I liked the sleeping under the stars part but was uneasy about the rapids. Ernie had been somewhat concerned about the rough, fast moving river, but he had been assured that the guides were the best.

As parents, we wanted to be versatile and decided to try a new activity that satisfied our son's adventuresome spirit. Looking back, I am so grateful that we overcame our concerns, for in the end we had another powerful example of God's care. Over the years, Ernie and I continued to say "thank you" to God for helping our son to safety that day.

Vacations on the Farm

We spent as much time as possible at our Round Lake Cabin Mansion, but after Craig bought his rundown house, Ernie and I chose to use our vacation time to stay with him and help with major improvements and household projects. We loved helping him and visited him for the three summers that he lived there.

I suspect that Ernie would say it was his favorite vacation spot, and I would agree. We helped harvest the vegetable garden, and I came prepared to can many quarts of the vegetables for the harsh and long winters of upstate New York. Meanwhile, Ernie and Stephen helped Craig with big tasks. They raised the sloping porch roof, installed new flooring, partitioned rooms, and cleared more land. There were eggs to collect and a pet pig that wanted attention. "Piggie" learned to stand on his back legs and put his front feet on the top of the barnyard fence so he could be pet, making noisy grunts for more tickles behind his ears. What a delightful way for us to work together and enjoy a fun and healthy two weeks while relaxing from the intensity of leadership of the State University of New York.

A Mennonite group of five families purchased deserted farms and moved into this depressed area, becoming Craig's very gentle and caring neighbors. They invited him to their homes for meals, and he helped them rebuild their broken-down barns and houses. They invited him to join them for their Sunday church services, which were held in a deserted one-room schoolhouse they were able to purchase and refurbish.

Through their kindness and example of true Christian love, Craig became a Christian. He says he knows that during his restless teen years his heart was searching for the peace that he had found there. As his parents, it was also our pleasure to become friends with these people who had come to mean so much to Craig.

A Silver Celebration

We shared many memorable moments at Chancellor House, but one I will never forget took place on August 26, 1975. The setting was the largest room in Chancellor House—the formal, grand living room. The momentous occasion was our twenty-fifth wedding anniversary. It was Ernie's idea to invite our extended family to a celebration ceremony where we would renew our wedding vows by repeating them to each other again. We had memorized the words of the vows for our August 26, 1950, wedding ceremony, and so we rehearsed the words for the August 26, 1975, ceremony.

Ernie dressed in his best dark suit and wore a boutonniere on the lapel. For several months I watched my calorie intake, in hopes that I could fit into my wedding dress. The dress was pressed to perfection and I was relieved to find I could get into it. Ernie ordered a bouquet with a white orchid and trailing white stephanotis blossoms between the gardenias, to match my first bridal bouquet. Beverly had practiced playing the "Wedding March" on the piano. I baked and decorated a small, three-layer wedding cake with a bride and groom on top.

The hour came, and our family gathered. Ernie waited for his bride of twenty-five years to enter and walk the length of the room, to her groom of twenty-five years, in step to the music played by our daughter. It was a holy, solemn and loving exchange of vows. Ernie said:

> I, Ernest, take you, Kathryn, to be my wife, to have and to hold from this day forward, for better or for worse, for richer or for poorer, in sickness and in health, to love and to cherish, until death do us part. What God hath joined together, let no man put asunder. This is my solemn vow in the name of the Father, Son, and Holy Spirit.

I then said, "I, Kathryn, take you Ernest, to be my husband . . . " and repeated the same vow to him. We both broke down with deeply emotional tears as we ended with the endearing promise, "until death do us part."

Those vows were willingly said, and everyone was ready to enjoy the anniversary wedding meal with toasts and gaiety and the traditional wedding cake. What a fond remembrance of Chancellor House! One that I will never forget.

An Island Retreat

For a number of Christmas holidays, our whole family went to Jekyll Island, Georgia—a warm place that put us into a state of supreme happiness along with the joy of Christmas. This pristine barrier island had miles of white sand beaches off the coastline. The waters were not warm enough for much swimming, but there was plenty of warm sunshine and a wealth of sea life and sea shells.

Our most fun was when the bunch of us would hop on our rented bicycles and together discover places and facts about Jekyll Island's rich history, exploring many of nature's mysteries that were unique to this oceanside paradise. It usually ended up with an exciting bike race or playing hide-and-go-seek.

How I dreaded the moment when I would have to think about packing up and leaving all this family fun and our comfortable rented cottage to return to Chancellor House. We all felt free and relaxed for the whole week we spent at this place, and I was free from the headaches I had begun suffering when we moved to the Chancellor House.

My headaches would return as we prepared to head home. In addition to the media attention and other public pressures, I struggled in my relationship with the lead housekeeper who took her job so seriously. She had a kind heart, but her need to control the household was very disruptive, and dealing with her was a challenge to my core values of staying upbeat and positive.

Before going to Jekyll Island, the stress seemed to be getting worse and was giving me excruciating headaches. One afternoon, Ernie and I sat on the porch and watched the waves almost magically splashing onto the beach with their calming, mesmerizing beat. I heaved a big sigh and said, "I can't leave this peaceful place and go back home to all the stress generated by the domineering housekeeper." He gently took my hand and with determination declared: "I'll find another job for her and present it as a promotion." I immediately felt a happy relief. When we returned home he planned a kindly transition that would benefit everyone.

Dear Stella then became the single housekeeper, and she was beloved by everyone for her sweet, gentle, and efficient ways. I loved helping her with the household chores. We had good times, like sisters. Finally, the family got to use the large kitchen. Stella was never critical, nor did she declare spaces off limits. We all felt relief and soon felt more at home at Chancellor House. It would never be our ideal home sanctuary, but it was getting closer.

Part II: Accomplishments in the Midst of Challenges

While we were struggling to make Chancellor House a home and adjusting to the changes occurring in our family, Ernie was making great strides at SUNY. Early on at Chancellor House, very exciting discussions were taking place late into the evenings among a small group Ernie called together to talk about starting a new college. He speculated for some time about the possibility of organizing—within the network of SUNY's traditional colleges—a nontraditional institution that would depend not on the rigidity of the calendar or class schedule but rather on the creativity of the students and the abilities of faculty mentors. This idea was partly an outgrowth of Ernie's response to the student turmoil, as many student protesters had asked for an education with more relevance and flexibility. This new approach would make it possible for students to design their own educational programs that were entirely relevant to their interests, but with well-thought-out faculty direction.

In deciding who to invite to those evening discussions about this innovative college, Ernie looked for scholars who could take a dream and give it shape and direction. He carefully chose a small team, and the first person Ernie mentioned to me was James Hall, saying Jim seemed to bring together all the necessary qualities. That small team soon moved out of our house to Ernie's office, and a SUNY planning committee was formed.

Ernie and I talked long into the night about what name would suit this new institution and initially decided on the name "University College." But then a little later, during a wakeful night, he realized that "Empire State College" captured the spirit and purpose of the institution. The tradition at SUNY was to name a campus after its location, and this new college would serve all of New York—the Empire State—so Ernie said Empire State College was the logical name. I too knew it was just right. The trustees soon endorsed it, and Empire State College was born.

It was a very bold move. But the board found the idea appealing and the governor agreed that the country would be greatly enriched if SUNY could build a truly diversified system of higher education. In time, even legislators liked the idea because it did not require funds to build a big new campus.

In 1971, Jim Hall was inaugurated as the first president of Empire State College, where he served until 1997. In a tribute to Jim Hall on the occasion of the school's twenty-fifth anniversary, Ernie wrote:

> It is truly remarkable that Empire State College, in its twenty-five year history, has had one president to give shape and policy direction and constancy. And I have unrestrained admiration for what he has accomplished and am absolutely confident that no one in America could have built so solidly and brilliantly this new college which has, during the past quarter century, emerged as one of the world's most distinctive and most prestigious institutions.

In January 1971, Ernie spoke with optimism in an interview with Richard Bonnabeau, saying SUNY was "coming out of a discouraging period. For three years, at least, the Board had confronted student unrest and legislative threats to close down campuses because of drugs and riots. So the very fact that an educational innovation had come along was refreshing."

Today I look back with wonder at the persistence and hard work of a large number of highly motivated, brilliant minds whose endless planning created a new college that has since become the archetype for other schools across the country.

Personal Triumph at Empire State

My heart holds a special fondness for Empire State. I had been trying for a long while to build up more college credits toward finishing my own bachelor's degree. Again, while living in Chancellor House, I revived that dream and went to talk to the dean of a small, private college in Albany. I gave her the record of all my college credits and asked if the college would accept these credits. According to my calculations I could have completed all requirements for a degree in one year. The dean of this college, which I won't name here, kindly listened to my reasoning, then sweetly replied: "Mrs. Boyer, we will be very happy to receive you in our freshman class in September," making it clear that I would lose all my previous credits and need to start over again.

I walked out of her office so discouraged. Ernie was also disappointed but explained to me that she probably had no other choice because of the rigid nature of the educational tradition she was working in, and he assured me there must be many other very frustrated people in similar situations. My experience made him even more determined to make education more accessible to the thousands of people like me.

Today there are more than 60,000 graduates of Empire State, and I was one of the first ones, graduating with a degree in health sciences. Although the unique nature of Empire State made it possible for me to complete my degree, the standards required to get approval for graduation were (and remain) very rigorous. Getting that diploma in my hand was truly a dream come true and granted Ernie a very special measure of satisfaction. Our son Stephen Paul and our grandson Gabriel followed me at Empire State. My heart continues to marvel at what my husband began.

Demonstrations and Confrontations

Of course, Ernie's job included many challenges as well as many accomplishments. One of his biggest challenges was dealing with students, as the period of student demonstrations continued well after Ernie moved from vice chancellor to chancellor. Tensions seemed to heighten when campus-wide student organizations planned for larger student protests on a number of issues, including demonstrations supporting impeaching President Nixon and opposing a tuition increase. More than once a group of students marched into Ernie's office, locked the door, and held him captive. On one occasion, they kept him there until morning.

I was always fearful that he might be harmed in these types of incidents, but Ernie would reassure me and tell me not to worry. While he was being held overnight, I got regular reports from wait staff as the hours passed. I knew in my heart that he was all right and handling the situation, so I prayed and was not overly anxious. When he was free to tell me about that close encounter with the students, it became evident this would be a turning point in his career as chancellor.

Those hours with the students helped lay the groundwork for the agenda that shaped his leadership as chancellor of the State University of New York. The students told him they shared nothing in common with him or with their professors, stressing that their education was not relevant to their lives and saying the curriculum was too rigid, too directed. In addition, they were angry about tuition costs. Ernie was a good listener, and agreed with many of their complaints, and together they found they had commonalities based on shared human experience, which would become a major theme in Ernie's later writings. Ironically, that long night that students held him captive, he also had the students as his captive audience. It was a ready-made classroom situation for a discussion about what makes an effective education that would allow students to relate what they learn to their lives. They had opinions and good ideas but also became eager listeners as Ernie talked about how together they were seeking meaning and purpose and the sacredness of life.

Averting a Home Invasion

There was an even more dramatic moment one day when a group of students caught me off guard and gave me a really strange fright. It happened late one day after all of the workers had gone home and things were quiet at Chancellor House. I was so happy to have privacy and was feeling free and relaxed until suddenly the doorbell rang at the back door, the one next to the driveway. I was not expecting anyone and was surprised by the interruption. When I opened the door I was very startled to find a dozen shaggy-looking students.

The all-male group was unshaved, uncombed, and their clothes gave off the immediate impression of being unwashed and even slept-in. Each one carried a backpack stuffed with a sleeping bag. I was immediately very uneasy and suspicious about their intent. The spokesperson blurted out that this house belonged to them and that they were all moving in—just like that. In that most frightful moment, my mind envisioned our family homeless as students moved in and camped out all over this clean and cared-for house.

Right at that very moment they took claim of the house that we never chose but by now had settled into. Several started to push through the half-opened door, and the others started to move in closer. I felt panicked and helpless, and I am sure I turned pale as I felt deep shock by their plan. But I was able to hold the door firmly and send off a speedy prayer and then gently, yet loud enough for them all to hear, explained that they were right—this state house was theirs, as much as mine. I went on to say that we were asked to live there, and that there were very few bedrooms and not enough room for them.

I then heard a voice from someone at the edge of the crowd say, "Let's go." More picked up on those words, "Let's go." It sounded like music to my ears. The main group of students suddenly understood and realized that we were fellow sojourners on this earth. Two of those near the door took hold of the bold leader and said, "Let's go." He did not resist, and they left as abruptly as they came.

With a pounding heart, I lifted the phone to call Ernie. My voice was quaking as I stammered out what had just happened. As I held the telephone to my ear, still shaking from my scare, I was thinking Ernie had been right when he paced the floor just before he was told he had been chosen as chancellor. At that moment, he had looked straight into my eyes and said it was an impossible job. After I got over my initial fright, I was very grateful for God's watchful eye and the positive outcome.

Winning Hearts and Minds

Many other times, student demonstrators would walk down the aisle of a crowded auditorium during a speech by Ernie or any other speaker and grab the microphone to yell slogans or lobby their cause. At one event, a group of students cornered Ernie and demanded to see the governor. Ernie said he would arrange such a meeting, all the while praying that it could happen. He and his staff knew Governor Rockefeller's top aide, and with Ernie's intervention, a rare meeting was arranged between the governor and the angry students.

Ernie went to the meeting and reported that Governor Rockefeller masterfully listened to their demands and calmed their frustrations with quiet answers. One student read an angry essay, and the governor thanked the student and asked if he could please have a copy. In the end, the students exchanged warm handshakes all around as they left the meeting.

There was a final climactic event about this same time. The board of trustees was meeting in a room on the eighth floor of a building in New York City where Ernie had an office and the university central office had a small staff. The meeting could not proceed because student demonstrators on the street below created such a serious disturbance. The trustees could hear chanting and loud calls through a bullhorn, all designed to get attention from the powers of the university.

Some of the trustees in that meeting on the eighth floor feared that the very survival of the university was at stake. Richard F. Bonnabeau described it as "a time of unprecedented turmoil" in *The Promise Continues.* Ernie left the trustee meeting and told the policemen standing guard in the hallway that he was going down to the street. They told him it was very unsafe and advised they would not go with him. Despite that response, Ernie went down the elevator and out into the street, alone.

He told me later that he simply walked into the noisy crowd and went up to a number of students and asked their names and questioned them about their families and hometowns. Taking the time to quietly move among many of the students, Ernie showed them respect, looking into their eyes and chatting. He did not tell them his name, but word spread throughout the crowd that there was someone among them posing as Chancellor Boyer.

The leader of the crowd, Andy Hugos, then jumped down from his stand, still holding the bullhorn. He recognized Ernie and introduced him as the chancellor and encouraged respect and peacefulness. After Ernie thanked Andy, he asked if he could please use the stand and bullhorn. Ernie, now in his amplified voice, told the crowd of hundreds of students that he wanted to hear their concerns and asked them to select a small number who could represent the group to come with him. Andy tells how some twenty-five students then followed Ernie to the eighth floor where they met with trustees and members of Ernie's staff. Arrangements were made for an official meeting in Albany with a group Ernie formed of helpful officials, including Elizabeth Luce Moore, chairwoman of the trustees. This whole event is a prime example of the power of Ernie's leadership.

It is interesting to note that Andy Hugos and my husband became lifelong friends, and in 2010, Andy was the speaker at a special event to recognize the Boyer Scholars at Messiah College. Years later the leader of these students wrote a letter to Ernie, thanking him for his life and for the witness Ernie offered during those turbulent years.

Advocating for Diversity

After many such events in the early to mid-1970s, things steadily returned to order. Throughout this difficult period, Ernie championed the rights of all students. In particular, he listened to the voices of the African American students and developed a conviction to serve as an advocate for them and to advocate for growing diversity on the SUNY campuses.

As the student protests decreased, Ernie could again focus on his many other urgent university responsibilities. It was still a young, developing university system that required attention and creative leadership. Ernie was in constant pursuit of the nation's best candidates for university presidential openings and tried to draw the world's top researchers to this growing, now highly recognized university. During this period, he hired Norman Manguni as the founding director of the State University of New York Press.

Ernie also demonstrated his innovative style by proposing another academic rank: university teacher. The designation of university teacher was prudently and sparingly given throughout SUNY to signify the best of the master teachers and to show that the university regarded excellence in teaching as a hallmark of success. He also initiated a five-year review of college presidents and negotiated the first undergraduate student exchange program with the Soviet Union.

Short Honeymoon, Long Struggle for Funding

I have related stories of events that occurred during the years we lived in Chancellor House, but I cannot really describe those years without discussing the reality of the serious fiscal crisis that hit the state of New York soon after Ernie became chancellor. Ernie described it simply by saying that the honeymoon period for the State University of New York ended shortly after he took over leadership.

Fortunately, Ernie had already begun plans for a new experimental college as one of his first initiatives—otherwise Empire State College might never have happened. Even so, for the idea to have a chance to succeed, he was forced to turn to his friends at the Ford Foundation and the Carnegie Corporation, receiving a $500,000 grant from each. Remarkably, on March 16, 1971, Governor Rockefeller noted his approval by writing, "This idea appeals to me so much, and I have included $200,000 for planning the experimental college in my Executive Budget." Ernie's first request for funds from the state legislature was rejected, but the next request was granted, thanks to an enormous amount of hard work from his excellent staff.

Each year the budget problems increased. On January 8, 1976, I wrote in my diary:

> Ernie went to the capitol yesterday to hear Hugh Carey [the new Governor] give the Annual State Message to the legislature. Other years Ernie was asked to draft a section on education. But this year there was no mention of education. At the follow-up luncheon at the

> Governor's Mansion, the Governor was friendly and told Ernie that he was sorry that education had to take so many cuts.

Perhaps the best way to demonstrate how the mounting pressure affected us is to continue with a couple of quotes from my diary. My January 8, 1976, entry continues:

> The news articles for the past days have been on how the University has to have the most lay-offs. Ernie resents this because he feels they are taking advantage of a healthy, efficient program. I must say that he keeps working really hard and believes that the University will survive, while he makes changes to improve it.

My next diary entry is from January 12, 1976. After describing the weekly, all-family dinner, I write again about the stress of Ernie's work responsibilities.

> After everyone left, Ernie took a nap. He felt depressed about facing another week. This is his sixth year as Chancellor and each year has become increasingly tougher. He feels the University has been treated unfairly with the budget cuts. I keep praying for the answer and I feel it will happen. Life is so wonderful and good.

A week later, I wrote:

> This week the miracle happened! Ernie is staying on top of the growing budget problems. He says he is worried about the human element and the morale, so in this one week he met with the 64 presidents, the faculty senate, the black caucus group, and the women's concern group. Then forty of the CSEA union group came here for lunch on Tuesday. For each group he gives out the spirit of hope. I was deeply touched and amazed at the encouragement I heard him give to the lunch group. But by Friday evening he was so tired. He has no time to rebuild his resources.

February 3, 1976:

> Ernie had a sore throat and felt bad before he left for the Board meeting in New York City. Now nine days later his throat still hurts and he is tired. Yesterday we had the worst winter blizzard in twelve years and he couldn't get to the doctor. We are scheduled to go to Cat Bay Island in the Bahamas, but at 4:00 AM Ernie woke- up from a deep sleep and said that this is the worst time to be gone because of the budget problem. In the morning he called Rita (his appointment secretary) and said to try to shorten the time away and find a place that has a telephone. Frankly, the place sounds like heaven—but this must not be the time for heaven. I don't care where we go but he must get away for a while. He got to the doctor who almost immediately diagnosed him and then confirmed with a very positive blood test that he has mononucleosis—a serious glandular fever with a great increase of mononuclear leukocytes in the blood. His resistance must be down because of his concern over the worst budget crisis in the history of the State University.

My diary goes on for pages about the weeks that followed. In reading through these pages I am reminded that during our great distress about his unusual illness and his anxiousness about the budget cuts, the very caring board chair, Mrs. Moore, and other board members stepped into the situation. Together, with the doctor's help, they ordered bed rest for Ernie. The very outstanding vice chancellor, Jim Kelly, came to the house to discuss priority issues, but Ernie was not allowed to attend the next board of trustees meeting—the first one he had ever missed.

After one week of rest, blood tests showed Ernie had improved enough for the doctor to give consent for him to fly to Lyford Cay, Nassau, in the Bahamas for a two-week rest in the warm sunshine. The trip was a most incredible gift from Jeanne Thayer, a longtime member of the university board. She arranged for Ernie, Stephen, and me to live in her beautiful home at the seaside under the care of her housemaid, who was a most outstanding cook.

The week after we returned from Nassau, I reported in my diary that Ernie's lymph nodes and spleen were normal and that he was "itching to get back full-swing." I noted that the illness gave him a chance to view the budget at a distance and he again felt the university could move ahead with strength and goodwill. In the diary entry I enthusiastically note that life is good and full of God's blessings for our life together—even in moments when the stress seems insurmountable.

A Beautiful Legacy

One of Ernie's most enduring legacies from these years, in my mind, is the one he left downtown Albany—home of the capital of the state of New York. The story begins with the plan that was approved for state funding to construct a large building to house the SUNY central administration offices in a wide, undeveloped area about five miles outside of Albany in the town of East Greenbush.

When Ernie first saw this isolated, open country, he felt in his heart that it was not right. Downtown Albany was depressed, with boarded-up stores and restaurants and nearly deserted streets. Ernie thought the plan to take hundreds of university personnel out of the city and across the Hudson River seemed to be ignoring a very serious problem.

The stately capitol building stood boldly on top of the hill, overlooking and facing what once had been the grand offices of the Delaware and Hudson (D&H) Railroad Company at the foot of State Street. Now, in 1973, these formerly grand offices were sadly deteriorating. Beautiful stone walls were crumbling; windows were broken; and the roof was badly in need of repair. Yet, Ernie already could envision how the D&H Building could appear if restored properly.

One Sunday, as we left our usual Friend's Meeting in Albany, instead of driving straight to our Chancellor House Mansion, Ernie drove to the D&H Building. We walked along the broken stone walkway looking for a place we might enter, when through a wide, dirty window, we saw a man with a green eyeshade sitting at a small desk. Stephen and I followed Ernie as he entered the door. The man, probably a hired watchman, said no trespassers were allowed. Ernie quietly explained why we were there and confided to him a bit about his dream of completely restoring it. The man's heart must have been moved because he said, if we were very careful, we could look through the building, but he was not sure the steps were passable because of many years of piled-up bat dung.

We continued on in spite of this warning, managing to climb the steps and moving carefully, watching out for broken floorboards, thick spider webs, and scurrying rats and mice. Ernie continued on up the narrow stairs into the tower, which we later learned was designed by renowned architect, Marcus T. Reynolds.

The space was huge, and Ernie clearly saw the incredible potential. Jim Warren, the vice chairman of the board of trustees and an Albany businessman, joined Ernie that week in another walk through the building. They talked to many others and then to Governor Rockefeller, who immediately understood how restoring the D&H Building to provide a much-needed space for the university central administration offices could also bring renewal to downtown Albany. The major renovation took two years and was completed in 1975. Ernie worked with the architects assigned to the project to design the tower area for the office of the chancellor and vice chancellor. He loved the view looking over the city on one side and the Hudson River on the other side.

All that is now in the long past, but several years ago I had the joy of going down State Street in Albany, and there, before my eyes, was the striking State University of New York/D&H Building standing beautifully and proudly—commanding the attention of all. To me it brought a flood of tears, of loving remembrances, and awe.

Not only was the D&H Building Ernie's legacy to the capital city of New York, but it also marked his legacy to the State University of New York. He gave SUNY seven years of earnest striving to help build a university system of world-wide distinction while offering his heart of caring, listening, and persistence.

Part III: Special Guests, Special Opportunities

Ernie's position as chancellor led to a number of opportunities and relationships that I could never have imagined in our early years together. As with most institutions of higher education, each member of the SUNY Board Of Trustees had social clout. Ernie and I did not try to play the social influence game but enjoyed each member as very caring and outstanding friends. The board members were appointed by the governor of New York, and as chancellor, Ernie served under their authority, so he made great effort to be thoroughly prepared for their monthly meetings since no major determinations for the university system were made without the board's approval.

Elizabeth Luce Moore, the sister of Henry Luce, who created *Time* and *Life* magazines, was an exceptionally effective leader as the board chairperson. She was unusually kind and thoughtful and also a close friend of Governor Nelson Rockefeller and New York First Lady Happy Rockefeller. Mrs. Moore very much wanted the Rockefellers to visit us at Chancellor House, partly because Ernie had invited artists from the SUNY campuses to exhibit their art at Chancellor House on a rotating basis. The governor was an art enthusiast, and Mrs. Moore wanted him to be aware of the excellence in campus-wide art activities that Ernie formally began in 1965.

Bolstered by Mrs. Moore's encouragement, Ernie and I extended an invitation midway through his tenure as chancellor to Governor and Mrs. Rockefeller and the twenty-six trustees for dinner at Chancellor House. Many evenings, as Ernie and I prepared for bedtime, we talked about how we would be able to actually pull off such an important event. We had no full-time events planner to work out every detail, but we did have a great staff, and I devoted much of my time to planning and finalizing arrangements. It was challenging and exciting.

The time arrived, and we were ready and full of anticipation. Our upstairs living room, bedecked with linens, china, flowers, place cards, and candles, looked beautiful and welcoming. Mrs. Moore had asked a board member to pray a blessing on the food and the evening. I have forgotten the menu, but I remember a leisurely evening of short speeches and lively discussions directed by Ernie. Near the end of the evening, Mrs. Moore whispered in my ear that she had told Governor and Mrs. Rockefeller that I would give them a tour of the house to show them the art hanging in the hallways and the various downstairs rooms. They were very gracious as I led them through the house, taking time to look at, analyze, and praise each piece of art.

Ernie and I had very much hoped that the governor would choose to buy at least one piece from a SUNY art professor. Instead, he stopped in front of a long-framed piece that included three of Stephen's finger paintings he had created when he was three or four years old. Pointing his finger at Stephen's art, Governor Rockefeller said to me, "I want to buy that one."

I was taken aback, but managed to say, "I'm so sorry, but that is the only piece not for sale—because it was painted by our son, Stephen. We treasure it." Governor Rockefeller understood and didn't press me on my firm decision. That special art piece has hung in all of our homes since that evening, more than three decades ago. It hangs in my home today as I write this memoir and serves as a constant reminder of how the smallest things can carry the greatest value.

The important and eventful evening ended well, and we were elated. At a time like this we could truly call Chancellor House "our house." It was perfectly adequate for what we asked of it that night.

Learning in the Mountains

For many summers Ernie was invited to conduct seminars at the Aspen Institute for Humanistic Studies in Colorado, where he engaged in intellectually compelling discussions centered on education issues. During the summer of 1975, Ernie led a workshop on state university systems, and presidents and administrators from all the state systems participated.

I had lived through years of constant exposure to all the issues. Yet I was curious about what I could learn and sat on the edge of the crowd. The program focused on such issues as recognizing the urgent need for the university to learn to live with creativity and constraint in a time of scarcity; broadening the concept of "student" to include learners of all ages; and examining aspects of student values, attitudes, and the Christian moral code. I was able to just get up and leave when the hours got long, hoping Ernie would soon adjourn the meeting so we could join with members of our family who were there with us in that beautiful setting.

These were bright interludes for us. Ernie so much looked forward to these experiences pursuing new ideas that he could take back home and apply to his work. It was also a refreshing break for us to be away from the expectations of Albany. But even here, at times, I felt saturated by academia; when alone with Ernie, I would say, "Let's take tomorrow afternoon alone with just our little family, and enjoy a mountain climb together." Hiking was my favorite thing to do. Ernie would do it and feel pleased with himself, but the next time he would say, "How about we swim this time?" That was his favorite activity.

There were many friends who loved to plan fun gatherings during these Aspen Institute evenings—skits, and other creative activities featuring the participants. Feeling young at heart, Ernie and I were once persuaded to do some kind of performance. Actually, Ernie had to talk me into it as he was much more of a performer that I was. Eventually, I did get into the spirit of it enough to go into Aspen with Ernie, where we bought two straw hats. We then made large, brightly colored cardboard rainbows and mounted them on the rims of our hats. Wearing these showy hats, we sang the tune "Somewhere over the Rainbow." The audience dealt kindly with us, but that was the beginning and the end of our show business career.

Misunderstandings and Painful Moments

Special opportunities and silly embarrassments were also a part of this life, which are both illustrated from this story that happened in Paris, where the university had an office and a staff. Ernie had been asked to travel to Paris to hold a seminar explaining the university's long-range plans; as the board of trustees had agreed that I would accompany him on these types of trips whenever possible, I went on this short trip to Paris.

It was an unusual but exciting experience because I had very limited exposure to the sophisticated world of a place like Paris, and I must have appeared quite naïve to our hosts. In fact, both Ernie and I were very ordinary people with plain and simple backgrounds, but I think Ernie avoided appearing that way because of his assured and open approach.

In my simple innocence, I made an appointment with a Parisian hairdresser the afternoon before a formal dinner. I could not speak the language to explain that I wanted a very simple style, and the stylist could not speak English. When all was over, I looked into the mirror and realized to my absolute horror that she had turned my long hair into an overpowering coiffure. With considerable embarrassment and self-consciousness, I made my way back to the hotel. By the time Ernie returned to the hotel room to get dressed for dinner, I was in tears. He was shocked at my strange appearance and together we tried to undo and redo my hair enough for me to join him in public.

That evening, I had to try my best to pretend to be poised and self-assured. As the time passed, I almost forgot my embarrassment because I became so enthralled with the endless array of culinary delights that were so exquisite to the palate and to the eye. The evening turned into a very pleasant occasion, full of delicious food and new friends.

That same year, the minister of education of Portugal invited Ernie to give the keynote address at a conference in Lisbon. We decided to use our own money to send Craig with his Dad, and I stayed home because it was a father-son trip. Ernie was eager to give our sixteen year-old son lots of fatherly, loving respect during his "hippie," acting-out years.

One evening the conference guests were invited to a reception and dinner hosted by the king of Portugal at the national palace. It was a formal, royal event in the grand setting of the king's palace with musicians playing background music in the polished, marble halls that reflected subtle lighting and hushed serenity. Ernie, in formal attire, and his six-foot, five-inch son with shoulder-length hair and dressed in blue jeans and tennis shoes walked into this stately setting to greet the king of Portugal.

Ernie properly greeted the king, and then turning to Craig, said, "Your Royal Highness, I'd like to introduce to you my son, Craig." Our not-so-well-dressed son very politely greeted the king, and together a proud and humble father and a very proud, self-satisfied son walked off together to the fancy dinner. They bought back the menu, in Portuguese, for me to see. I have lovingly saved that May 1972 memento as I have saved and cherished the memories of my husband's wisdom and love for each of his children.

Privileged to a Special Invitation

There is another category of events that perhaps comes under the classification of *privilege.* I can tell of one evening that definitely fits that category: attending the wedding reception following the marriage of U.S. Secretary of State Henry Kissinger to Nancy Maginnes at the Nelson Rockefeller Estate—the famous 2500 Foxhall Road, on the banks of the Hudson River.

I can't recall clearly how we got there, but I do vividly remember how overwhelmed Ernie and I were from the moment we approached the impressive entrance. Ernie and Dr. Kissinger had both served on the National Commission on the Financing of Postsecondary Education during Richard Nixon's administration. It so happened that they were seated side-by-side during their regular meetings in Washington DC. As a result of the relationship that Governor Rockefeller and Ernie shared, we were honored to receive an invitation to this wedding celebration.

Ernie always remembered a face, and as people stepped from the limousines pulling up to the entrance of the Rockefeller Estate, he would whisper their names to me. It was quite intriguing. When Barbara Walters walked in, she took Ernie by the arm and said, "Let's go and get seated." She startled both of us, but she rushed off to someone else when Ernie tried to introduce her to me.

We were ushered to a beautiful, wide terraced, garden area where rectangular tables for eight were elegantly set for the multicourse dinner. As we were escorted to our seating area, I was feeling nervous about who I might be sitting next to and whether I would be able carry on a conversation with that person. Ernie would not be able to brief me because he would be seated next to someone else. I was on my own, and it was certain that I would be seated next to someone who was accomplished and most likely famous.

It turned out that my name card was next to the name card of Ross Perot, who I knew was a Texan and one of the richest men in the country. Fortunately, I had just that week read a news magazine article about Perot, which described his distinct personality and the very successful business he founded—the Electronic Data Systems Corporation—that turned him into a multibillionaire. The news article also noted about how he was still driving a twenty-year-old Chevy, so I asked him about the car, and he was pleased to talk about it and tell me of his thrifty policies. He talked about many of his ideas, all of which he seemed to believe were absolutely right. Our conversation ended up involving the whole table, including Ernie. Long after that evening, he continued to contact Ernie to test some of his plans to improve schools in Texas.

It was a long evening of "toasts" to the bride and groom. But before we left, Governor Rockefeller told us that since we had shown him the art hanging in Chancellor House, he wanted to show us the art hanging on the walls of his house. What a collection and what a treat! I cannot begin to name them, but I remember pieces by Monet and Delaunay and many other artists who we had previously seen only in books or the best art museums. Then Governor Rockefeller took us to the rear garden area to see the lights that had been installed to shine on the rapids tumbling over and over on the river. The three of us stood there completely enthralled, looking at God's breathtaking, astonishing creation.

It was an evening of friendship and warmth and we left feeling that we were blessed to have been there.

Part IV: Seeing the World

Ernie and I shared so many fascinating, unforgettable times during the years he was chancellor. One memorable experience occurred in 1975 when Ernie and I traveled to Moscow with the full cast of the musical version of *The Wizard of Oz*. The theatre group was made up of SUNY students, under the direction of Patricia Snyder, the founding director of the State University of New York Children's Theater. Patricia had come to Ernie with the idea, which seemed an improbable idea to some, but to Ernie thought Patricia Snyder's idea was brilliant.

Accordingly, Ernie went to work getting the legislative approval to fund this innovative, artistic program. Ernie always welcomed people with fresh, creative ideas, and this promised to be such an unusual undertaking because it was a first of its kind. As it turned out, the group was invited to perform at the elegant Bolshoi Theater in Moscow, and members of the SUNY Board of Trustees chose to join Ernie and me as we made the long flight from New York City to Moscow. We were all eager to support our student performers.

On the night of the event, a huge crowd of Russian citizens jammed into the large theater. The performance was in English, but with all the fast-moving, exciting action including the Lion, the Tin Man, and the Scarecrow, the audience seemed spellbound with delight. The climax came when the SUNY cast sang in Russian, "Somewhere over the Rainbow," and at the curtain call the crowd applauded and stomped their feet for about twenty minutes. There was hardly a dry eye in the Bolshoi Theatre as people reached out to strangers and hugged them tightly and smiled though their tears. This performance came right in the midst of the Cold War, and Ernie and I and all the students were deeply moved by the sweet, unexpected uniting of hearts and sharing of love across two very different cultures during this time of political tension.

Once again, common ground expressed itself, mightily. Ernie and I both felt the hand of God expressing His loving approval.

Whirlwind Trips

Travel experiences for Ernie more typically were like the time in June 1974 when he went to Germany after being invited by Stephen Muller, the president of Johns Hopkins University, to speak at a higher education conference and work with a German group regarding problems in higher education in Germany. Ernie really wanted me to go along, but we agreed it would be best for me to stay home this time because our first grandchild was due to be born soon and several of our children were arriving home for the summer. In addition, his schedule for this trip was planned too tightly for my liking, meaning we would not have time together to share in the thrill of seeing even a little bit of this European country.

As I relate his schedule, you can easily understand why it was not the best trip for me to share with him. Ernie left Albany on a very early Monday morning flight to New York City where he spent the day in meetings before taking the overnight flight to Germany. He later told me that he may have slept an hour on that flight since he was working on his speech almost the whole time. He arrived an hour before he had to deliver that speech at the opening of the conference. True to Ernie's "can do attitude," he took just enough time to refresh himself by taking his usual hot bath before he was to speak.

Later, when we talked, Ernie didn't mention he was going without sleep because he knew I would be very disapproving. Nonetheless, he kept going on adrenaline, and his body responded in amazing ways. After his speech, he spent the whole day in back-to-back discussions of various problems in higher education. He told me the time was well spent because he found Germany's difficulties were far harder than anything he faced with SUNY.

The next morning my dear husband flew to Paris to meet with SUNY staff. The director of the SUNY Paris office had informed him they did not want him to send a substitute, insisting on what proved to be a daylong meeting. That evening he hosted a dinner to honor their diligent work and left Paris very early the next morning for Kennedy Airport.

His frantic schedule did not end there. After he returned from Paris, Ernie was scheduled to meet me at the Binghamton State campus, where the plan was to have dinner at the home of President and Mrs. Sig Smith, after which Ernie was to give the commencement address for that campus. A trustee couple drove me the four hours from Albany to Binghamton. Ernie's flight from Paris was delayed, but the SUNY plane was at Kennedy Airport to meet him, and he arrived in Binghamton just in time to use the Smith's guest bathroom for his refreshing hot bath so he could appear as if he had a normal day. At this point, he had been up almost twenty-four hours, but he was ready to enjoy the dinner and put on his cap and gown to march with the graduates in the commencement procession.

Echoes of the recent student demonstrations could be heard at the commencement ceremonies. When the graduates marched in and were seated, many of them set off loud poppers with paper streamers. When people were introduced on stage, there was booing and more poppers would go off. When Ernie got up to speak, he said he felt as if he was still in Paris— celebrating Bastille Day. The students seemed to like that and clapped, cheered, and sent off another display of poppers and colored paper streamers.

I was seated so that I could easily see many rows of the student graduates, and it was obvious to me they had no intention of listening to a commencement speech. Within two or three minutes after Ernie began, however, the disturbances all stopped, and the graduates started to listen, respectfully. I was intrigued, and began specifically watching the graduate wearing a Mickey Mouse hat instead of his graduation cap; he had been very intent on sending off poppers and passing them around to others. At first he ignored Ernie's speech, continuing to talk and disturb others, but then something Ernie said caught his attention, and he began listening. Amazingly, this student was the first to start applauding and rise to his feet at the end of the speech.

Tears welled in my eyes as I observed Ernie's patience, warmth, and sensitivity to this spirited audience. The whole week had felt like a marathon, and I had felt totally out of touch with Ernie and was upset he had been too occupied to find a telephone to get in touch with me while he was in Europe. I very rarely complained because we were in this together, but this time I felt that his travel and meeting plans were ridiculous. But as the crowd rose to their feet after the commencement address, I felt proud and overjoyed. I was feeling uplifted just knowing that this was the same man I had exchanged marriage vows with some twenty-five years before.

After the commencement was all over, the twin-engine university plane was waiting to fly us back to Albany. I love remembering that spectacularly beautiful ride home. The moon was full and bright orange, and it seemed to hold just on the horizon as we looked down on it, like a gift of peace and inspiration to the two of us all alone in that little seating compartment.

We were so happy to know that Ernie had no international travel and no more commencement speeches for the whole next week. Three of our four children were home for the summer, and Ernie would be home early for dinner all week—a simple blessing that left us both feeling overjoyed. That week we spent warm evenings sitting in lawn chairs beside the pool while the young folks swam. Ernie and I dreamed together and felt so thankful to God for each other and endless blessings.

The Forbidden Kingdom

After the "Wizard of Oz" experience in Moscow, other doors of opportunity deepened Ernie's interest in international education. The most unusual of all came out of the blue—a Monday morning surprise. Ernie's office received a phone call one morning in 1975 from the Washington DC Chinese Liaison Office. The officer told Ernie the two of us had been invited to visit China and that we would be granted visas to come as guests of the People's Republic of China. This was a few years after President Richard Nixon's 1972 groundbreaking visit to China, which had ended twenty-five years of China's isolation and clearly marked the beginning of normalization between the two countries.

We never knew why Ernie received that invitation, but Ernic thought the Chinese may have been attracted to the rapid development happening at SUNY. We were intrigued and honored to go to this country that few had been able to visit for a quarter of a century and looked forward to this mysterious adventure, which turned out to be a most interesting experience of intrigue, delight, and some bitter grief.

Our Chinese hosts expected our visit to last about three weeks. Ernie managed to clear sixteen days on his calendar, and we tried to decide on a plan for Stephen, who was then eleven. We wanted to find something special for him to do during our time away, which would be in June when his school would be out for the summer. Craig's little farm was the most appealing choice, with Grandma and Grandpa Boyer as a backup.

As we approached what was then called Peking, a city of seven million people, the city looked as if it were practicing for a World War II blackout. It was scary to be landing at a big city airport in such darkness. I remember Ernie looking out the window and anxiously wondering out loud whether anyone was expecting us, saying, "We have no name and no letter of introduction." The air terminal was large, severe, and dark, and the only lights at the entrance were over a very large picture of Mao Tse-tung. But as we went down the steps of the plane, we heard someone politely call, "Dr. Boyer, Dr. Boyer."

Such happy relief! We immediately felt sincere warmth from the party of ten high-ranking officials from the National Ministry of Education and from Tsing Hua University who were waiting for us at the very spot where the plane came to a stop. After a brief greeting in the darkness, we were led inside to a softly lit, formal guest lounge, where we were served tea. Wei Zhang, who spoke excellent English, introduced himself as our guide and then introduced us to the others in the welcoming party. Each smiled broadly and gave a little bow.

After polite inquiry about our long trip, they escorted us to a long, black limousine with a large number "1" displayed on the hood that would be used throughout our visit. From then on, it was as if we were visiting family, with seven or eight people traveling with us wherever we went. On the long drive from the airport to the Peking Hotel, we quickly realized that a glow of lights would be considered wasteful. There were no streetlights; in fact, we saw no lights anywhere. During our sixteen-day visit, we discovered there was no waste in China, which explained why the stewardesses on our Chinese Airline flight washed the dishes after they served our meal.

Right from the start, there were puzzling surprises, such as the extreme luxury of our three-room hotel suite and balcony. Yet, looking down from our third-floor balcony, we saw not a single automobile. But there certainly were bicycles, traveling eight or ten across. Watching the bicycles traveling wheel-to-wheel, almost silently, was like watching a flowing river. Ernie and I stood there side-by-side, contemplating this sight that was strangely poetic and captivating yet so alien to our modern thinking.

Our Chinese hosts had set many things in motion for our visit. Our beloved guide, Wei Zhang, was the vice chairman of Tsing Hua University. He was highly educated, with a PhD in engineering from a German university, and was fluent in German and English as well as his native dialect of Chinese. Wei Zhang traveled with us everywhere we went, as did Mrs. Au, a young teacher of English and the mother of a young daughter. She called Mr. Zhang "Professor Zhang," so that was how we also addressed him. He seemed to approve. The two of them even took rooms on the same floor of our hotel to be nearby and always available to us. They seemed to know that we wanted to see schools, universities, students, hospitals, communes, factories, and, of course, the Great Wall. We did it all, and nothing we did or saw was like anything we could relate to life in America.

The Cultural Revolution had profoundly affected all of China. The people who had desk jobs went periodically to what was called "cadre schools," where they dirtied their hands doing manual labor, like feeding pigs or working in the fields, while studying the *Little Red Book*—the theoretical guide to Mao Tse-tung's revolution. Dr. Zhang arranged for us to visit the pig farm where he had been sent to work for two years. We noticed he appeared unusually agitated as he showed us around this large farm and told ourselves those two years must have been a terrible time for him. He was told that he was being retrained from an aristocratic mindset, to a mind ready to serve the people wholeheartedly—a political indoctrination.

We also visited what the Chinese called universities in four major cities but never met a "president" or "dean." Instead, we were always introduced to a "responsible person," or a "leading person," or "a member of the coordinating committee." The way the Chinese assigned these leadership roles appeared to be a method to broaden participation but also to keep power fluid by preventing authority from becoming firmly fixed.

The institutions were almost unrecognizable as universities to the American eye. They had been closed in 1966 and reopened in 1970 with students who had been chosen by their fellow workers in the factories or fields. The students spent their time working and studying Mao's revolutionary theory—mixing theory and practice, as they called it. Teachers often went to teach in the factories and fields. The campuses were plastered with student posters containing criticisms or questions such as, "Which best fulfills the theories of Marx and Lenin–the campus or the countryside?" It was common to see a group of students standing together and talking loudly and gesturing as they tried to prove some revolutionary political idea. A number of times, Ernie asked our interpreter to listen and tell us the point of their debate. The students were flattered with the attention and welcomed Ernie's participation, which was very limited because of the language barrier. A smile, however, was always the great communicator.

I asked our guides if we could visit with some female students and possibly go to a girl's dormitory. They immediately obliged, and we headed off with the usual crowd following along as we were taken into the girls' area and down a hallway with doors all open to identical, clean, and orderly rooms. I concluded that this was how they lived because there would have been no time for a warning to clean up for visitors.

We stopped at a room where two girls were sitting and reading at a small table that stood against the wall. Communicating through an interpreter, they explained that four girls lived together in this space, a room six feet by eight feet. The floor was cement with no carpeting, and there was a picture of Mao on the wall. The room had bunk beds, two tiny tables, and four chairs.

There was a small closet where hung four towels and four dresses, all alike—one change of clothes for each girl. Canvas book bags were arranged on a shelf, along with four tin cups containing toothbrushes and toothpaste. There were four combs and ribbons and rubber bands. All the girls wore their hair in braids, and they told me that the girls from the north held their braids in place with rubber bands and those from the south used ribbons. The schedule posted on the wall showed where they were to be every hour of the day. Lights were turned off at 10 o'clock each night.

"Do you get together to talk and share with other students?" I asked. They said, "Yes, very often, and we always talk about affairs of the state." It then seemed appropriate to ask if there were male and female romantic relationships, as Ernie and I had met while in college. After each gave a little giggle, one said they talk to male students but only about affairs of the state. Unfortunately, we did not find out about romance or marriage policy, except Dr. Zhang said they had marriages.

They then explained that two of them were peasant girls from the farm and two were factory workers. All four of them had been chosen by their fellow workers to come to the university. As we left, students from the other rooms gathered around us and applauded.

By this time it was noon, and we moved on to the vast dining room, where about a thousand students ate at a time. Since there were no chairs, each stood to eat at waist-high tables, filling their bowls with rice scooped from a bathtub-sized container. A vegetable, a meat dish, and steamed bread were added. The students liked to watch us and applauded when we ate some steamed bread—their special food.

We were told repeatedly that the students considered it a great privilege to be at the university. It was a happy time for them because all their basic needs were supplied and they were assured success, with no academic tests or graduation requirements to cause them concern.

Again and again on each of our sixteen days, we saw something completely alien to our experience. The day at the Peking University Medical College was surely one of those days. As SUNY chancellor, Ernie was responsible for the overall administration of a number of medical centers and was especially interested when a Peking medical college "leading person" gave an overview of the 600-bed hospital, which was basically run by committees. He could not help but compare it to the highly structured organizational way hospitals worked back home.

A most unusual pleasure was offered when we were taken to the surgery area and told we could observe any operation. Most were complex surgeries such as bone transplants and tumor removals, and we discovered that acupuncture was the anesthesia used for all patients. One was a seventeen year-old boy who was having an appendectomy. We watched them place the acupuncture needles in the boy's body, quickly make the incision, and remove the appendix—with almost no bleeding. We watched the whole procedure and talked to the patient, who kept smiling and saying he felt fine. When the operation was over, he just got up off the table, walked to the stretcher and climbed up on it, shook hands with us, and again said he felt fine.

What we saw seemed almost like a miracle. We checked back with two other patients, and both said they were doing well. By now you are probably saying that you have to see it to believe it. Even for me, while I was seeing it, it was unbelievable. There were similar stories about dental surgeries and childbirth.

At the beginning of our last week in China, our hosts planned a trip so that we could have two days of rest, which we very much looked forward to. Only Dr. Zhang traveled with us on the seven-hour train ride to a very beautiful vacation spot. After we boarded the train, Dr. Zhang said, "Just follow me and I'll tell you where to sit." He clearly wanted us to understand and follow his directions. We followed with our bags, and he selected the side of the train with three seats in a row where no one was seated in front or behind. He directed me to the window seat, while he seated himself on the aisle and Ernie in the middle. It was an old train that moved very noisily down the tracks. Dr. Zhang appeared to be attentive and alert to the other passengers.

During the monotony of the long ride settled among the passengers, he leaned in close toward me and Ernie and whispered, "There is something I want to tell you. We are constantly being bugged, but because of the noise of the train and my low whisper, this is the only chance I will have to tell you the truth about what is really happening in China and what has happened to me." He continued by saying, "The Red Guards broke into our home, destroyed all the furniture, broke all my wife's prized dishes we brought back from Germany, and took me off to the pig farm for re-education. I never saw my dear wife again." At this point, tears were rolling down his checks. We wanted to sob with him, but we knew we had to be cautious to protect his safety. He trusted us in revealing the reality of the very dark side of Mao's "Cultural Revolution," with its disastrous and often brutal political and social realities. After Mao's death in 1976, his successors quickly reversed the course and repudiated many of those efforts.

We had traveled thousands of miles and consistently heard the same message: "We are building a new China, a China that is run by the workers and the peasants." Dr. Zhang's whispered comments on the train conveyed a different message. Although we keenly felt the anguish of the hidden sadness within the heart of Dr. Zhang and many others, we left with goodwill and deep gratitude for the exceptional kindness and warm friendship we experienced everywhere we went. As a farewell at the airport, one delegate said, "May the friendship between the Chinese and the American people last as long as the Mississippi River flows into the sea." Ernie responded, "Yes, I wish that too, and just to be safe, I suggest we include the Yangtze River, also."

Importing Ideas from China

After we returned, Ernie wrote and spoke often about his fascination with and questions about Chinese society, its people, and its institutions. One dramatic example of the differences in our cultures was the contrast between the motto of the State University of New York, "Let each become all he is capable of being," and what we had been told was the motto of Chinese universities, "Let each student prepare himself wholeheartedly to serve the people." SUNY's motto expressed a commitment to serve each individual, while the Chinese prepared to serve the whole society.

Ernie wondered how SUNY could continue to celebrate the individual and also face up to the challenge of working together to reach out and serve others. Some of what we witnessed in China he related to the purposes and procedures of higher education. For instance, he asked if liberal education should exclude preparation for worthwhile work, whereas in China, practice was primary.

Ernie found many other ways to consider what we observed. He wrote about administrators moving from their own pivot points of power from time to time, to meet the people and to participate in the work of the enterprise they directed. He then decided to experience that concept more himself. Ernie often made trips to the various campuses, but this time he arranged for an extended stay on a campus and spent a night sleeping in the men's dormitory. The next day he spent time alongside the maintenance workers, campus security, and the lower administrative ranks. I recall how he happily relished the adventure and returned to his desk with a new sense of what his job entailed.

A Chance for Sabbatical

In June 1976, we were given a chance for an extended overseas trip when Ernie received an invitation to be a visiting scholar at the University of Cambridge. The SUNY Board of Trustees granted him a sabbatical leave for the fall semester so that he could take advantage of the offer. When completed, he was to return to his chancellor responsibilities. What we did not know was how those plans would be completely interrupted. Later, as we looked back, we understood a little more about the meaning of Solomon's words in Proverbs 16:9, "In his heart a man plans his course, but the Lord determines his steps."

As plans moved forward for the sabbatical, we packed our bags with clothes for the chilly and damp English fall and early winter weather. We were very excited, and totally unaware that the Chancellor House Mansion chapter was about to close.

CHAPTER 15

HOUSE 17
The English Sabbatical Mansion

Cambridge, England
1976

"We thank thee for this place in which we dwell, for the love that unites us, for the peace accorded us each day, for the hope with which we expect the morrow."

—Robert Lewis Stevenson

In September 1976, Ernie, twelve-year-old Stephen, and I arrived in Cambridge, England, to damp and chilly air. That chill was not an indication of what we were to experience in our hearts or daily contacts during the autumn and early winter months of Ernie's sabbatical. On the contrary, we felt very welcomed and so warmly received by the University of Cambridge and, in particular, Wolfson College—one of the 31 residential colleges comprising Cambridge.

Richard Whitford, the executive assistant in Ernie's SUNY office had traveled to Cambridge to finalize our relationship with Wolfson College, known to be one of Cambridge's friendliest colleges, where Ernie had been invited to be a visiting fellow. It was arranged that Jack King, the Wolfson college bursar, would be Ernie's contact at Wolfson; Ernie and Jack became devoted friends, and his Scottish wife, Ruth, became my special friend. She liked to cook her delicious Scottish food for us, and we would all sit around their table and talk late into the evening. Peace and relaxation, with interesting conversations, was exactly what we needed.

Jack and Richard Whitford had found us a perfect second-story rental with two bedrooms, a large living room with a dining area, and a convenient yet rather small kitchen. We were surprised and delighted by the coziness and simple charm the minute we saw "the flat," the British term for what we thought of as an apartment. Since we wanted to fit in, we also called our new home a "flat."

It was carefully and neatly equipped with everything we needed. We had brought nothing but our clothes, so we were thrilled to find in the kitchen cupboards whatever we would need to prepare meals and to set a nice table for the three of us and any guests.

As much as we found the flat homey and pleasing, we had to adapt to some British ways. For one thing, it was the practice in most homes to always have a window open several inches, even on the coldest days and nights. That was difficult enough, but the hardest adjustment was not having any heat in the bathroom. At first we admired the luxurious touch of heated towel racks in the bathroom until we realized this was more a necessity than luxury. I guess we had a positive attitude, because we quickly got used to the differences and felt at home and content.

The landlady was gracious and helpful, walking with me to the next street over, where all the little shops were lined up, and introducing me to the various shopkeepers. I needed to shop almost every day because things were on a much smaller scale. Our refrigerator was very small, and groceries were packaged about half the size to which I was accustomed, meaning I needed to go to the little food shops frequently.

We were amused by the milkman who stopped his tiny, opened-ended truck close to our door every morning and placed two pint-sized glass bottles of milk at the bottom of the outside stairs. At the same time he picked up our empty bottles. Our address at 19 Croft Lodge, Barton Road, was on his regular daily milk delivery route.

Living a Dream

One of Ernie's big dreams was to have a chance to write. His responsibilities as chancellor of the State University of New York demanded most of his time. Yet, so many ideas were running through his mind that he longed for a block of uninterrupted time to capture this mental activity onto paper.

Through a series of carefully planned steps and the help of Martin "Marty" Kaplan, a very bright, newly minted Stanford University PhD, everything was falling into place for Ernie's dream to come true. During the previous summer, Marty had worked as Ernie's assistant at an education workshop in Aspen, Colorado, which resulted in the publication of *The Monday Morning Imagination.* When Ernie was granted the sabbatical, he invited Marty to join him in England as a collaborator. Marty, being a good writer and clear thinker, was a perfect match to work with Ernie and help him complete a writing project during the short months of the sabbatical.

Marty and Ernie would get together several times during the week, and I sometimes caught parts of their discussions about the core curriculum in higher education and their even deeper conversations about what it means to be human or what it means to be educated. During these months, the writing was completed, resulting in *Educating for Survival,* which was published the next year, 1977. This book, being among the first of Ernie's writings, reveals some of his basic thinking about education's deeper purposes.

This opportunity to write and the hospitality Ernie experienced at Wolfson were true joys. The thrill of Ernie's more relaxed schedule and the fulfillment of his goal made us feel so very grateful and blessed.

Purple Ties and Jugged Hares

At that time the home schooling concept was not accepted, and Stephen was required to be enrolled in a school. The school choices were very limited, but King's College School of Cambridge was the school where he could be enrolled. The school had great fame, in particular, because of its Boy's Chapel Choir dating to the fifteenth century. Stephen was not a chorister and, at first, was not warmly accepted. He frequently had stomachaches and missed school. He gradually adjusted and managed those months of school, trying to endure even the unheated and simple, stark classrooms.

To make matters worse, he had to wear a purple jacket and a matching purple necktie, which was part of the school uniform. Stephen grew up hating to wear ties. As soon as school was over for the day he would take off his tie and stuff it into his jacket pocket. One day when he was riding his bicycle back home from school, his tie problem was uniquely remedied when the tie fell out of his pocket, got caught in his bicycle spokes, and was torn beyond repair.

A few letters remain that Ernie and I wrote to our children back in the United States. I have one that I wrote to Beverly, now a student in Columbia, Missouri, on October 25, 1976:

> It's Monday morning and we're raring to go after a big weekend. We all work so hard all week and then put work aside for pure pleasure. Saturday we rode across the city on our bikes to do some brass rubbings. It was our first attempt, so we did small ones, but rather successfully. It's tedious because your fingers, arms, and back get tired as you patiently go over and over the brass figure with the hard wax to get a smooth look. One of the largest and most famous brass pieces dating to the year 1289 is in an ancient cathedral in a small village, only two miles from our flat. People from all over the world come to rub it—Sir Roger de Trumpington, a famous British landlord. We had hoped to get an appointment. He is very large but we could complete it in one day or a long afternoon if all three of us worked at the same time. Then yesterday we took a local bus for a trip sixteen miles north of Cambridge to the town of Ely, where the largest cathedral in England was built in 1234 and with its repositories of centuries of worship. It is such an elaborate spectacle and a genius creation architecturally. Two days later we had a fancy dinner party in our flat for two friends. Dad played the old fashion phonograph (with the side wind up handle) that he bought in the Cotswolds on our last weekend trip. The records are so great because they send us into another era.

Other weekends we went to Stratford-upon Avon, Blenheim Palace, and the Salisbury Cathedral. We learned much history and marveled over and over about every place we went. There is another treasured letter Ernie wrote to one of the children:

> Saturday we traveled to London—a one hour train ride from Cambridge. We shopped, visited museums and went to the Agatha Christie show, "Mousetrap." Yesterday we bicycled around town and went to Evensong at King's College chapel to hear the Boys Choir—magnificent. Steve has adjusted to school and just loves this city with its bookstores, parks, flowers, chapels, and colleges.

I envied the way Ernie could write without wasting words and still be able to say it all.

We celebrated my forty-eighth birthday at a restaurant during one of those travel excursions. Ernie told me to choose anything on the menu without consideration of the price, so I chose the more costly and exotic menu listing, "jugged hare," more because it sounded like something that I could only order in a British restaurant. I knew hare was rabbit, but the waiter would not clearly explain what jugged meant or how the dish was prepared. It was served very attractively on my plate with gourmet complements and was unusually flavorful and delicious.

Back in Cambridge we asked an amused Jack and Ruth King to explain why the dish was called "jugged." I started to feel ill when they explained that the rabbit is hung for long enough to allow it to be infested with maggots and left to decay. If that is true, I'm happy that I did not know what I was eating. But it is a birthday that I have never forgotten.

Being away from our three older children on Thanksgiving Day was a sad sacrifice we had to make during this sabbatical. However, Marty was determined that we needed to have our own traditional American Thanksgiving even in England. He invited us and other friends to his little flat where he managed to prepare the very best roast turkey and all the trimmings. He assigned me to make two pumpkin pies, and I had to go to four food stores to find enough canned pumpkin because the cans were so small and no store had more than two cans.

Marty was so right. As much as we loved our time in England, somehow it felt good to be reminded that we were also happy with our own traditions. The roasted turkey, as the defining part of the customary Thanksgiving holiday, was certainly a special warm spot in the sabbatical.

Birthing a Paper and a Passion

Even now my mind bubbles over with so much happiness when I recall that sabbatical time. Here we were in this bucolic spot of gardens, ivy-covered walls, and quiet academic courts. Ernie and I felt God had given us overflowing blessings. Many days were worshipful days—especially when we went to the Evensong at the grand chapel of King's College where we were inspired by the sounds of the boys' choir echoing through those hushed spaces.

I was able to use my time during this semester in a way that was just as much of a blessing for me as Ernie's writing focus was for him. I was nearing the end of my studies at Empire State College, and one of my academic assignments was to write a major paper comparing midwifery practices in England with maternity practices in America. My Empire State College faculty mentor requested from the British Midwifery Association that I be granted privileges to observe and work with the District and Cambridge City Midwives. The request was approved, and I received overwhelming acceptance and a warm welcome among the many midwifery services.

I could hardly contain my joy as I rode my bicycle along the busy downtown Cambridge roads leading to the Mill Road Maternity Hospital. The first time I bicycled there, Ernie rode beside me to show me the way. After that I was ready to do it on my own, and I did it many times. In one of my letters to the children I wrote about one of my days at this very special hospital:

> There were four babies born within the period I was on the labor and delivery wards on Tuesday. There were no doctors around. Each woman had a midwife who managed the complete birth process. Every birth was unbelievably simple and beautiful. Tomorrow I'm

> taking an early morning bus and riding eighteen miles to the country, doing home visits (prenatal and postnatal) with the district midwife there. I'm having a ball!

One of the supervising midwives was my guide who helped me obtain a number of contacts along with wide exposure that helped me gather much valuable information for my research. She would even call me in the middle of the night and come to our flat to pick me up and take me with her to a home birth. Her skills and wide scope of knowledge and wisdom made her my heroine and professional role model. To this day we still exchange letters every Christmas, and I will always treasure her gift of Christian generosity and friendship.

In England at that time, 1976, every woman was assigned a midwife. It was recommended that midwives deliver first babies in the hospital, but any subsequent births were most often home births. All the births I witnessed were calm, under very competent control, and without technical intervention. Births I witnessed in England were in great contrast to the practices that I was familiar with during my maternity nursing work in the United States.

I remember an incident that took place in the Mill Road Maternity Hospital that was awesome when I witnessed it and is still awesome when I remember it. At four o'clock, which is afternoon tea time, an elegant tea cart with a white tablecloth, silver teapots, and china tea cups and saucers, was pushed down the hallway by a white-uniformed tea server. I was in a labor room with a midwife and woman in labor. Her husband was sitting on a chair close to her side. The tea server stopped at the open door and asked the couple if they wished to be served tea. The laboring woman answered that they would enjoy having their afternoon tea and then informed the midwife that she was going to take time out for tea and a biscuit. The sweetly connected husband and wife smiled and had their tea together. It appeared to be the perfect formula because within a half hour, the woman gave birth to a pink and glowing baby girl.

Midwives also supervised the mothers with the baby care, giving thorough attention to breast-feeding and the teaching of mothering. When I talked to the mothers, they seemed to assume that mothers everywhere got the same special pampering that they enjoyed.

When I was not working alongside the midwives, I would go to the city library and work on my term paper. I had dreamed of becoming a midwife, and by the time the semester ended, I was beginning to feel a strong determination to prepare for a midwifery career. Ernie was so very proud and pleased that I had accomplished something entirely satisfying.

He felt the same gratitude as I did toward everyone's kindness to me. He had met my supervisor, Mrs. Goodbody, when she invited us to her home to meet her family and share a typical meal of English veal pie with the surprising china blackbird heads peering out though the pie crust. Ernie thought we should host a luncheon event to say thank you to her and about twenty of the midwives who had so kindly welcomed me to work and learn from them.

It was quite a big undertaking to make all the arrangements, but it turned out to be a sweet and sad good-bye event for me. I managed to say my heartfelt thanks to these dear friends with Ernie at my side as my loving supporter and encourager. I was deeply touched that he came up with such a thoughtful idea and then presided over the very lovely event.

Educating across Borders

Ernie and I were able to spend three days in Moscow about halfway through the sabbatical—an unbelievable experience. I was aware that it was a very special gift for me to accompany Ernie as this was a historic event especially for that point in U.S. and Soviet relations. Ernie met with the Soviet Minister of Education to complete the details of an agreement and the formal signing of the first exchange agreement between Moscow State University and the State University of New York.

The agreement, which called for an exchange of ten graduate students and four faculty members each year, was the first agreement of its kind between Moscow State University and a university in the United States. There was much excitement about the agreement because in 1976 any contact with the West was very big news in both the Soviet Union and the United States. The Soviets credited Ernie for the agreement and planned a beautiful formal banquet following the signing to honor him. I felt my role was to try to graciously respond with appreciation.

The following day Ernie spoke at a Conference for the American Bicentennial, the only Bicentennial program in the Soviet Union, which was held in a large university auditorium filled with Russian students and faculty. He got a standing ovation, which he said was an act of respect for America, but my wifely heart knew it was something more.

For the entire trip and through various encounters, we were keenly aware of the display of friendship between a university in the Soviet Union and a university in the United States in the midst of the Cold War, which was similar to the friendship shown during the "Wizard of Oz" performance several years earlier. Ernie liked to believe that education had a great responsibility toward working for peace and a better world, and this visit was a poignant reminder of the success that can come when one fervently believes in that aspiration.

A Refreshing and Fruitful Time

As the sabbatical was coming to the end, I believe we all were amazed at what we had accomplished. For Ernie and Marty, it was the satisfaction of completing their book writing. Stephen was going home with a selection of brass rubbings, and I had finished my term paper and said my final good-byes to my midwifery friends. Ernie was still enjoying cherished friendships as a Wolfson College Fellow, once more attending the formal, antiquated High Table dinner where everyone was required to wear black academic gowns. But, he was also preparing himself to deliver a final farewell speech and express his deep appreciation.

This was a U.S. presidential election year, 1976. The day of the election we were touring Stonehenge, another of our marvelous explorations of England. The mysterious Stonehenge structure on Salisbury Plain seemed so distant from happenings in the U.S. That night Marty, Ernie, Stephen, and I watched on the hotel's television as Jimmy Carter was declared President of the United States. It was a surprising outcome, and we were totally unaware how his election would have a surprising effect on our lives.

The four-month sabbatical was an amazing gift that refreshed our minds, souls, and spirits. We were so thankful to feel renewed as we said our good-byes and walked away from our English Flat Mansion, a temporary home that warmly touched our lives.

Christmas in Chancellor House

We arrived back at Chancellor House in time to prepare for Christmas, and a wonderful time with the whole family eased many of the sentimental longings for our life in Cambridge. We had so much to tell the family, bragging about all the brass rubbings that we had brought back, framed, and given as gifts that year. We thought we had created the perfect Christmas gift for everyone. Perhaps we presumed too much because of our enthusiasm; however, a few of those rubbings still hang here and there though somewhat aged and faded.

Returning to the large number of things that were waiting for him, the demand for Ernie's immediate attention at the Chancellor's Office was all-consuming. But the sabbatical had left him energized and primed to return to what he loved to do.

I also was ready to complete a few requirements necessary before my graduation with a Bachelor of Science degree. Finally, that dream of many years was coming to completion. It truly seemed amazing that Ernie's vision for Empire State College was being fulfilled in my upcoming graduation.

Stephen was back in his school, finding it great to be with his friends again and not being required to wear a tie and jacket.

Then came a phone call from a member of Jimmy Carter's nominating committee. He was looking for someone to fill the position of United States commissioner of education. Ernie told the caller that he was not interested and turned down the invitation to go to DC for an interview. He was committed to and happy at SUNY, and he also told me he did not want to get involved in the politics that would come with such a job. I was happy about his determination.

That evening I was on the telephone talking to Ernie Jr., who had returned to Maine with Pam and their one-and-a-half-year-old son, Nathan, after celebrating Christmas with us at Chancellor House. We were just ready to say good-bye when I remembered the phone call. I said, "Oh, by the way, Dad had a call today from someone on Jimmy Carter's nominating committee looking to fill the top education position. But, don't worry, he told them that he wasn't interested." Ernie Jr. said, "What do you mean that he's not interested; he's been at the chancellor job long enough and a change is due."

I explained that his Dad did not want to work for the government, but told him I'd get Ernie on the phone. Ernie Sr. took the phone and explained his reasoning for not wanting the position. Finally, after a long conversation, I heard him say, "Okay, I'll go for the interview, but I will not accept any offer." It was his thoughtful compromise with his son.

When a second call came from Washington, Ernie agreed to go for an interview, partly to honor Ernie Jr.'s reasoning. During the interview, in his usual tactful style, he said he could not give an answer without talking to his family and the chairperson of his board of trustees, Elizabeth Luce Moore. He called me after the interview and was feeling relieved, assuring himself that he could refuse in a phone call when he could report that there were objections from his family and the board of trustees. He then boarded a plane to fly back to Albany. In the meantime, without his knowledge or consent, word went out on the Associated Press Wire Service that Ernest L. Boyer had been chosen as the next U.S. commissioner of education.

The first I knew of this was when the housekeeper, Stella, came to me with a concerned look on her face and asked what was going on outside on the front lawn. I hurried to look out and was horrified to see television news and newspaper vehicles parked on both sides of the street, with many journalists setting up tripods with cameras and lights. Others were standing around with microphones or notepads in hand. What was the meaning of all this extraordinary strangeness?

My frantic call to Ernie's executive assistant sent the SUNY central office media staff into action. They immediately discovered what had been reported by AP. Staff went to meet Ernie at the airport with the news. What a shock! And what was he to do? He just wanted to get home so that the two of us could think about the idea together. Harold, Ernie's faithful driver, found a way through an unused alley so that Ernie could enter Chancellor House from the rear and escape the spotlight on the front lawn.

Ernie came in the back door very shaken. He and I needed to be left to privately reflect on what had happened, why it happened, and most of all, what would he do about the impossible situation? At the time there was no calm, only confusion in our minds. But I clearly remember the very decisive moment when he turned to me and said, "There is only one explanation; it must be God's plan and that is what I'm to do." We said a prayer asking for God's will.

We had been through hard times before, but this was the hardest. Heading the federal Office of Education was far from Ernie's dream job. Leaving the State University of New York where he devoted so much of his time and energy for more than a dozen years was deeply painful. Emotional farewell events with Ernie's most beloved staff, campus presidents, faculty leaders, student leaders, best friends on the board of trustees, and state legislators were now before us.

But there was no turning back, and we prepared to move on to new experiences. Family and friends, including Jack and Ruth King, our dear Cambridge friends, accompanied us to Ernie's confirmation hearing in Washington. The short sabbatical months and the seven years at Chancellor House Mansion were about to end.

I am still amazed at how we learned to make that house into a home and how we found ways to make it feel comfortable for the whole family. Now the abruptness of having to leave Chancellor House was unsettling. Ernie may have had less time than I did to dwell on it, but I had to set my mind to the task of separating all of our personal things from what belonged to the state, and I was so grateful for the inventory Ernie had required when we moved into Chancellor House.

By the end of January 1977, Ernie had to transfer his loyalties to Washington DC and the Office of Education. It was frightening to suddenly find we had no home, but we were grateful that we could use Chancellor House as long as we needed while we worked out all the details of moving. Our close friend, Father Timothy Healy, president of Georgetown University, gave Ernie a guest apartment on the campus to use until we could find a house to buy. Stephen and I stayed in Chancellor House while he continued in school, and I concentrated on the complicated particulars of carefully going through the large house and deciding what to pack. Stella and I packed box after box, a sad chore for both of us as she loved our family and we loved her.

It seemed like it would be easier for Stephen to stay in his Albany school to finish out the school year. However, it was not long until he wished for the family to be together, so we began to seriously concentrate on house hunting. The task of finding a house that we could afford was not easy, especially since Ernie's salary in his new position was greatly reduced. Perhaps it was unusual, but Ernie never negotiated a salary; he always accepted what was offered and never made money the issue of any job.

In our early years we had lived happily with less; surely we could do so again. I was especially looking forward to living in a smaller house where I could stand at any spot, call to someone, and expect them to answer. In the large and many-roomed Chancellor House, it could be a chore to track down someone just to take a phone call.

Our real estate agent immediately understood our concerns and had an uncanny way of knowing what to show us. Without wasting time, she showed us 7016 Benjamin Street in McLean, Virginia. It was the perfect find, and now we were eager to move. Ernie could give up the Georgetown University apartment, and we could all be together in our own home once again.

To economize, we rented a U-Haul truck to move all of our belongings from Chancellor house. Craig came home to help Ernie carry the furniture and boxes and pack the truck parked in the driveway. Again, the press came to document this whole scene, which they apparently found worthy of the front page of the Albany paper. They seemed to think it was strange for the past chancellor and the new U.S. commissioner of education to be loading up his family belongings in a U-Haul truck.

When everything was loaded and the house checked one last time, we drove away from Chancellor House slowly, looking back with mixed emotions. Ernie and I drove our car, and Craig drove the U-Haul truck with

Stephen sitting beside him. The boys seemed so grown-up, and we knew they could handle this big responsibility.

Everything was going smoothly until it became very windy about halfway throught the trip. When we came to a thruway with a toll, Ernie paid the toll and drove on, thinking Craig would do the same. Eventually, he realized Craig had not come though the toll booth. We pulled off and waited and waited. What to do? We had no way to contact them.

We were fearful and worried, but we were consoled by praying as we started out without them. We kept straining to see them somewhere in all the traffic until Ernie and I arrived late in the evening to our newly purchased yet empty house. We spent hour after hour looking out the living room window, watching for Craig and Stephen.

We could not remember ever experiencing more anxious hearts. With prayers of pleas, we hung on, waiting and waiting, as this was long before the time of cell phones and GPS. The boys had directions, but Craig had never even been to Mclean. How could they find our house on a narrow side street in the darkness? There was certainly no one to ask at this hour.

Finally, we thought we saw some lights. They suddenly turned into bright lights and then, without a doubt, we heard the sounds of a truck motor. Ernie and I ran out of the house, running as fast as we could go to the end of the driveway and out into the middle of the road—waving our arms in great jubilation. They were safe! It was 3 a.m., and we embraced our boys with the greatest of relief. They had managed to safely arrive with the loaded U-Haul truck and smiling faces, and we were safely together at our new home.

The boys had astonishing stories to tell. Because of the winds, the truck was not permitted on the expressway, and they had to find their way, using only smaller roadways. They told about a narrow road that ended with them driving down a railroad track. We were always most thankful to God for their guardian angel that night for giving them protection and safe directions.

Here we were at a different house and a different life. We would have to make many quick adjustments, but we knew God was with us.

CHAPTER 16

HOUSE 18

The Warm Heart Mansion

McLean, Virginia

1976–1983

Part I: Out of the Mansion, Still in the Spotlight

"The nobler part of all the house is the heart."

—J. Rutter

The whole family agreed. After seven years of living in a state-owned house with limited privacy, it felt good to return to a home we could truly call our own—a place where newspapers and books spilled over in the living room and an occasional slipper peeked out from under an oversized chair.

We quickly realigned our thoughts and emotions and accepted our move to Washington DC as something providential. We felt we were meant to be in that place at that time and that Ernie was meant to serve as the United States commissioner of education. Stephen was thirteen, about to become an eighth grader. I was two years away from half a century—still youthful, and ready for a change. Even so, we all missed Grandma and Grandpa Boyer, as they still lived in Albany, just one street over from Chancellor House.

At age forty-eight, Ernie was presiding over an organization with more than 3,000 employees and an annual budget of approximately $9 billion that funded more than 100 education programs. Those efforts ranged from preschool to the postdoctoral level, as well as international programs and student financial aid for proprietary, public, and private school students. As chancellor of the State University of New York, he had led the largest university system in the United States, with sixty-four institutions and more than 350,000 students. I thought that job had been daunting!

I struggled to begin to imagine what life would be like with Ernie filling this new job that seemed impossibly complex. Ernie, on the other hand, was ready to take action and did not feel uncertain. He viewed the work as giving him new inspiration and providing him a platform to meet some critically important challenges on behalf of our nation and its people. He believed that with care, compassion, and careful planning, all Americans could be given the opportunity to earn a good education. He later talked about how his work as commissioner added more clarity to his mind on a broad range of educational issues.

For instance, during his term as commissioner he realized with stunning force how the poverty crisis impacts educational opportunity for so many. He began to understand more clearly just how wide the gap was between the privileged and the disadvantaged. As commissioner, he was responsible for the administration of the Title I program of the Elementary and Secondary Education Act ESEA. The ESEA was enacted on April 11, 1965, under the leadership of President Lyndon B. Johnson as one of a number of sweeping programs in his War on Poverty. The premise of Title I is that equal access to education is a natural right of all children, no matter what their race, creed, color, or geography. This sweeping legislation was the Johnson administration's way of trying to amend some of the injustices caused, in particular, by segregation and discrimination.

However, it was also by no means a giveaway or handout as high standards and accountability undergirded the legislation. Subsequently, the Bilingual Education Act and the Education for the Handicapped Act became amendments to ESEA. Title I was the beginning of the reawakening of America to the plight of its disadvantaged citizens, and none of the principles or precepts of this legislation were antithetical to Ernest Boyer's philosophy and vision. In contrast, he viewed it as a privilege to administer the ESEA Act.

Cozy, Comfortable, and Charming

The house we found was actually just across the Potomac River in Virginia, giving Ernie a twenty-to thirty-minute commute across the Woodrow Wilson Bridge, past the Jefferson Memorial, and finally to his office in the United States Office of Education Building on Independence Avenue. We cherished our house at 7016 Benjamin Street in McLean, in an area known as the Langley Forest. our home was on a narrow, quiet road within an easy walk to a wooded area with trails leading down to the Potomac River and views across the river to the John F. Kennedy Center for the Performing Arts and the noted DC skyline.

The house was infinitesimal compared to the stately expanse of the Chancellor House. Yet it had everything we needed all on one level. To Ernie it was both aesthetically pleasing and practical, and it was small enough for me to perform a thorough weekly cleaning in half a day. There were three bedrooms, and one doubled as an extra bedroom and a study. The master bedroom and bath were a little larger than the others, but none of the bedrooms were particularly spacious. Stephen enjoyed having his own bathroom, and we found the house was comfortable, practical, and thus very cozy.

In essence, we loved our new home, inside and out. A pleasing entrance faced the adjoining lot, with steps leading to a covered portico. This was the front of the house, which was reached by walking down a long sidewalk from the driveway. To the right of the entrance was a dining room and a connected, efficient, and well-planned kitchen. To the left of the entrance area was the living room with a lovely white marble fireplace and a wide doorway leading to an expansive family room, which overlooked a landscaped lawn and sidewalk to a stone patio.

From the kitchen-dining area, French doors opened to the stone patio and a step down to a large wooden deck. This area was the feature that persuaded us to buy this compact but charming house. Sitting on the deck, we overlooked a bank with many trees and a side lawn that had many landscaping possibilities for Stephen, who was developing a keen interest in plant life.

We were also pleased to find this modest house because for the first time in a long time, we were responsible for a mortgage and the accompanying expenses of running a house. When Ernie was chancellor of SUNY, those costs were covered by the State of New York. Now, living on a considerably reduced salary (the federal government's pay scale at that time was relatively low), we had to plan carefully and maintain a strict budget. Thankfully, Ernie calculated we could cover all the costs for this home and still have some extra for savings.

There were bigger houses and new additions being added to existing houses on our street. However, we felt content and blessed with what we had purchased, and quickly turned this house into our mansion. I must confess there were rarely books and newspapers spilling over, nor was there ever a slipper peeking out from under a chair. However, it was cozy, relaxing, and most importantly, ours. There were no maids at the ready or polite houseboys who stood by to do our bidding. Fancy electric floor buzzers were things of the past. But Ernie or Stephen could hear me call from any part of the house, and I could hear their spontaneous laughter and chuckles, or penetrating silence telling me my family was engrossed in study. That little house gave us so much joy and will forever remain a mansion in my eyes, not so much for what it had, but for what it offered to us. I thus think of it as the Warm Heart Mansion.

Blessing of Nearby Family

Thinking back, I now know our greatest blessing was that Beverly and her husband moved to McLean shortly after we arrived. They were able to find a nice house to rent just around the corner from our Warm Heart Mansion. Will got a teaching position at nearby Fairfax Junior High School, and Beverly's loving and amazing help made it possible for all of us to thrive.

It was so special that Stephen's older sister was so close by during those years. She was not working on a degree at that time and was eager to help make our stressful days easier as I also took on new challenges. She was there each day when Stephen came home from school. He was once again experiencing the adjustment of new school with all new classmates, and Beverly was full of empathy as only a caring and sensitive sister can be. Ernie and I had to rely on her, and she knew she was needed. It was not unusual for her to even have meals prepared for us, along with Will's dinner, when we all arrived home at the end of a long day.

We also were thrilled when another generation of our family moved to be closer to our new home in DC. While we had been in England during Ernie's sabbatical, Grandma and Grandpa Boyer stayed in their rented house close to the Chancellor House Mansion. They missed being close to family, but Grandma wrote to us weekly about the details of what was proving to be their rather uneventful life. I tried to faithfully respond to her letters but fear I may not have proven as successful as I hoped.

They were thus understandably upset when we suddenly moved from Albany to Washington DC and did not want to continue to live in Albany after we moved. To be closer to us, they moved to Baltimore where a special friend was a pastor of a Brethren in Christ church. They had moved from their home and their cherished church in Dayton more than ten years earlier. Now they were thrilled to have the opportunity to again worship where they immediately felt at home.

Baltimore was a long and difficult drive for them to come to visit us in McLean, Virginia. As a result, we conscientiously set aside as many Sundays as possible to drive to Baltimore to go to church with them and then spend the afternoon together. They always took us to the same restaurant, which was their favorite, and we politely accepted what proved to be the rather bland choices on the menu.

We loved to be with Grandma and Grandpa Boyer, and nothing made them happier than to see us show up at church on a Sunday morning. We also liked worshiping in the church where we too felt at home. Craig, who was still living and working in Zanesville, Ohio, near his Mennonite friends, came home frequently, which also made his grandparents especially happy.

Explorations and Creations

Part of what also came with our move was the idea of adding a dog to our family. Ernie and Stephen went to the pound and promptly came home with a shabby, mangy-looking, medium-to-small-sized fellow with the sweetest, happiest face. They fell in love with him at the pound when he seemed to politely beg to be chosen. With lots of loving attention, he thrived at the Warm Heart Mansion and quickly responded to the name, Benny. He turned out to be an excellent choice as a loyal and faithful companion for Stephen because he was always ready for an adventure.

Benny and Stephen explored the wooded trails in Langley Forest together. On occasion, Stephen wrote (and published for family and friends) accounts of the adventures and discoveries he and Benny had in that undeveloped area. Ernie and I saw this activity as a blessing because it gave our youngest child a chance to practice his writing skills and afforded him an opportunity to record his thoughts and observations.

One wintry Saturday, Stephen, Benny, Ernie, and I trudged through the snow for what felt like miles. We started out in Langley Forest and followed along unmarked paths, looking for the "source" of the Potomac River. Stephen had researched this topic prior to our adventure. He knew everything about the Potomac River from its 383 statute miles' length with a drainage area of more than 14,000 square miles, to its nickname as the "Nation's River" because it was such a rich blend of America's history and culture. He knew that the river forms part of the borders between Washington DC and Virginia and upstream between Maryland and Virginia. His curiosity thus led him to want to know exactly where the river's source was located. We were excited that Stephen was so intensely interested in this topic, and when we looked at him poring over geological and geographical records we thought of him as a junior scientist/explorer.

And so on that Saturday, the four of us set out to find the source of the Potomac River. We were all explorers, doing what parents around the world have done with their children from the beginning of time. Maybe we were just amateurs, but, despite the cold, it certainly was a day of pleasure that allowed Ernie and me to smile and give thanks to the wondrous ways of the Almighty. However, after many hours of tramping through the snow and sludge, I began to think we would never find the source of the Potomac River. My steps began to lag; cold and hungry, I simply could not muster the energy to keep up with Benny, Stephen, and Ernie.

Just when I was about to assert the executive privilege that all mothers have, I heard two excited voices. Stephen and his Dad were yelling to me that they had found it. Believe it or not, the source of the Potomac River was in the exact place where Stephen's research directed us. It was very exciting, even if the source looked like a pretty insignificant beginning for the famous Potomac River. The hike back home, propelled by satisfaction and excitement, seemed much shorter. Stephen and Benny ran way ahead. Neither Ernie nor I had done any research on the source of the Potomac, and I'll never be 100 percent certain that we actually located it on that cold day. Regardless, with the faith only parents have in their children, we hold in our hearts that we did indeed find what we were looking for on that day.

Seeking to satisfy another one of Stephen's curiosities, Ernie and Stephen also started drawing architectural plans for a greenhouse designed as an attachment to the family room. As I mentioned previously, Stephen had a real interest and skill in growing plants and experimenting with propagation, which met at this point with Ernie's considerable interest in architecture. One challenge proved to be finding a builder who could follow their complex plans, which included everything from controlled temperatures to proper ventilation and had room for blooming plants and tables for starter plants.

Right off we agreed the contractor had to be our nephew, Jeffery Boyer. Jeff, then twenty-four, was the son of Ernie's brother Bill and my sister Esther, making him a very special double cousin to our children. He had finished at the top of his high school class and then decided that he would educate himself instead of going on to college; several years earlier he had successfully built the deck at our lake cabin. We knew Jeff was smart enough that he did not need an architecture degree to masterfully build the greenhouse. Much to our satisfaction, he agreed to take on the project, which Jeff saw as an exciting challenge.

And so what had once been a study that doubled as a guest bedroom became Jeff's room away from home. He lived with us for months, working with precision and expertise to bring this project to fruition. We all took great pride in watching this super-talented young man turn a dream into reality. When Jeff's project came to an end, beautiful plants thrived inside the greenhouse, and new azalea shrubs were started and used for plantings in Stephen's developing garden side lawn. It is also interesting to note that more than thirty years later, that greenhouse remains proudly unchanged from its original design, even though several different owners have made major architectural changes to the house.

Constant Media Scrutiny

As when Ernie was the chancellor of SUNY, his position as a high government official in the nation's capital meant the press was always lurking around, looking for a story. There was thus never a feeling of freedom from the constant scrutiny of the media, and Ernie learned the hard way he had to be careful when he used humor during a press conference.

That lesson came when he answered a question about teaching the metric system in U.S. schools during what would become the country's failed attempt to switch to the metric system. Ernie related a humorous anecdote about driving in England and his efforts to convert kilometers into miles. The next day there was a newspaper headline and story about the new commissioner of education opposing students being taught the metric system, which was not at all Ernie's position.

The persistence of the press, however, did not affect Ernie only but touched the whole family. Although Stephen was a student at the local public junior high school, radio reporter Walter Winchell said the U.S. commissioner of education was sending his own son to a private school. People had faith in Winchell's reporting, which seemed to touch off a contest among members of the press as to who would be the first to find Stephen for an interview. But Stephen was on the lookout for the press and at least once tricked them by hiding in the school's restroom. They never found him, and he was able to avoid a dreaded interview.

However, Stephen's grandpa called Walter Winchell and told him what he had reported was false and that it was Winchell's duty to report the truth. The next day, Winchell issued a correction and a half apology. While Winchell's associates in the press were then off to their next story, we knew they would be back.

Part II: Delivering a Dream

After the sabbatical, when we had moved back into the Chancellor House Mansion, Ernie came up with a radical idea about how I could fulfill my dream to become a midwife, planning for me to enroll as a midwifery student at the New York State University Downstate Medical Center in Brooklyn. To me it seemed like just an impossible dream, but he was determined and even talked of renting a little apartment for me to use, assuring me that he and Stephen would come to visit on weekends.

His radical plan was seriously interrupted when he was called to serve in Washington, but about this same time we were astonished to learn there was a new nurse-midwifery program opening at Georgetown University. We also learned that all university-based midwifery programs were admitting only a very small number of students from hundreds of applicants. Still Ernie somehow believed I could become one of the students in the first class at Georgetown.

Once we were settled in our Warm Heart Mansion, I worked up enough courage to place a call to Marilyn Schmidt, the program director at Georgetown. She told me the university had funding for ten students and that the class members had all been selected out of 350 nurse-midwifery applicants. Nevertheless, she told me to come for an interview. I had no reason to feel hopeful, but she kindly received me.

During the interview she told me new government money was being granted for two additional students, but letters had already been sent out to the hundreds of disappointed applicants who had not been accepted. Still, as the interview proceeded, I clearly felt a glimmer of hope. She was in need of two students. Interestingly, besides me, there was one other late applicant, Fran Ventre, and we were both admitted.

I shortly received a letter of acceptance from Georgetown University for their midwifery program and was also notified my class would begin in four months. How amazed and thrilled I was! But I was also scared. Ernie was truly overjoyed. He understood my dream and wanted to see it fulfilled.

I felt honored my husband would be so supportive of my dreams during such a busy season in our lives, but time after time Ernie reminded me it was part of our mutual commitment to support each other's hopes and dreams. There was something about the way Ernie explained things that helped me see that what I did almost automatically was exactly what any good spouse, man or woman, would do to support his or her partner's well-being. I thanked God for having such a supportive spouse, and I know he felt the same way and offered the same prayer about me.

Ready to Walk Out

That September day in 1977 stands out in my mind more clearly than most days. My classmates and I were told to come to the medical education building at Georgetown University for orientation. Eleven young ladies and me, a forty-eight-year-old-woman, sat nervously around a conference table. Abruptly the door flew open, and the beautiful young director, Ms. Marilyn Schmidt, came rushing into the room with an armload of books.

She piled them on the table and curtly said, "The nurse-midwifery program at Georgetown University is the most difficult—mentally and physically—of any department. If you are not capable of living up to these high standards, do not come back tomorrow." Right then and there, I almost threw away my dream. I looked around and it was clear she had completely scared all of us. I drove home having fully decided that I was not going back.

That was my decision, that is, until Ernie came home that evening. When I told him what happened and that I was going to have to give up my dream because I was not going back to that impossible program, he calmly told me I was going back and that together we would trust God, one day at a time. And so it was that leaning on God with trust and faith, I went back the next day and every other day until graduation.

Our class soon bonded together as a team, and we always looked out for one other. The program was demanding and stressful, but I loved learning and putting my learning into practice. Most of the clients we served came to the large District of Columbia General Hospital on Massachusetts Avenue where we practiced (and which sadly closed in May 2001). Our clients were often very young teenagers with extremely poor nutritional habits who had received no prenatal care before they came to us to give birth.

As a student, I had an ongoing dream about ways to reach out to these young girls. It was my dearest hope that by trusting God one day at a time, as Ernie always said, and with determination, I would complete the program. Then I would find a way to help these young women and the babies entrusted into their care. Such a challenge would become one of the true joys of my life.

Delivering My Own Granddaughter

Shortly before I graduated from my nurse-midwifery program, I had the chance of a lifetime when Beverly gave birth to her first child and our third grandchild. She had her regular prenatal check-ups with a nurse-midwife at the maternity center and been assured of a normal delivery. Beverly insisted she did not want to give birth at the hospital or even at the homey, inviting birth center but dearly wanted to have her baby at home—surrounded by the familiar and the love of family.

When she started labor, the midwifery backup doctor was notified. I was about to graduate as a nurse-midwife but had only participated in hospital births during the education program. With the backup support from the midwifery practice where Beverly received her prenatal care, a faculty member came to assist me. I felt prepared and so overjoyed to be asked to deliver my own grandchild. Ernie and I had two grandsons and were now secretly hoping for a granddaughter.

Our son-in-law, Will, helped Beverly with the breathing exercises they had learned. Soft music was playing, and the lights were low, and at 10:33 p.m. on May 7, 1978, precious Leah Kathryn had a sweet, gentle birth into the hands of her grandmother Kathryn. Nothing could have been more thrilling for me as I received this baby and welcomed her with God's blessing of love and overwhelming joy! I have to confess Ernie and I also celebrated having a granddaughter to complement our two grandsons.

Ernie wrote an op-ed article that he never published but I kept about the terrible anxiety he suffered during this home birth experience. He would do anything for his precious daughter, but he had a huge problem with the idea of Beverly delivering her baby at home. He wrote:

> Whatever gland that goads the flight instinct was pumping overtime. I wanted to run from the reality of birth. I felt I had to use the telephone. My car keys burned in my pocket: I wanted to rush Beverly to the hospital. Instinctively, in spite of her own wishes I preferred to turn her over to machines, to medication, to strangers.

He then goes on to offer:

> But the time has come to renegotiate our social contract with our inventions. It's time to assert the strength of every individual and the boundless resource we have in one another.

He ends the piece by writing that we left at midnight. "Mother and daughter are doing fine. And Grandpa is beginning to recover."

Baby Leah was nurtured and caressed by the whole family, but her Papa (as Ernie was called by the grandchildren) was downright doting, and I'm thinking Uncle Stephen and Nana (me) were also.

Graduation and Celebration

About a year after I first arrived in Washington and only a few weeks after delivering my granddaughter, I completed a major goal that was as noteworthy for Ernie as it was for me: I became a certified nurse-midwife. It would never have been possible without Ernie's constant encouragement and support. He fully kept the promise he made to me on my first day of class when he told me he would be there to help me, along with God, to face that challenge one day at a time.

The graduation for the Georgetown University Nurse-Midwifery Program was set for 2 p.m., Saturday, May 27, 1978. That announcement appears simple enough. However, when I now read Ernie's calendar for Thursday, May 25, 1978, and Friday, May 26, 1978, I wonder why I was not sitting on pins and needles worrying if he and Stephen were even going to make it to my big graduation day ceremony. I guess I had learned to live with Ernie's tangled and overbooked routine and somehow trusted all would work out as he believed it would.

On Thursday before my graduation, Ernie and Stephen left Washington for Bangor, Maine, where they were met midafternoon by four school officials and Ernie Jr. The opportunity to combine Ernie's official work with a chance to be with precious family in Maine was too wonderful to turn down. It was a terrible sacrifice for me not to go to be with our three darling grandsons—four-year-old Nathan, two-year-old Gabriel, and two-week-old Julian. However, I was frantically finishing one last requirement. I had taken time off already for the birth of now three-week-old granddaughter Leah, and so had to miss the family visit in Maine to be ready for my graduation.

Ernie and Stephen stayed overnight and most of Friday with Ernie Jr.'s family, celebrating the birth of baby Julian, before flying to Albany, New York. Patricia Snyder, director of SUNY's Empire State Theatre Institute, had asked Ernie to attend the opening production of "Peter Pan." Ernie accepted the invitation to show respect for the amazing efforts of the student performers and support for the institute, and also because it would be an evening he and Stephen could enjoy together.

On Saturday morning, my graduation day, Ernie and Stephen boarded a flight in Albany that was scheduled to arrive at Washington National Airport just one and a half hours before graduation began. There were no cell phones then, so all I could do was watch the entrance to the hall where graduation was being held, longing to see them appear. Like in a great story, Ernie and Stephen arrived in time, looking relaxed, found their seats with the rest of our family, and cheered as I walked across the stage to receive my diploma.

I am almost embarrassed to reveal what happened the very second the graduation ceremony ended. I fear readers will think our plan was foolish, although to Ernie and me it was an act of newfound freedom now that I was finally free from the midwifery program's demands and able join Ernie's busy but exciting life. So, as soon as graduation ended, Ernie and I left for the airport, where we actually made the 4 p.m. flight back to Albany. There we rented a car and drove to the Rockefeller family's estate in Pocantico Hills to celebrate Nelson Rockefeller's seventieth birthday at an 8:30 dinner.

Mrs. Rockefeller's staff arranged for us to stay that night at the lovely Tarrytown Hilton Inn, and the next day we were off to Hamilton College in Clinton, New York, where Ernie gave the commencement address and held a press conference. That afternoon we flew back to Washington, arriving home in time to begin a family celebration of my graduation that lasted all the next day.

I had met my big goal of completing my midwifery education before my fiftieth birthday, and my heart and all my family were full of celebration and joyous thankfulness. I was especially grateful to my husband, Ernie, for the sacrifices he had made in his own schedule and life order to help make my dream come true.

Making a Difference in Young Lives

After I graduated from the nurse-midwifery program, I worked as an intern midwife at the District of Columbia General Hospital, a position I wanted even though I knew the work would be challenging and demanding. The urge I had experienced as a student—to someday find a way to help the many pregnant school-age girls—was stronger than ever. Most of these girls were repeating the life experiences of their own mothers and grandmothers who had started having babies as teens and then dropped out of school.

The typical pattern was a household without fathers and mothers living on welfare. I felt these girls should be given an opportunity to break that cycle, and my hope was that this midwifery position would allow me to bring dignity and meaning to the lives of these young people. Helping these girls to master infant care, including understanding the importance of good nutrition, and providing services so these teenagers could continue their education—even go on to pursue a higher education—were components of the vision that stayed with me. My most ideal vision was that through counseling young girls would be spared the tragedy of the youngster I'm about to discuss.

I clearly remember one night when I was working in the hospital admitting area. It was after midnight when a fifteen-year-old girl walked in alone. She did not look particularly pregnant, but since she was complaining of pain in the abdominal area, she was sent to me, the midwife on duty. My examination found she was in active labor. She had never had any form of prenatal care and admitted to me she had tried to hide her pregnancy by dieting—eating mostly potato chips and diet sodas. I gathered she did not want the baby, but I calmly helped her through her labor and delivered a tiny baby girl.

I had many concerns for this young mother and for her low-birth-weight infant. The girl even needed encouragement to think of a name for the precious child she had just birthed. I worried about the future of her child because the mother, in her ignorance and immaturity, had provided almost no protein or other nutrients her baby needed to develop healthy brain cells or grow overall. It was so sad to think this young mother's lack of information and understanding about the importance of proper prenatal care could have destroyed her child's potential. This girl, just five years past her tenth birthday, was just one of hundreds of youngsters in the area who were experiencing or destined to experience the same predicament. I believed I was called to help make a difference in their lives.

Federal Interventions

In the evenings, I would tell Ernie all about my work frustrations, and we would talk over possible solutions. He started to focus on the broad problem of children having children all across America, not just the disadvantaged babies in Washington DC. He felt any education solution should extend

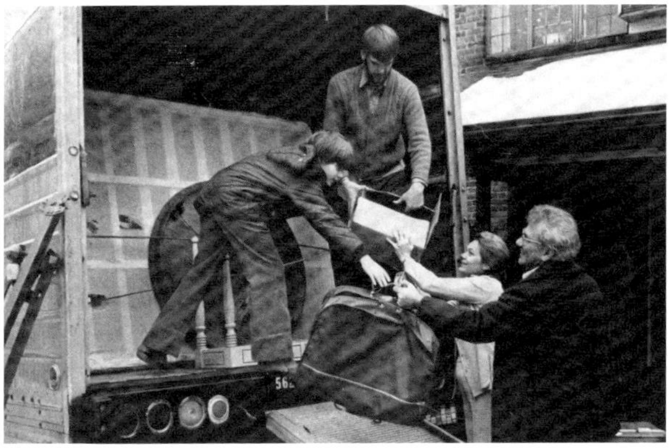

Personal Photo of the Boyer Family

Ernie and I packing the U-Haul truck, along with Stephen (Paul) and Craig, as we prepared to move from Albany, NY to McLean, VA.

Photo Used with Permission of the Ernest L. Boyer Center Archives, Messiah College)

Ernie with Jean Kennedy Smith (left) and Vivienne Anderson (right) at the Very Special Friends Arts Festival, Kennedy Center for the Performing Arts, Washington, DC.

Personal Photo of the Boyer Family

Craig and Flora at their wedding in Belize.

Personal Photo of the Boyer Family

Flora's family home in Belize.

Personal Photo of the Boyer Family

The greenhouse Ernie had built onto the Warm Heart Mansion in McLean, VA.

Personal Photo of the Boyer Family

Professor Chang in front of a seemingly endless rack of bicycles during the trip Ernie and I made to China.

Personal Photo of the Boyer Family

Ernie and I with Madame Professor Hao Keming (far right), "Director-General of China's Most Important Arm on Education Policy-Making and Education Reform," along with two other education officials from China's Communist Party.

Personal Photo of the Boyer Family

Ernie in his office at the Carnegie Foundation for the Advancement of Teaching in Princeton, NJ.

Personal Photo of the Boyer Family

The front door of the Family Home Mansion in Princeton, NJ.

Photo Used with Permission of the Ernest L. Boyer Center Archives, Messiah College

Ernie and I speaking with children. He loved to get down on their level when talking with them.

Photo Used with Permission of the Ernest L. Boyer Center Archives, Messiah College

Ernie with former United States President Jimmy Carter and Messiah College President D. Ray Hostetter at Messiah College.

Personal Photo of the Boyer Family

Ernie and I with United States President Bill Clinton and First Lady Hillary Rodham Clinton at a reception at the White House.

Personal Photo of the Boyer Family

Ernie and Nathan taking a break from their hike in the Cotswolds. While we were in England on this trip Ernie discovered a lump in his neck that turned out to be lymphoma.

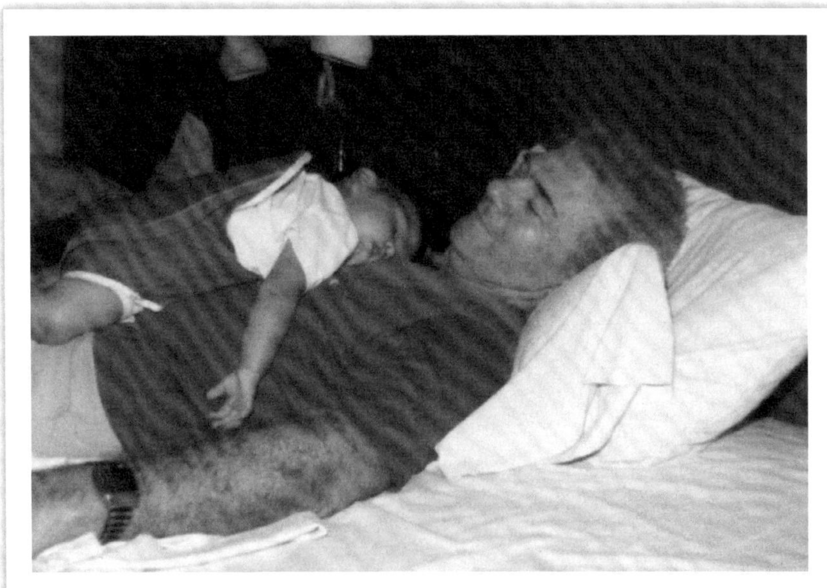

Personal Photo of the Boyer Family

Baby Anna, Craig and Flora's daughter, asleep on Ernie.

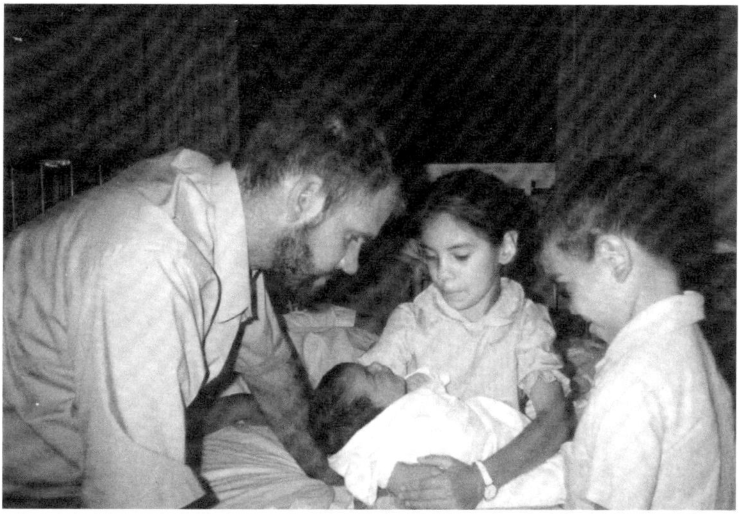

Personal Photo of the Boyer Family

Craig showing Andy to Andy's new big brother and sister. Ernie believed we needed to head to Belize in order to be of assistance to Craig and Flora when Andy was born. He was right and fortunately we arrived just in time for me to help deliver Andy.

Personal Photo of the Boyer Family

Ernie and I with our grandchildren (Craig and Flora's children) in Belize. Ernie was undergoing chemotherapy for lymphoma at the time.

Personal Photo of the Boyer Family

Ernie and I on a trip to South Carolina shortly before he died.

nationwide, and thus a Federal Office of Adolescent Pregnancy Programs was established with Lula Mae Nix as director.

Through that office, grants were given to schools across the country to develop education programs to decrease the number of teenage pregnancies and to keep girls in school if they did get pregnant. Many high schools opened outstanding programs that began to have amazing results. I was thrilled and proud of the nationwide movement Ernie initiated as an outgrowth of our shared experiences and concerns.

At the same time, I continued to concentrate on the Washington DC area. With grant money and help from Lula Mae Nix's Federal Office for the Prevention of Teen Pregnancy, I worked on developing a comprehensive program to reduce the number of teen pregnancies through education, to teach proper nutrition for those already pregnant, and to help these young mothers finish their high school educations. Our goal was to have these teenage mothers not only learn how to be successful parents but also how to be successful citizens.

Cities in Schools Program

I was fortunate to be able to connect with a strong inner-city youth organization, a nonprofit agency called Cities in Schools, Inc., that was started by a friend, Bill Milligan. The Washington DC director, Maurice Weir Sr. applauded the comprehensive program I launched, which featured the use of certified nurse-midwives to provide prenatal care and deliver babies. We rented a facility large enough to include school classroom space and hired a city high school teacher whose salary came from the school district. We operated a prenatal clinic area, a kitchen for nutrition and cooking classes, and programs that included social services and spiritual counseling. There was also a scheduled program for teen fathers.

A second midwife was hired to deliver our students' babies at Georgetown University Hospital and the District of Columbia General Hospital. A fine daycare program was already operating in the same building, which made it possible for the student-mother to bring her baby to the care center and then go a few doors down the hall to her school classroom. Adding to the happy atmosphere were rocking chairs in the rear of the classroom where a mother could sit to nurse when the daycare worker brought the hungry baby to her. This allowed the nursing mother to still be a part of the classroom studies and not miss out on any of the instruction.

I loved the very capable, dedicated, and compassionate staff I was able to hire. We all worked together in loving relationships and shared in the thrill of the many positive results. Sometimes, I would join the social worker on her home visits and was pleased with so many of the effective results I was witnessing. I was the only white person on the team, but my colleagues did not seem to notice. They just affectionately nicknamed me "Big Mama," a title I still cherish.

My degree was being put to good use as God had placed me just where I needed to be. The challenges were real, but together we were striving to make a difference in the lives of these women and the children they would raise. Ernie, to his credit, had helped me fulfill this dream, and I was committed to helping him fulfill his own. Settled in at the Warm Heart Mansion, both of us were fully prepared to be of complete support to one another as we worked to follow God's leading regardless of what changes might come.

Part III: Grueling Schedule, Enduring Accomplishments

It seems to me now that we had a completely impossible schedule during those years. I recall how much I wanted to give Ernie my daily, loving support. But my midwifery studies were too grueling for me to be fully aware of his daily responsibilities.

At the beginning of his appointment, Ernie said he wanted to reaffirm the centrality of education in America and to say what was right about our schools. It was time to counter critics who seemed more intent on cutting budgets than on educating children. And, it was time to declare that education has been and must always be one of America's priorities.

Ernie supported and praised teachers and enjoyed speaking at national and state teachers' conferences. I often heard him say to them, "You've been asked to adjust your curriculum to countless passing fads; you've been expected to teach effectively every day, to help solve social problems, and yet, despite these added obligations, you carry on your work with dignity and skill." He told teachers that they had chosen the noblest of professions as they taught and trained young minds.

Four Days in February

In the Boyer Archives at Messiah College are large binders filled with Ernie's daily calendars given him daily by his executive secretary, Ruth Worsley.

Before I put pen to page in writing this book, I read hundreds of pages from those daily appointment books, struggling to figure out the complicated comings and goings of my husband during this time. I confess, looking back at these schedules reminded me of the quiet fear I often harbored that this overcrowded schedule would injure his health. By way of illustrating, I offer four days in February 1978, beginning with Thursday, February 9, 1978.

That morning started with an 8 a.m. breakfast in his office, which was his weekly Thursday morning meeting with three to six Christian friends who were also government employees, plus Bill Milligan, a friend of President Carter's family. Each week they took forty-five minutes to read from the Bible and discuss how they each tried daily to be accountable to God and maintain their integrity amidst the crushing political demands of their positions. Then they prayed for the work, the employees, and the efforts at the Office of Education.

Following this time of prayer, there was a short staff meeting about the duties of that day before Ernie headed to Capitol Hill for a hearing before the House Committee on Education and Labor and a Senate Committee on Human Resources.

Noon to 3 p.m. was reserved for desk work and phone calls before his driver, Arthur, a gentle and thoughtful man, took him to National Airport for a flight to Columbus, Ohio. Ernie met there with the Ohio superintendent of public instruction and later that evening was given the Ohio governor's award for his "Contribution to the Field of Education" at the Newspaper Association dinner. He left Columbus on an early-morning flight the next day and by midmorning was back in his DC office, meeting with Cora Beebe, the well-respected and efficient budget director for the Office of Education. Before a meeting with the director of the Right to Read Program, Ernie was interviewed and photographed by UPI for a feature article on people in Washington DC.

Ernie's schedule notes he was to leave for home at 5:30 p.m. But when it was time to leave, he called me to say several people were waiting to talk to him about Jesse Jackson's "Push—Excel" program, focusing on inner-city youth and their need to pursue excellence in education. Of course dinner waited another hour or more. I suppose Stephen and I did what we must have done many times before—stole some nibbles and continued with our own work until we could all sit down to dinner together. Sharing dinner, however long it had to wait, was sacred in our house, as it is with many families even today, and provided all of us with a time to reconnect.

Saturday brought a change that included Stephen and me. Ernie's happiest times were when his work could include family in his duties, even if it was brief. I remember this Saturday, February 11, 1978, as a fun-filled one that started at 7 a.m. when Arthur arrived at the house to drive us from McLean to Williamsburg, Virginia. Ernie was scheduled to deliver the major address at the College of William and Mary's 285th Charter Day Convocation and to receive an honorary doctorate. Because it was a Saturday event and we tried to save weekends for family time, Ernie accepted the invitation as a family group—that also included Arthur. After the luncheon, Stephen and I left the college and used the three hours while Ernie was busy at the convocation to visit the restored Colonial Williamsburg, the original capital of Virginia.

We were back home by about 7 p.m. The trip was a day of sight-seeing for me and for Stephen and was done in twelve hours. There was no rest, however, for Ernie, who had to keep up the pace in order to attend a dinner in downtown Washington in honor of the former commissioner of education, Terrell Bell and his wife. I had also been invited, but had sent regrets, knowing I needed to stay home with Stephen.

That was only day three of the four days I'm trying to untangle. Certainly, by now there must be exhaustion, but Ernie did not focus on that. Unfortunately, we did not get to go to Baltimore to spend Sunday with Grandpa and Grandma Boyer that week because Ernie's schedule required him to drive himself to the Dulles Airport for a noon flight to Los Angeles. That same evening, West Coast time, he would address the Annual Convention of the National Association of Secondary School Principals.

I cannot resist also giving you a preview of Monday, day five. After the long flight back to Dulles Airport, Ernie drove to his office to make sure everything was ready for a meeting the next morning with Congressman Al

Ullman of the House Ways and Means Committee regarding the Education Reauthorization Bill.

Igniting a Flame

Those five days provide a glimpse into the scope and intensity of Ernie's efforts, but it does not reveal all of his work. Day-by-day, Ernie was charged with leading 146 separate programs, from federally insured student loans to programs addressing our nation's tragic legacy of segregation and discrimination in education. For example, Ernie told me of a time early in President Carter's administration when the president instructed all agencies to prepare a "zero-based" budget. The goal was to go back to square one and "prioritize" all federal programs from top to bottom.

In response, Ernie scheduled a weekend retreat with his senior staff to debate the merits of each of the existing programs. He wanted to make the retreat a cordial time for the staff away from the office, to be able to respectfully work together to complete this intense assignment. He was most impressed when Cora Beebe argued eloquently that the Native American Indian Education Program should be the "number one priority." She had discovered in her budget research that a shameful neglect of federal support for the education of Native Americans and insisted that the federal government had both a legal and a moral obligation to help Native American children who were suffering under the prejudicial conditions our nation had tragically imposed upon them.

Ernie found her research and her argument compelling and moving. In fact, he was so troubled by America's unwillingness to respond adequately to the needs of our Native American population that he used his influence for the next decade and a half of his life to pursue opportunities for them. Later, Stephen picked up the torch. (By this time he was going by his middle name, Paul, and from this point on I will refer to him as Paul). He served as an instructor of journalism at California State University at Sacramento and has written two books on behalf of Tribal Colleges and Native American Colleges, in addition to publishing the scholarly *Tribal College Journal* for eight years in the 1980s.

All his writings are under the name Paul Boyer (not to be confused with his uncle Paul S. Boyer, who served on the faculty in the history department at the Universities of Massachusetts and Wisconsin and has also authored a number of books). One could say his father, Ernest L. Boyer, inspired our nation to look anew at the education of tribal peoples. However, Ernie would likely also be quick to note that such inspiration begins in many ways at home, and he would be extremely proud of his son, Paul, and what he has done with his writing.

Entertaining, DC Style

Ernie's work rarely ended when he left the office, and our lives became deeply permeated by the unrelenting political atmosphere of Washington DC. It was not unusual to be invited to two or three cocktail parties a week. Sometimes Ernie discerned it was necessary to attend, and he was most happy if I could go with him. I loved to go and went whenever my duties allowed.

These parties were an interesting study for me, and I was intrigued by watching people as they arrived and following their movements after they took a quick glance around the crowded room. They would politely greet people while moving swiftly to the one or two individuals they had sought out upon entering the room; often they had come to the party specifically to lobby for a particular cause. Under the pressure of busy daytime schedules, these events were often the only way to take care of some pressing issues.

Ernie, I must confess, would act the same as the people I just described. I had met enough of these government officials by this time that I could help with the spying or could alert Ernie if one of the people he was hoping to speak to was making moves toward the exit. We would often leave one party and travel to another similar event somewhere else in the city. He could clear up some important agenda issues in one evening, and we could enjoy some time together. We called it our own unique version of a date night.

We preferred, however, to open our home for hospitality and friendship. With new friends in this new job and in this new city, we decided to send out dinner invitations. It was not easy, but in between my midwifery studies I managed to fit in the preparation of home-cooked meals for our guests. We anticipated a lovely evening of eating, conversation and laughter, as at past dinner parties.

But one particular evening proved to be a big letdown. Ernie and I felt like it was a failure because the guests treated the evening as simply a continuation of their political business. I confess I thought they never even noticed I had cooked my best for them and seemed barely aware that they were in a dining situation versus a cocktail party. Ernie always thought of dining as a relaxing opportunity to enjoy friendship, but that time it did not work. We eventually gave up on that kind of entertainment in DC and reserved such times simply for family and friends.

Creating a Special Kind of School

It is very true that Ernie honored and admired many people in Washington, and felt that almost all of his government colleagues were people of integrity who were dedicated to serve and to do what was right. But early on, during his first year as commissioner, he was asked by the head of one of the departments for a meeting with her and some of her staff. She began the meeting with a deeply shocking question. "Mr. Commissioner, could you please tell us why we come to work every day here at the Office of Education?" It was a shockingly direct and pertinent question that called for a direct answer. At that moment, he tried to educate them about the overall goals and responsibilities of the programs in the Office of Education.

However, the question stayed in his mind and, in a short time, he came up with an exciting response that would turn out to be one of his most creative plans. He decided to start a school within the Office of Education where all employees would take classes that would teach them how their work made a difference and why it was so important, hoping to bring purpose and joyful enthusiasm to their work. He named it the Horace Mann Center in honor of the nineteenth-century American educator-reformer, who was often called the "Father of the Common School."

I always thought Ernie was a born teacher, and I applauded when he decided to return to the classroom himself as the head of this initiative. He wanted to teach a course on the use of clear language. He told a news reporter the class was "to flush gobbledygook out of the agency." The *Washington Post* then ran an article with a headline; "The Boss Teacher Comes Back to the Classroom."

The article offered illustrations of samples Ernie brought to the classroom. One was a letter with one sentence that rambled through thirty-eight words to say "we have no money" in order to turn down a request for grant funding. Another letter described students as "the raw material we are in-putting." Ernie said he wished to remove the cloak of impersonality from memos and letters so they would not reinforce the attitudes that bureaucracies are faceless, obscure organizations. He loved teaching, and those classroom sessions livened up his highly scheduled day.

The Horace Mann School became a vital center not only to educate the employees but also as a focal point for lectures and symposiums Ernie chaired with distinguished educators and national leaders. These events, which explored major issues in education, were important highlights for the Office of Education and I always tried to find a way to attend and share them with Ernie. Some of the notable guests I remember include Senator J. William Fulbright, Daniel Boorstin, Charles Frankel, Benjamin Mays, and Congressman John Brademas. Their presence, Ernie's leadership, and the way Ernie's colleagues invested in these sessions elevated the level of conversations concerning education taking place in Washington DC.

The education commissioners from each state, called the Chief State School Officers, were answerable to Ernie, and he planned way ahead for their regular visits. The Horace Mann School was an especially fine setting to host their productive meetings, and he insisted on attention to such details as seating and lighting. Ernie's staff was enamored by his high demands for proper settings to honor all guests and attendees, and I understood how they felt because I was often in awe of the way he would change the furniture around at our house to please his eye or to prepare a room for an event, even one as simple as reading stories to our grandchildren. His aim was to help people feel connected to each other and to the speaker.

Faith to Meet the Challenges

More than thirty years later, when I look back at those days, I am surprised we had enough of whatever it took to deal with the high-pressured lives we led in Washington. Ernie had the weight of America's public schools on his shoulders. I was wrapped up in my studies at Georgetown. Together, we did all we could to be the parents for our children that God had called us to be.

Each night during our evening prayers, Ernie always said a special thank you to God and asked for His protection. We also asked for forgiveness for individuals such as reporters who, in their thirst to land a story, often twisted the truth. By God's grace, our prayers were almost always answered. We sought to do the best we could to put our faith into every decision we made as a family and into our efforts to serve the needs of others. Such challenges are not easy but are entirely necessary for God's creation to flourish as He first intended it.

Part IV: Black Ties and Burned Steaks

After a while, Ernie and I began to feel as if we had found our way in the nation's capital. In a place so complicated and so highly charged, however, we knew any successes we were having came by virtue of God's grace. Ernie's position put him in frequent contact with the top leaders of the country, which could range from simple business meetings or quiet conversations to elaborate celebrations, and Ernie felt called to demonstrate God's grace in all those encounters.

His daily calendar pages include frequent notations that he had been cleared for all gates at the White House. For example, on March 21, 1978, Ernie's driver, Arthur, was told to enter through the northwest gate. Ernie was then escorted by a White House uniformed attendant to the Roosevelt Room, where a group was gathered to honor the National Teacher of the Year, Elaine Barbour, of Colorado.

Ernie spoke briefly to the individuals gathered there and then escorted Ms. Barbour to the Oval Office where President Carter received the honored teacher. Ernie left his office for the White House at 1:30 p.m. and was scheduled to be back in his office by 2:30 p.m. In that one hour of his busy schedule, Ernie presided over a most memorable moment in the life of a dedicated teacher.

One month later, he again met in the White House Roosevelt Room to administer the oath of office to the commissioner of presidential scholars.

Ernie attended other outstanding events at the White House, and each time he described it as a singularly extraordinary privilege.

One Enchanting Evening

I delight in recalling a very formal White House black-tie reception. When we arrived, our presence was announced to President and Mrs. Carter whose casual friendliness as they greeted us eased my tension. That evening, we were honoring five performing artists: Marian Anderson, George Balanchine; Fred Astaire; Richard Rodgers; and Arthur Rubinstein. From the reception everyone traveled to the Kennedy Center where we were privileged to dine with these world-famous artists who would be on stage following the elaborate dinner. Dinners with famous people were exhilarating and yet also made me feel somewhat on edge.

By now, I had enough experience to not be as nervous as I was when we first went to Paris and attended that formal French dinner. There I had pretended to be poised, but now I was more self-assured and more comfortable, although dining with Arthur Rubinstein and his colleagues kept me on my toes. Mr. Rubinstein charmed all of us sitting around his table with stories that showed his love of life. This same enthusiasm was later evident on stage in his robust and glorious piano renditions.

From the Kennedy Center dining atrium, we walked to the Center's Concert Hall for a once-in-a-lifetime event—to see these five artists on stage and watch as they received from President Carter awards for "lifetime contributions to the American culture through the performing arts." President and Mrs. Carter usually sat in the President's Box with their honored guests, but on this night they were right up front with the rest of us.

Whenever President Carter was not using the President's Box at the Kennedy Center, the seats were offered to certain government officials and their families. It was a delightful perk that we used to treat family and guests. We could sit together in an area that housed enough seats to accommodate approximately eight or more people. Off from the seating area was a small kitchen with a refrigerator that was always stocked with cold beverages. One very remarkable performance stands out in my mind, when we and our guests sat in the President's Box watching the performance of a one-man show by the outstanding actor, Alec McCowen as he recited from memory the entire Gospel of Mark.

Finding Friends in High Places

Despite the pervasive cynicism of our current age concerning individuals called to public service, Ernie found a number of friends he greatly respected in the United States Senate and House of Representatives. Because he was not closely identified with a political party, he easily worked with either side, especially the legislators on the education committees. Ernie found bipartisanship was not only possible, but downright necessary.

To this end, I will offer two examples although more could certainly be noted. First, when a Republican senator (whose name will go unmentioned) made a comment at a hearing that reflected a racially prejudicial attitude toward one of Ernie's assistant commissioners, the staff member was deeply offended. Ernie made an appointment to meet the senator for lunch because he knew what had been said at the hearing was not right and needed to be addressed. He also knew the senator was a Christian and would not willingly want to harbor an attitude that could make him say words laced with racial bias.

The open discussion Ernie and this senator had over lunch led to the senator asking forgiveness from the staff member and requesting a change of the language in the formal record. The offended assistant commissioner was vindicated, touched, and grateful, and Ernie's respect for this senator also deepened as a result of this interaction. Both Ernie and the senator were thankful for a friendship that allowed them to openly discuss this incident in a warm and kindly manner and that friendship lasted for Ernie's lifetime.

The second incident involved a speech Ernie gave at the National Conference on Higher Education entitled, "The Chaos of College Curricula." On March 21, 1977, *The Washington Post's Sunday Outlook,* printed the full text of the speech. Later, a senator, whose name I have now unfortunately forgotten, quoted large sections of the speech on the floor of the Senate. He requested his Senate colleagues read the entire article and said, "I ask unanimous consent that the entire Boyer article be printed in the official *Senate Record*." I suspect the senator was touched by Ernie's words such as, "Our life is just an instant in a long stretch. Yet we spend time fighting one another and laying waste our earth. We must better educate to make the human spirit more sensitive."

These two incidents may be special examples, but it is heartwarming for me to relate such gratifying moments in the nation's capital. Public service, while a constant challenge, is necessary for the health of our society. In order to nurture that health, we need people who can cross party lines, work behind the scenes with charity, admit faults, and keep their eyes fixed on the largest possible goals. With God's grace, we can certainly find the will to address our gravest challenges and bring light to people living in the darkest of places.

Barbecue with the Vice President

Vice President Walter Mondale was perhaps the government official Ernie appreciated the most. His wife, Joan, was also outstanding and known as a national advocate for the arts. She was herself an excellent artist and craftswoman. Ernie was interested in art education in the nation's schools and promoted this cause in various ways. One widely publicized event was the "Arts in Education Forum" at the Kennedy Center, and Mrs. Mondale was an important participant. At the same time, at the request of Jeanne Kennedy Smith, Ernie served as chairman of the "Very Special Art Committee" at the Kennedy Center.

Vice President Mondale and Ernie saw eye to eye on many issues. During an early afternoon meeting in Mondale's White House office, Ernie sought counsel on a government issue. They ended the meeting with a casual conversation in which Mondale invited Ernie and me to come to their home for dinner that evening, saying he would barbecue steaks and Joan would prepare baked potatoes and a salad.

The vice president had to give Ernie very specific driving directions since their home was in a location unfamiliar to us and we had no technology at the time to tell us the way. Mondale was the first vice president to live in the mansion at the Naval Observatory—Number One Observatory Circle. Ernie, being a good driver and having a very clear sense of direction, was able to drive right to the gate.

More than thirty years later, I remember that evening clearly, even though I have forgotten some details about the setting, although I do remember it was beautiful. The evening was warm, and when we arrived, Mr. Mondale was busy trying to light charcoal on an ordinary grill. Mrs. Mondale greeted us warmly and invited us into the lovely home, where her crafts and her art were tastefully displayed, revealing fine artistic skills. Our conversation moved through a variety of areas as Mrs. Mondale gave the background for each piece of art. The vice president was enthusiastic about his wife's accomplishments and added his viewpoints.

The time was unhurried and comfortably relaxing. Although we were fairly new acquaintances and their daily lifestyle did not coincide with ours, their own ease made us feel at home and affirmed. Ernie loved these kinds of evenings with friends and easily showed he was having a good time.

Once we moved outside to the pleasant patio area, the vice president declared the coals were ready. He was intent on getting the steaks done just right, but the fire must have been too intense and the conversation too absorbing because before he was aware of what was happening, the steaks burned. He was very apologetic as we all sat eating together in this idyllic setting, enjoying a warm friendship, and trying not to dwell on the overdone steaks. In the end, Ernie and I wondered, "How many times does one get to eat steak, prepared to perfection or not, with the vice president of the United States?"

A Test for Governors

While on the subject of interaction with highly recognized government officials, there is one more occasion that merits mentioning. Every year while Ernie was the commissioner of education, the two of us were invited by President and Mrs. Carter to the White House to meet with the governors who served as members of the Governors Council. The annual council reception was a valuable opportunity for Ernie and me to be introduced to these governors.

After being announced and greeted by President and Mrs. Carter, we moved along the line to greet the honored guests. At these receptions for governors, Ernie and I liked to play a little game to evaluate the ones who we thought were the most effective and impressive public servants. It was a simple test and fun game to play. First, we tested their handshake. Was it firm and clearly sincere or weak and lacking interest? The next test was the smile. Was it warm and gladly given? But the most important test was eye contact. In essence, did the person look you in the eye? I'm pleased to report that all but one or two passed our three-part test with flying colors. Sorry, but I won't divulge the names of those governors who did not pass.

Chatting with a Princess

Even though we attended many events with many important people in DC, getting an invitation from Secretary of State Cyrus Vance to an upcoming event both pleased and surprised Ernie. The occasion was a formal reception to honor Her Royal Highness Princess Margaret, the sister of the Queen of England. According to custom, the invitation read, Commissioner Ernest L. Boyer and Mrs. Boyer are invited to ________. This was a great honor for Ernie and me.

We had never experienced as many security measures as were in place on that particular occasion. Once we were cleared to enter, we were directed to an adorned room with a warm-colored plush rug and matching draperies, which appeared to be a proper setting for a princess. As we waited for our turn to greet the guest, I could not take my eyes off of the princess, who was beautiful and clearly had mastered her role to perfection. I watched carefully as the other female guests curtsied, trying to determine if the way I had practiced bending my knees and lowering my body was the proper technique.

However, I found Princess Margaret to be so lovely and gracious that she accepted all greetings with charm and so managed to greet her with relative ease. I do not remember if Ernie bowed. Obviously, it was not something he was stressed about or I would have remembered. Being formally introduced allowed Princess Margaret to engage Ernie in a brief discussion comparing American schools with British schools. He interested her when he told her how Paul had been a student at the King's College School while Ernie was a Fellow at Wolfson College in Cambridge, England.

Art with an Emperor

We had another encounter with royalty much later when Emperor Akihito and the Empress of Japan in 1994 visited the U.S. for the first time, and Ernie and I were asked to host this couple for a full afternoon. We were told they were interested in the "Very Special Arts" program that Ernie had chaired at the Kennedy Center, and particularly wanted to learn about the unusual program with art classes for adult individuals with disabilities. The teachers in that program were exceptionally talented and compassionate, making it a true success.

The Emperor and Empress asked to see the artists at work and to meet the teachers, a request that brought unbelievable excitement to the Kennedy Center staff, the "Very Special Arts" students, and the program's board of trustees. On the afternoon of the visit, students, many of whom were paralyzed and used wheelchairs, were set up with their art materials so they could demonstrate how they were able to unleash their creativity in spite of their respective disabilities. Their art was beautifully displayed, and to this day, it is hard for me to imagine the joy and encouragement it was for these special artists to have their talents and their lives recognized by the Emperor and Empress from Japan.

On that day, Ernie and I were asked to stand at the point where their limousine would stop at the Kennedy Center, welcome them, and serve as their hosts. We both had given much thought to what we should wear, and to this day I envision Ernie's perfect-fitting dark navy business suit and my navy blue silk-blend suit with accompanying navy shoes. We stood there together as we watched with every nerve geared in expectation. When the Emperor and Empress arrived, it seemed as if they wanted to be the ones greeting us, offering us their traditional, Japanese bows; we bowed in return. The Empress wore a stunning kimono with a colorful broad sash; I was so taken by her appearance that I cannot remember what Emperor Akihito was wearing.

The couple spoke English but also had a translator and displayed high interest and eagerness to learn about the art program from these exceptional artists. Ernie had a short welcoming program, which was highlighted by Senator Ted Kennedy's son, Ted, Jr., also giving a welcome.

The artists were busy concentrating on their art pieces, which were in varying stages of progress. I walked alongside the Empress as she moved among the working artists, many of whom painted with brushes in their mouths due to their paralysis from the neck down. She took her time, talking with each artist while watching him or her work. Ernie directed the Emperor, who took in all the activities with ease while also asking Ernie about his role as commissioner of education.

The royal couple was quick to congratulate and encourage all of these courageous and gifted artists, and as they departed, Ernie and I felt a deep sense of appreciation for the ways they had affirmed the abilities of these outstanding artists. We also sensed a connection with the couple and were touched when they sent us a gift of a delicate and beautiful Japanese porcelain vase, which is now on display at the Ernest L. Boyer Center.

Part V: Sharing DC Life with Our Family

Many of our unique experiences like the visit with the Mondales and our encounters with the Emperor and Empress gave us a chance to share fascinating stories with the rest of the family. Ernie's parents in Maryland loved hearing tales of our time in Washington. Ernie was a good storyteller, but his mother often translated his anecdotes to mean that her middle son's life was too intense and that there must be a way to slow things down.

She was right, of course, but she was careful not to overly criticize. After all, she was proud of her son, and she and Grandpa Boyer enjoyed joining us at a number of events. Ernie was always watching for opportunities when his parents and other family members could be included in his schedule.

He was especially excited to receive six tickets for the annual National Prayer Breakfast on February 2, 1978. It was a thrilling experience for Grandma and Grandpa Boyer, Beverly, and Paul to join Ernie and me for this significant event. It was especially exciting to Ernie's father, who kept up with national and world news and was interested in political personalities. He was familiar with and recognized many of the leaders seated at the platform breakfast table.

The message was given by James Wright, the Speaker of the House. President Carter also spoke and included some remarks concerning the ongoing energy crisis—an issue which certainly merited prayer as gas lines at service stations and gas shortages were becoming an all-too-familiar part of daily life in America. We were also fascinated by the sheer size and logistics of the event, which included a banquet setting with many tables set for a breakfast of several courses served by uniformed waiters.

Finally a Farmer's Wife

Ernie would often receive an honorary degree from a college or university that invited him to give the commencement speech. It happened enough that we, as a family, no longer took the time to formally celebrate each one. However, the degree he received after addressing the fifty-first national convention of the Future Farmers of America, was in my opinion a very big deal. Ernie was awarded 140 honorary doctoral degrees in his lifetime, but this particular degree pleased me more than any other.

Growing up on a farm, I naturally hoped to someday marry a handsome, prosperous farmer, have children, and settle into being a good farmer's wife. By now you know that dream did not come true. While I dearly loved Ernie and respected his commitments as an educator, I did like to tease him that I was going to try to turn him into a farmer.

So it is not hard to understand that when the request to address the Future Farmers of America came to his desk, he was determined to accept that invitation—no matter what. He was determined enough that he declared he would cancel anything else to be able to participate, playfully explaining to me that this event could possibly make him a farmer. And that is exactly what did happen.

It was a very large and grand convention event with lots of pageantry, and Ernie was given the royal treatment, with drums and a marching band escorting him to the stage so he could be honored with the "Degree of Honorary American Farmer." After it was over, Ernie was eager to get home to proudly hand me a beautiful wall plaque reading, "This certifies that Ernest L. Boyer was awarded the Degree of Honorary American Farmer." I could hardly believe it—I was married not only to a handsome farmer, but also to an officially certified one!

Ernie was thrilled to know he had more than fulfilled my farm girl dream—without ever turning a shovel. For years that plaque hung on our kitchen wall, and now it is proudly displayed at the Ernest L. Boyer Center at Messiah College.

Speeches and Interviews

It was important for Ernie's office to put out press releases and for him to meet regularly with the media to keep the public informed about the significance of education in their lives. In particular, educators and families at that time were very interested in issues such as bilingual vocational training programs along with the availability of funds for the education of disabled students and improved education of children of immigrants.

Robert Hochstein was chief of the office of education's media staff and was masterful at keeping abreast of all that was going on in Ernie's office and in nationwide education issues. Bob had an uncanny sense about what was newsworthy, and Ernie totally trusted Bob's judgment. In particular, Ernie was fascinated with reporters who conducted television and radio interviews and sometimes did not want their times together to come to an end. Because interviewers did a lot of background work, the conversation usually turned into a fun and stimulating time for Ernie.

I am thinking especially about a *Today Show* segment when Bob Abernathy interviewed him about what defines an "educated man." It was a most fascinating subject for Ernie, and Bob proved to be equally captivated. Ernie's monthly schedules show he made numerous speeches, and I felt privileged whenever I was able to sit in the audience and listen to my husband. For example, it was a special honor for Ernie to be scheduled to speak at the National Press Club, and he made sure I had a reserved seat for that event. He worked hard at writing that important speech. After it was over Bob Hochstein told Ernie the speech was "a home run," which captured my sentiments far more elegantly than I could have.

Fifty Is Nifty

In 1978, Ernie and I both celebrated our fiftieth birthdays. Birthdays obviously come each year, and they typically did not cause Ernie concern. But he suddenly realized that the fifty-year landmark seemed somehow very significant. Thoughts of how his saintly grandfather William H. Boyer lived in the second half of his life and how he touched the lives of so many people truly challenged Ernie. Like his Grandfather Boyer, he wanted to make his years beyond fifty count for the eternal. These deeply meaningful thoughts absorbed him as his birthday was approaching, and he frequently communicated these thoughts to me.

My fiftieth birthday did not consume my mind that way, but I understood his thoughts and wanted to help him. One practical way was, of course, to celebrate. I told our children that their dad's fiftieth birthday would be the ideal time to give him a big surprise party. With their enthusiastic agreement, we went to work on the plans.

So I suggested to Ernie that it would good to host a big extended family reunion during the time when Ernie Jr. and Craig were planning a visit home. I hoped all this would appear as happenstance and not reveal the true reason why all the children were coming home, so I asked Ernie to help me with the invitation list, which included family members on the Boyer and Tyson sides of our family. I sent out invitations and asked people to come prepared to offer poems, verses, or stories of encouragement in Ernie's honor and include some high points of turning fifty years old.

Everything worked like a charm. Ernie was totally surprised, only catching on when folks wished him a "Happy Birthday" and a cake with fifty candles appeared as the centerpiece of our celebration. Our four children put their creative minds together and wrote and acted out a humorous, dramatic program called "Fifty is Nifty," and Beverly bravely sang the Beatles' song, "When I'm Sixty-Four" as part of the show.

The crowd of thirty to forty family members had traveled great distances, coming with their own original fiftieth birthday suggestions and encouraging words as gifts. I was also surprised when our children unfurled a large banner across the entrance of the driveway announcing Ernie's fiftieth birthday on September 13, 1978, and mine on October 16, 1978. Thanks to my esteemed children, I could no longer hide my age. Ernie, to his credit, never tried to hide his.

Being together with family and friends seemed so natural to us, and Ernie took great pride in listening to the words of advice that he got from friends and families. Like his Grandfather Boyer, he was now ready to commit his remaining years to the individuals and communities God had called him to serve.

Another Country, Another Child, Another Birth

Family circumstances naturally keep changing. Craig, our third child, had moved to Virginia to teach at a Mennonite high school. Shortly thereafter he was presented with an opportunity to teach at a church mission school in Belize, where he met a lovely young Mayan woman whose name was Flora. They fell in love, married, and in due time discovered they were going to have a baby.

Whether in China, Russia, England, or Belize, cultures and practices differ. Craig soon came face to face with a major difference, the kind that had life and death consequences: in the Belizean culture, expectant fathers deliver their own babies. That is the tradition, the expectation, and the way things work. Ernie and I wanted Craig to bring Flora to the United States to have the baby. But Flora resisted, not understanding why she could not have her baby in their little house next to the mission school. Her mother, her mother's mother, and generations of women gave birth in their country under the hands of their husbands.

Our fears mounted as Flora's determination increased. No prenatal clinics were in her area. Being a trained midwife, I fear I knew too many worst-case scenarios. After considerable periods of prayer and discussion with Ernie, I flew from Washington to Belize four times to make sure that everything was set for a normal and safe birth and on June 7, 1982, I helped with the birth of another of my grandchildren.

I remember the thrill of receiving baby Anna Kay, as I said, "Come to your Grandma, you beautiful little Indian baby." Like her Mayan mother, she had lots of black hair ringed with black fuzz along her hair line. With blessings and thanks we celebrated that evening with Flora's precious mother, father, and Flora's ten brothers and sisters. The only one missing was Ernie, the other proud but lonesome grandpa, sitting in McLean, Virginia. He was very sad to not be there for the important celebration of the arrival of Craig's first child and our sixth grandchild.

Part VI: A Move Without a Move

In the fall of 1978, a number of media reports indicated that Ernie was stepping down from the commissioner of education post to become president of the Carnegie Foundation for the Advancement of Teaching. On October 27, 1978, *The Washington Post* reported, "Sources say that Boyer has accepted the post to succeed the retiring Clark Kerr in one of the most prestigious jobs in education." The reports were only half right. The Carnegie Board of Trustees had selected Ernie, and he had accepted, but the agreement was that he would continue in his government position until 1980.

The rest of the truth is that it was a thrill for Ernie, and similarly for me, to know that his dream job was waiting for him when his tenure with the federal government ended. This was no small victory, and it offered unusual opportunities. Ernie looked forward to leading the Carnegie Foundation, a financially independent organization, so that he would be able to speak to the issues of higher education and public policy unencumbered by politics. In addition, based on his experience as commissioner of education, he had hopes of expanding the foundation's portfolio by examining the interrelationship shared by institutions of higher education with primary and secondary schools.

Although he fully planned to continue in his government position until 1980, an unexpected change in the law forced him to take his leave earlier.

The National Commission on Federal Ethics Law was establishing the Ethics in Government Act of 1978, which would restrict contacts between former federal officials and the agencies for which they worked. The law was to become effective on July 1, 1979. For years, the Carnegie Foundation had worked closely with federal agencies, and those arrangements would need to continue. Ernie was now advised, however, that his role as president of the Carnegie Foundation would be negatively affected by this law, so he felt his only choice was to resign as commissioner before it took effect.

Ernie was sorry to have to write a letter of his early resignation to President Carter, who accepted it with regret, knowing Ernie was the sixth high-ranking health, education, and welfare official to resign because of the law and its July 1, 1979, deadline.

To this day I am thrilled to read what President Carter said about my husband's years of service as U.S. Commissioner of Education: "Boyer passionately articulated the need for policies to give children who needed it a helping hand. He called for greater access, equity for all students, and excellence in all the nations' public schools." President Carter also offered, "To increase efficiency and service to students, Boyer cut red tape in the colossal federal education agency and reduced the number of forms schools and colleges had to fill out to receive grants. He convened forums to get divergent groups talking again about how to improve schools and enhance learning."

I was especially happy the now former president wrote, "I am proud that we more than doubled federal support for schools, providing special funds to districts with large numbers of disadvantaged students." He also noted:

> Boyer won the respect of people at every level of education, from preschool to graduate school. Teachers, students, administrators, and parents all learned that he understood and sympathized with their hopes and needs. He earned their trust, and believed that it was essential for the educational system as a whole to regain the trust of the American people.

Ernie took "great pride and satisfaction" in those words.

New Job, New Lifestyle

Ernie took the title of president of the Carnegie Foundation for the Advancement of Teaching on the same day his resignation as United States Commissioner of Education went into effect—July 1, 1979. He was eagerly looking forward to this new position, which was his choice and his choice alone, making this a different kind of transition than he had made into many of his previous positions. Ernie and I felt his new title was a great blessing for many reasons, including the fact that Ernie had been told he could establish his office for the foundation anywhere he chose.

This was a wonderful gift for us because we were determined not to move from the Warm Heart Mansion at least until Paul had finished his last two years at McLean High School. Moreover, we were happy in our house on Benjamin Street, and I certainly did not want to have to resign from my very favorite position of directing the Cities in Schools Adolescent Pregnancy Program, with its many positive results of uplifting the lives of at-risk teenage girls.

I was able to contentedly continue my work since Ernie happily established his office in Washington DC, renting space in an office building at 1785 Massachusetts Avenue, NW. He now was answerable to a twenty-five member board of trustees, and he promptly began by working on proposals designed to chart new paths for education, hiring the best researchers and writers to help him work through the plans and ideas that had been brewing in his mind for years.

Our lives changed in ways very much like they had when we moved from Albany to England. We discovered we were once again able to plan relaxed family visits and build in undisturbed personal time. We bought a Washington DC tourist guidebook, determined to catch up on all of sites that surrounded us that we'd not had the time to visit yet. One weekend we made reservations at the Watergate Hotel—a five-minute walk from the Kennedy Center and leisurely walked around DC, hand-in-hand. We were both overwhelmed by the magnificent architecture of this city that was built on a swamp. And following the guidebook, we enjoyed learning more about the history of the nation's capital.

Considering Princeton

Ernie and I gave plenty of thought to where we wanted to live after Paul graduated from McLean High School. Amazingly, invitations had come from five different colleges and educational institutions, asking Ernie to move the Carnegie Foundation to their location. In the end, we were, however, most attracted to the offer from Princeton University. The president of Princeton, William Bowen, showed Ernie a very attractive three-story building on Thurlow Terrace, a part of the campus. The luxurious, older-style house had a lot of charm and was the perfect size for a staff of twenty or more. President Bowen also said the university would share in the cost of a complete renovation. In addition, Princeton offered Ernie the faculty title of senior fellow with the privilege to teach at the Woodrow Wilson School of Public and International Affairs. While we did not know a great deal about that portion of New Jersey, Ernie and I set about reading and talking with friends and acquaintances familiar with the area.

We also remembered one remarkable incident from a much earlier visit to Princeton that we had tucked away in our minds. We had found ourselves on the Princeton campus on a spring day back in 1955. Ernie had been asked to take a deanship at St. John's College in Annapolis, Maryland. My mother was babysitting Ernie Jr. and Beverly while Ernie and I visited the Maryland campus. Returning to my mother's place in Pennsylvania, we drove through Princeton. Coming into town and driving along Elm Road, we found everything to be lush and green and bright with countless spring flowering trees.

It took our breath away, especially since we were visiting from California, which I still found to be quite brown. Suddenly, we both spied a turtle slowly crossing the road. We stopped our car to watch it, almost believing that our watchful eyes would protect the turtle from speeding cars—several of which almost ran over it. We decided it was not safe to leave the turtle along the road, so picked it up and took it to my mother's house, away from fast-moving cars.

Before we left New Jersey on that long-ago trip, we had found the Princeton campus and stopped to have lunch at the charming Princeton

University Inn. In 1955, it was also a women's dormitory with a dining room open to the public. While we lunched, our little turtle waited patiently for us in the car. During our luncheon, Ernie firmly declared that he wanted to retire in this quaint hamlet, although retirement seemed like it was a long way off at that point.

When President Bowen offered Ernie the opportunity to move the Carnegie Foundation offices to Princeton, we both recalled that magical day in 1955. We remembered what we had done to save that turtle and the joy it had brought to Beverly and Ernie Jr. back at my mother's house as they watched him lumber here and there and then pull inside his shell-like house, away from the prying eyes of the children.

We knew this would be a move like none other and were thus quite excited. However, there were still the heartaches of what we were leaving behind. There was a sadness as we left our friends, the area, and the Warm Heart Mansion. It was especially sad for me to say good-bye to the beloved staff and the thriving program I had helped to launch. So many adolescent girls' lives were being changed because of our work together. They gave me a farewell party complete with a gift of a large, gold heart that said, "We love you, Big Mama."

Looking for the Final Mansion

Decisions by one part of the family touch the lives of other members of the family. Our move from McLean, Virginia to Princeton, New Jersey was certainly a time of consequential family changes. Grandma and Grandpa Boyer needed to make a decision about staying in Baltimore or following us to Princeton. They chose to do neither, deciding it was the right time to move into a retirement community.

A lovely two-bedroom cottage was available for Grandma and Grandpa Boyer at the Messiah Retirement Community near Harrisburg, Pennsylvania, and Messiah College They had so many friends at the retirement center, and it would be a fairly easy drive for them to come to Princeton. What made this an even bigger blessing was that my own mother was already living there. Having them all at the same place was wonderful for all of us.

The other big change was being separated from Beverly and her little family, particularly two-year-old granddaughter, Leah. Leaving them and having to give up our almost daily contact was most difficult and makes me sad to think about even now.

One thing that kept us moving forward was the hope of finding the right house so that we would never have to move again. Ernie was now fifty-three and wanted to stay on as president of the Carnegie Foundation for the Advancement of Teaching until his retirement. We expected we would have many more grandchildren to add to our current four, so we knew we would need a house with enough space for a growing family.

Naturally there was a transition period for the move to Princeton. Ernie would travel from Washington to help direct the remodeling of the Carnegie Foundation headquarters on the Princeton campus and also to help look for a suitable house for us to buy. We traveled together to Princeton, and while he dealt with the remodeling, I would look at houses with a realtor. Paul was now a high school graduate, making plans of his own, and not very involved in this house search.

As we were looking for our nineteenth house, we realized we had become experts at evaluating what was best for our family's needs. We looked and looked but could not find the right home. However, we really did not want to build. A Princeton friend then gave Ernie a tip about a couple who were considering selling their house. I had not joined Ernie on this Princeton trip and was a bit surprised that he and the friend boldly went to the house. The older couple who owned the home seemed pleased that these two gentlemen were interested in their house, even though they had not yet hired a realtor. Ernie was given a thorough tour, and then he called me and asked me to get the next train from Washington to Trenton, where he would meet me so we would go to see the house together.

He did not tell me the house had won his heart as he wanted to get my unbiased opinion. My first impression was that it was not a special house. But when Ernie elaborated about why he thought it was the right place, I knew his reasoning was exactly right. He pointed out that it was an unusually well-built house and had many possibilities for exciting renovations and additions.

If Ernie had not chosen to be an educator, he most likely would have chosen architecture, and he already had visions of what he wanted to add to this house. Whether it was innovations in education or innovations in house renovations, I was always intrigued, amazed, and pleased with the outcomes of Ernie's visions. As our long-term home, it was the perfect buy. We were pleased with our choice as we said our good-byes in McLean and moved to our new address at 222 Cherry Valley Road, Princeton, New Jersey.

By this time, Paul had finished high school, I had said my farewells to my beloved teenage girls and my colleagues at The Cities in Schools Midwifery Adolescent Pregnancy Program, and Ernie had packed his last box from his DC office. He was leaving some things behind in a smaller office that would remain in Washington, where Bob Hochstein would manage the public relations affairs for the Carnegie Foundation for the Advancement of Teaching.

The move from Washington DC to Princeton, New Jersey, was uneventful and characterized by joy. It was from this Family Home Mansion that Ernie and I would make many plans and welcome many precious family members over the years. From here Ernie would drive the three miles to his office on the Princeton campus. From here I would rush off in the middle of the night to the birth center when a midwifery client would call, telling me she was in labor.

Here is where Ernie and I would settle in before bedtime to have devotions and pray together. He always said a prayer of gratitude for God's plan of salvation and then he would say, "Please help us to trust you more." I recall asking him why he always asked for more trust because I thought he was already trusting God daily. He said when times are good, trust is not difficult, but when troubles come, it's great to know God would acknowledge our prayer for more trust and be close at hand.

CHAPTER 17

HOUSE 19

The Family Home Mansion

Princeton, New Jersey
1983–1996

God the Father, Creator hand
Bless this house and this land.

—Swiss House Blessing (1737)

In September 1983, the moving van arrived at 222 Cherry Valley Road, Princeton, New Jersey. This house was truly going to be the family home for everyone. It was the place where all of our grown children and their children would love to gather as often as possible. And after major changes, it was also a house that could fulfill almost any need.

Almost as soon as the moving boxes were unpacked, Ernie found an architect who was willing to let him help with the drawings for the many remodeling changes he envisioned. The most dramatic change was to open up and enlarge the entrance space. Following Ernie's instructions, the contractor arranged the work so that the remodeling mess was restricted to a limited area of the house at a time.

Ernie knew I did not look forward to the disturbance of tearing down walls or putting up a skylight. He felt a little guilty and apologized about his plans for redoing whole sections of the house, but I had agreed to these changes before we bought the house and knew the end results would make up for the short-term disruptions. Furthermore, I loved to watch Ernie's pleasure and satisfaction as the work progressed.

There was a keen sense of celebration at the Family Home Mansion. We were truly settled here and knew we would not be moving again. This security made us want to transform the house into a place that would fit any family circumstance, which helps to explain all the major remodeling and additions that we underwent.

The remodeling projects were done in intervals over a number of years with enough extended breaks to have many family events and fun-filled summertime visits from grandchildren. The winding brook of rushing water that ran through the property created an exciting place for the grandchildren to play together. Another children's gathering spot was at the long rope swing. They would catch hold of the rope while standing on top of the high hill at the edge of our backyard, and swing way out and then jump off on the return swing.

I watched with nervous fear when Ernie decided to put up the rope swing and when he courageously climbed up the tall tree and then worked his way out along a high branch where he tied the rope securely around the branch. He knew how to tie a safety knot, but still tested it by taking many rides himself. After his trial tests were done, everyone felt safe and wanted to join the fun.

Take a Tour of the Family Home Mansion

The only way I can really describe the Family Home Mansion is to lead you on a tour around the finished house. First, follow me along the outside walkway until you reach a stone porch, which leads to a wide, covered entrance area. When you enter a polished stone area, take two steps up to the foyer; notice the skylight. To the left is a bedroom wing with two guest rooms. Straight ahead is the master bedroom area with two open rooms—one is a sitting room furnished with a love seat and the twin reading chairs Ernie and I use along with a desk area. The other room is a larger bedroom with a door that opens to a large outside deck facing the back lawn, which leads into the wooded acreage.

Now follow me back through the front foyer into the living room, which includes a space at the far side of the room that Ernie designed to fit a table suitable for hosting a small dinner group. This living room, with the extended space, can hold twenty to forty people, depending on how we arrange the furniture. The wide door on the other side of the room leads to the dining room that can seat twenty when we extend the table for family gatherings.

I should tell you that when we bought this house, the dining room wall was the end of the house, but from the first time Ernie saw it he visualized this area to be the perfect spot to add a family room, or more accurately, an all-purpose room. You can see here a wall of built-in cupboards for activities and toys for our fifteen grandchildren. The wicker furniture makes it feel a bit like a sunroom, and these two brightly upholstered couches can be used for beds when family and friends come for overnight or weeklong visits.

The door leading outside opens onto a sizable three-level deck, which was part of the addition project. This is our favorite spot for family meals and birthday parties in warm weather. It can also be used as a secluded spot to sit quietly on the glider to rock a baby to sleep, or to just sit alone enjoying the flowers and the rustling of trees swaying in the wind. The kitchen windows overlook this deck and the landscaped backyard and tall trees.

Let's go back in; there is another section of the house, and it will only take a short time to walk through it. This glass wall nearest to the entrance foyer toward the living room continues up a full set of stairs to Ernie's study and library. Here is his large desk, two couches that convert to beds, his adjustable lounge chair, and shelves overflowing with books. The skylights help it feel open and cheery. The big windows on the west wall were Ernie's idea so we could watch the glorious sunsets.

Return down the stairs to a platform, turn right, and descend about seven more steps to enter the large room directly below Ernie's study. Off of this room there is an oversized bathroom with a laundry and utility room with plentiful shelves and counter space. Before the latest house addition, these particular rooms, both upstairs and downstairs, were a large garage. When we bought the house, we were attracted to an attached cozy one-bedroom apartment that had its own entrance. Even when we were converting the garage into an upstairs and downstairs there was no disturbance to the apartment.

Using Every Inch of Our House

I wanted to describe the layout of the Family Home Mansion in great detail because as the next twelve years unfold in this chapter, every part of the house has its own story to tell.

The attached apartment was filled every summer when our missionary son, Craig, and his family came from Belize, Central America. By coming home to Princeton in the summertime, they avoided the intense tropical heat of Belize, where Craig directed teachers and taught at the Mennonite church school during the school year.

Craig's family enjoyed living at our home in Princeton during the summer and liked having the apartment as their own living area. Ernie and I loved having them come with their children. They could extend the apartment living area into the adjoining large space with the extra bathroom and utility laundry room.

"All's Well That Ends Well"

When we moved from Washington DC to Princeton, I decided to take a long break from my midwifery practice. I wanted to take time to organize and settle into our Family Home Mansion, and I also wanted to have the chance to help Ernie fix up his office. Those exciting plans were suddenly and abruptly threatened when the director of the new Princeton Midwifery Birth Center pulled up into our driveway just as we were unloading the moving truck with the things we had brought from our Warm Heart Mansion in McLean.

She hastily told me the center desperately needed me to immediately begin helping them with office prenatal care visits and to be on call to deliver babies at the birth center. I tried to explain my plan to take a long break from midwifery work, but she said the center would have to close if I didn't agree to begin working because of a serious shortage of certified nurse-midwives in the area.

Ernie became aware that we were engaged in an intense conversation and stopped unloading the truck to politely listen to the conversation. Being a calm, thoughtful problem solver, he helped me negotiate a firm, reasonable plan. In short, the agreement was that I would begin working at the birth center in three months, but that I would only work part-time.

That night when I slipped into bed after saying my prayers, I thought about the unobtrusive way Ernie had joined our conversation. With gentleness he sought to help me accommodate the birth center director while also thinking of me and my wishes. He and I both wanted a plan that would allow me to accompany him on his school and campus visits and to have more time together. The words that came to me as I fell off to sleep were Shakespeare's: "all's well that ends well"; and my own: thank you, Ernie, and thank you, God.

For years thereafter I did prenatal, post-natal, and gynecology office appointments two days a week and took calls for baby deliveries one weekend per month. I thoroughly enjoyed this work as it was what I had dreamed about doing. Ernie had helped me accomplish this goal by being so supportive of my studies in the Georgetown University Nurse-Midwifery Educational Program and by helping me to work out an agreeable arrangement with the Princeton clinic.

Spirit- and Fun-Filled Sundays

For some years Ernie, and I had been involved with the Quakers, attending silent Friends Meetings, focusing on the Holy Spirit within us. After arriving in Princeton in 1983, we decided to worship at the Dutch Reformed Church just a few miles from our house. Sitting in the pew our first Sunday there, we clearly knew there was a divine presence. I remember how Ernie was awed and deeply moved by the sermon and many sermons thereafter. We attended regularly, and both Ernie and I always left the service feeling spiritually blessed and inspired.

One Sunday, the church bulletin listed the closing hymn as *Breathe on Me, Breath of God.* We had to leave the service a little early that day, but Ernie said he wished we could stay and sing that song because it was very meaningful to him. We ended up singing it together in the car as we drove away:

"Breathe on me breath of God, fill me with life anew." That memory and the peace of that hymn has sweetly lingered in my mind and heart throughout the years.

We also looked forward to Sundays for another reason. We had developed our own fun routine by going to the same simple little restaurant for an omelet and whole wheat toast after church. We became such a Sunday midday fixture at the little café that the waitress always gave us the same table and the cook was standing by ready to prepare the omelets just the way we liked them. This was our leisurely time of the week, and I would even dare to drink a little bit of coffee. The waitress knew exactly how to make me a cup that was three-fourths water, one-fourth coffee. During our leisurely Sunday brunch, Ernie would indulge in a full strength cup of coffee.

When we finished eating the omelets and were slowly sipping our coffee, we began the fun little ritual that we had created just for this time. Ernie would check the time on his watch and then tell me to start. For fifteen minutes, I would talk and Ernie would carefully listen; he was not allowed to interrupt me with even a single word. After my fifteen minutes were up, we would discuss what I had said. Then it was his turn to talk, without interruption, for fifteen minutes, followed by a discussion about what he had said to me. Since we were not a nagging, argumentative, or a complaining couple, we engaged in these discussions just for fun. Neither Ernie nor I took ourselves too seriously but kept an attitude of playfulness as we would stretch our minutes by discussing childhood relationships or just talking about the events from the past week and seeking advice about dealing with certain situations. Ernie and I enjoyed light banter and knew that love needs attention to grow and flourish.

One Sunday when it was my turn to take the second fifteen minutes, I did not have anything pressing to offer. Then I remembered how Ernie and I used to spend time entertaining our children in the car when we took family trips. So, I spent my fifteen minutes telling childhood stories and reciting some of our favorite silly rhymes like:

> Bill Grogan's goat was feeling fine
> ate three red shirts from off the line.

Bill took a stick, gave him a whack
and tied him to the railroad track.
The whistle blew, the train drew nigh,
Bill Grogan's goat was doomed to die.
He gave three groans of awful pain,
coughed up the shirts
and flagged the train.

Ernie could easily outdo my silly stories, or he would add his own rhymes, while our friendly waitress stood off, listening and smiling at our playful exchange.

This weekly brunch time together was always rewarding. We profited by maintaining ongoing fun and open communication. We knew it was important to keep doing this regularly and staying closely connected because our lives were often too full of work and separate activities.

Sad Good-Byes

My mother had been living at Messiah Village Retirement Center for ten years when Ernie's parents moved into a two-bedroom cottage at the same retirement center. After they lived in the cottage for about six years, Grandma Boyer's Parkinson's disease developed to the stage where she needed much more care and needed to move from their cottage into the nursing care unit at the retirement center. Every day Ernie's father stayed beside her, caring for her and often pushing her around in a wheelchair as her Parkinson's disease progressed until she could no longer walk or converse. Still, he sweetly watched over her care.

We were with them on Grandpa Boyer's eighty-seventh birthday. Only a few days later, we were notified that he had suddenly become critically ill and been admitted to the hospital. We arrived at the hospital just an hour before Ernie's father's spirit went to heaven and his eternal reward. Ernie deeply loved his father and pleaded for him not to die. He repeatedly told him that he loved him and then put his arms around his father as he took his last breath. Ernie was deeply grieved, and I too was heartbroken because I loved him as my own father. He had told me many years earlier that since my own father died when I was only three months old, he would like to fill in as my father—and he did, loving and caring for me as a father. He was very dear to me and I grieved for him, along with Ernie.

At the close of the funeral for Ernie's father, our daughter Beverly was pushing her Grandma's wheelchair, when she said with deep sadness, "We cannot leave Grandma here at the retirement center hospital without Grandpa." We all must have had those same feelings, but when Beverly spoke those disquieting words, Ernie and I immediately started to discuss a plan—we would care for Grandma in our home. We immediately hired someone to do extensive remodeling to prepare a room in our Family Home Mansion that could be equipped like a hospital room. Ernie worked with our dependable contractor to convert our garage into a large bright room with an adjoining bathroom and utility/laundry room to keep all of the nursing care supplies. The contractor worked on a fast schedule, and we were able to transport Grandma to the lovely new space in our home within record time.

Ernie's mother lived for two more years in our Family Home Mansion. Carla, our niece, who also dearly loved her Grandma, came from California and moved into the adjoining one-bedroom apartment to gave Grandma special care. Carla, Beverly, and I took turns filling eight-hour shifts of nursing care. Beverly, who lived near us once again and was also caring for her new baby, Julie, would take the day shift, bringing little Julie with her every day and letting her play or nap on the bed beside Grandma. This brought big smiles from Grandma as she watched Julie. Grandma was eighty-nine years old, but she was not too old or disabled to smile.

Ernie and I took the night shift and also directed all of Grandma's care, so each week I would print out the weekly care plan. The work was strenuous because Grandma could not do anything for herself, even turn over or change her position in bed. She could not stand up or walk and had lost her ability to speak so could not tell us what she needed. She would cry out day or night.

Carla, Beverly, and I were all registered nurses, so we knew how to respond to Grandma's needs, such as how to turn her while changing the bed linens and how to lift her into a wheelchair. Ernie learned how to take care of many of these nursing tasks too so he could help to care for his mother. Together we usually took the night shift, but sometimes Carla or I took the night shift alone when Ernie was traveling. However, he tried hard to manage his schedule to be home to take his night duty of turning his mother every two hours to preventing her from getting bed sores.

All of us were keenly tuned into all of Grandma's needs, and she received the best of care. I completely retired from my midwifery work during this time to be available for her care and to do whatever was needed in the very busy household. As we all worked together, Ernie and I talked about how important it was for the family to give love and understanding care to a precious and aging mother and grandmother. She was a very gifted woman with a brilliant mind who had spent much of her life caring for others. Now it was the time in her life that we wanted to give back to her. All the while, she was showing us what it meant to grow old.

During this time, I attended a Bible Study Fellowship class one morning each week. One week I invited my class to come and sing hymns for Grandma. Many in our group had lovely voices, and when they sang, it must have sounded like a heavenly choir to Grandma because her face glowed with joy. She knew the words to the hymns and although she did not have the ability to speak, she would sing along. We also had family sing times for her, and our son-in-law, Dale, would play the piano that we moved into her room. It was great to see Grandma so happy during these wonderful singing times.

Grandma Boyer died peacefully on December 8, 1990. We grieved because we all loved her and had a strong attachment to Grandma. Carla, who had given so much loving care to her beloved grandmother, moved back to California with a grieving heart. Beverly still talks about her special endearing memories of her Grandma Boyer and the privilege of caring for her.

I too loved her deeply and grieved her death. I had loved her from the first time I saw her when I was only sixteen years old and she sweetly accepted me as Ernie's girlfriend, telling him he should invite me to their family Thanksgiving Day dinner. I often let her know that she was a model Christian mother-in-law who so fully blessed my life.

She was a very important love in Ernie's life too, as he adored his mother. To him she could do no wrong, and he often told her that she was the perfect mother. She gave him much love and always understood him perfectly. Her death left a big void in his life, and Ernie and I felt it was an honor to have cared for her in our Family Home Mansion.

Part II: Creating Change Through Carnegie

Bringing the staff of the Carnegie Foundation for the Advancement of Teaching (CFAT) from Washington DC to the Princeton University campus was very exciting. The office spaces were assigned, and enthusiasm was high as the staff felt privileged to work in the beautifully remodeled house at 5 Ivy Lane. Neither Ernie nor I ever heard any complaints about the extra work of moving, even though it was a major undertaking to transfer all the research project materials. Ernie had been president of the foundation for three years before the move, so much work had already been accomplished.

Ernie's large office on the Princeton campus became a masterpiece of hospitality, decorated to show respect to everyone who entered. His desk was a simple piece of mahogany with a polished top and distinctly manufactured table legs.

On the wall beside his desk hung framed portraits of three people who Ernie greatly admired: Albert Einstein, the genius physicist; Helen Keller, the writer and lecturer who was blind and deaf from infancy but learned to speak and read and use her handicap as an opportunity; and Albert Schweitzer, a theologian, musician, and medical missionary in Africa. Ernie welcomed the chance to talk about each portrait whenever a guest or scholar asked about them, and many who entered his office ended up being inspired.

In the center of his office was a mahogany work table large enough to place eight to twelve comfortable chairs around it. He spent many a workday sitting there, preparing for meetings with the board of trustees or the college board, or writing speeches events at institutions such as Yale University in New Haven, Connecticut and Maricopa Community College in Phoenix, Arizona.

Ernie worked long and hard, and we had a long-term understanding that we built together. I completely understood his high performance standards, and I shared his vision. However, I admit I did not like it when his work in that office went on for too many hours. Although I recognized his passion for his work at the foundation, I had a growing concern that he was overextending himself, perhaps more than ever.

Focusing on Reports

I find it noteworthy that the plans for CFAT's future that Ernie had proposed to the board of trustees during his first year as president were being fulfilled. In truth, I can say that those plans and purposes continued throughout his fifteen-year presidency, but there is no simple way to talk about the ongoing work of the foundation. However, I can say that the main focus was the preparation of Carnegie essays, which were written on topics significantly related to the purposes and quality of higher education.

Later, secondary, elementary, and early childhood education were included in the research because Ernie believed one level of learning related to every other. He liked to say that "education is a seamless web"—one of his original ways of describing the inextricable links among the various levels of education.

The Carnegie reports were written for educators but also for the general public, with the goal of getting educational issues on the national agenda in order to bring about reform. After each major report, which truly was more like a book, was published, a national CFAT Colloquium would be held for a wide variety of leaders, and these attracted wide coverage from the media. After these meetings and news reports, Ernie would give speeches, write articles, and provide interviews on the topics—prompting widespread discussions, debates, and action among education and political leaders.

The research and the resulting books attempted to highlight what was working and what was needed to foster overall improvement in the nation's schools and colleges. Ernie and his colleagues would diagnose problems and prescribe remedies in the Carnegie reports. It could take several years to complete a report and then prepare to begin another major study. Seven specialized major reports were completed before Ernie's earthly life ended, and it still seems sad that he never had a chance to complete the two additional reports he had planned—one on medical education and one on international education.

Living in a Cycle of Reports

During our years in the Family Home Mansion, our lives revolved around the cycle of each stage of the various reports.

Stage One: Researching

In the first stage of the process, Ernie would select the best team of about twenty researchers to spread out across the country for several months and thoroughly investigate the particular type of institution being studied, such as high schools or undergraduate colleges.

This part of a new project did not require Ernie's full focus, so during this time he was always heavily booked with speaking engagements related to the previous report. This period was thus filled with travel, and I tried to arrange my responsibilities so I could travel with him. Over the years, we shared the joy of getting to know many extraordinary schools and colleges. It was particularly fascinating to get acquainted with the faculty, students, academic programs, and administrators at each educational institution.

Ernie was also asked to speak at dozens of state and national educational conferences regarding the topics of the CFAT reports. I think I'd choose that phase of the cycle as my favorite because I was able to share these unusual experiences with Ernie. He frequently said that an event, or even a particular moment, was only fully enjoyed when he shared it with me.

Stage Two: Writing

In the next stage, the research teams would return with their reports, and Ernie and the staff would review them. After these discussions, Ernie would start to pen the report, scrawling his ideas on yellow paper tablets. The work of writing was exhilarating for him as he was able to create and refine his ideas, but there was one major problem—his handwriting was extremely hard to read, particularly because his left-handed style presented unique challenges for anyone trying to decipher it.

Years before, when we were courting, Ernie would write to me every day during the three years we were separated when I was in nursing school in Pennsylvania and he was a student at Greenville College in Illinois. We were engaged to be married during those three years, 1947 to 1950, and I had no difficulty reading his love letters. In fact, his penmanship was so beautiful that I never missed any words with their sweet meaning and love.

However, when he was writing the Carnegie Foundation reports in the 1980s, his handwriting had changed so much that I could not decipher many of his words, which was partially because he had developed his own shorthand. He would write the first three letters of a word before his mind raced ahead and led him to the next word. Thankfully, Ernie was very blessed to have Dawn Ott Berberian on his staff. She easily learned his shorthand and could read his left-handed scribble and transcribe it on a computer. Dawn worked with Ernie for many years; he called her an angel, and I would add that she was a magical angel to be able to decipher his difficult scribble.

Ernie's writing process was engaging for me because he often wrote at home very early in the morning and late in the evenings, and we would often discuss his developing ideas. I remember those times fondly because he took such joy in discussing his vision and explaining to me how he came to see a particular point of view and how he intended to write about that topic.

Stage Three: Revising

The third stage of developing a CFAT report was my least favorite. I learned this was the time for me to plan things independently because Ernie and his team would be going through the finished draft in a rigorous page-by-page review that seemed painfully slow to me.

Ernie would put together an expert team who would sit in his office around his polished mahogany conference table for long hours, sometimes late into the night, reading each page to make sure that the manuscript represented his thoughts and visions and presented them the best way possible. He would ask other leaders in education to read and comment on his work, including the members of the foundation's board of trustees. If the book was long, it could take months before he was ready to write his eloquent summary in the final chapter. Ernie kept me well informed about the progress of the reports, which were always a vital part of our daily life.

Occasionally, he would ask one or more of our children to come to his office in Princeton and join the book discussions, as he valued their opinions. He even loved to have a grandchild come and sit with him and the scholars at that large polished conference table, saying he learned a lot from their young minds. Ernie was a doting grandpa who always looked for opportunities to be with his grandchildren.

Everyone knew that when discussions around that conference table got heated, Ernie could relieve any tension with his wit and humor. Everyone who knew him appreciated his thoughtfulness and the way he could use a lighter touch. He could issue a rebuke in humor, without giving the other person a chance to take offense. These many years later, I ask myself just how much those times influenced his staff, our children, and grandchildren. I believe he inspired them and passed on to them his ethical and Christian moral principles along with something of his own stamina.

Stage Four: Publishing—and Beginning Again

The final and most rewarding stage of Ernie's work was when he sent off the report to be published. This would be followed by Ernie crisscrossing the nation, speaking at conferences to educators, government officials, parent groups, a wide range of boards and corporate executives, hundreds of college campus events, and commencement speeches. So many groups wanted to hear Ernie speak that he had a full-time appointment secretary just to handle the demands.

Moreover, he gave countless television and telephone interviews and responded to a large number of letters and calls, particularly after each report was released. Although Ernie was the most visible CFAT spokesman, he always applauded his excellent staff and the countless scholars across America who had joined together to produce the research in an effort to achieve educational reform.

This stage of the report process also coincided with the first stage of a new report when teams would fan out across the country to collect research. As I noted above, this was my favorite stage because I often got to travel with him. Ernie was eager for me to be able to arrange my schedule so we could share this time, and it was wonderful for both of us. I was happy to lose my life into that of my husband's during that season. My interests were those of my husband, and I counted it a great privilege to share his life. For us, this was a God-ordained part of our marriage partnership during those years.

Taking Care of Ernie

While he was engrossed in these stimulating stages of creating Carnegie reports, it took a special effort for Ernie to think about resting his mind and body. He would occasionally take a break due to strong urgings from me and pleas from our children, but I knew full well that his mind could not really let go of an in-process manuscript. Even when he was making an effort to relax, he would have his manuscript within reach.

I remember when he would try to take a break, hoping to relax right in our own Family Home Mansion. When the weather was nice, we would start with a leisurely Saturday morning breakfast that was free from manuscript talk out on our back deck. I tried to extend those relaxing breakfasts as long as possible. Then Ernie would sit in one of the lawn chairs we had placed on the wooden deck, and I would sit in the chair next to him, angling our chairs to be hidden from direct sunlight, but hoping to catch the warmth of the sun shining through the large trees surrounding the back of our home. His favorite form of relaxation was sitting in the deck chair with manuscript in hand and me sitting nearby listening to him read a draft of the latest chapter.

His writing style was clear and readily understood by educators and laypersons alike. Sometimes, assuming the layperson's role, I would question him about a paragraph or two, suggesting he rephrase it so every reader could follow his logic. He always listened and welcomed my suggestions. At the end of such a weekend, we loved going out to a restaurant for a candlelit dinner. He would feel refreshed after our more leisurely day, and I felt pleased because I thought he was trying to take care of himself. As his wife, this was my natural concern. The family was also happy when they thought he was responding to their pleas to be mindful of his health.

The Spirit of Community

This memoir is not meant to be an academic book, and yet the years of Ernie's Carnegie presidency were dominated by the reports he was always in the process of writing or discussing. Each book was a vibrant part of his reasoning and beliefs. For example, after the compelling impact of the book on high school reform, he wrote *College: The Undergraduate Experience in America*, which was published in 1987. He put the nation's undergraduate institutions under his critical yet caring eye. I remember some of the issues and questions that were explored included "Were the important undergraduate courses taught by the most respected and gifted teachers on campus?" As in his report on high schools, he argued that students needed to be engaged in community service, helping others.

Because of those two books, "The Best of America" citations for 1990 in *U.S. News & World Report* acknowledged Ernie with its "Excellence Award in Education," calling him "a major force in education reform." After the release of the *College* report, there was a very high demand for Ernie to speak at colleges, universities, and education conferences in America and overseas. These were very enriching years for me and Ernie, as I usually traveled with him. We loved to share our observations and impressions after each of these education events, and I often recall many of them with pleasure to this day.

Shortly after these reports were published, some unusual circumstances brought another important book to publication. Although Ernie always considered how institutions of higher learning could strengthen a spirit of community, he had not formulated a plan to write about community. All that changed when he took a phone call from a president of one of the nation's Ivy League institutions who explained that he and four other Ivy League presidents wanted to come to talk to Ernie at his office. When they came, and Ernie was taken aback by their unexpected request. These university presidents straightforwardly asked him to write a book about how to create a spirit of community on their campuses. Each president told of concern about the growing tension between races, reporting that white, black, and Asian students had organized themselves into separate worlds. One president confessed that he had been around for a long time and that he was more worried at that time than he had been during the campus tensions in the late 1960s and early 1970s.

Ernie's underlying belief was that every problem had a solution so he set his mind on honoring their request, making it a priority for a season. I was fully aware he was preoccupied day and night and that it was hard for him to focus on anything else. When we were alone, that was what he talked about, often thinking aloud. For the two nights after his talk with the university presidents his night sleep was restless. The third night, after I fell into a sleep of exhaustion, I woke briefly about 3:00 a.m., aware that he was pacing back and forth across the room.

At 5:30 a.m., when I again stirred from my sleep, I realized his pacing steps were more spirited. With excitement in his voice, he said, "I think I've got the solution. Can I tell you the six principles that I believe could define the spirit of community and can help solve the crisis on the campuses? Tell me if you think it would work." I sat up in bed and listened as he quickly ticked off the six principles of community that he had created and finalized during that sleepless night: a purposeful community; an open community; a just community; a disciplined community; a caring community; and a celebrative community. In the end, I think he was influenced by the remarkable Oakleigh neighborhood community spirit we enjoyed in 1964 when we lived in Santa Barbara. Those very same community spirit principles were very much alive there.

Just like the troubled university presidents who came to see him, Ernie was concerned about the general student attitude on campuses. He was eager to get the book written and published. He went to work to organize the campus visit teams and the research staff, and he started to draft the text. That report, *Campus Life: In Search of Community,* was then published in record time in 1990. The book stirred up a lot of interest, and he received hundreds of invitations from campuses and conference organizers to speak to large audiences about the principles of community.

By this time, Ernie decided I should plan and direct his speaking schedule. It was a difficult task as many of his invitations to speak had to be declined because there just were not enough days or hours to honor so many requests. I would work and rework his calendar to honor as many requests as I thought were reasonable. However, many times disappointed program organizers would manage to get a call through to my husband. Unfortunately, he did not know how to say "no" as well as I did.

As often as possible, Ernie and I traveled together to these campus visits, and we were delighted to see that many leaders found creative ways to use the six principles to make their institutions more vibrant. For example, one large university had the art department design and construct sculptured centerpieces for each table in the large dining room, using the six principles of community. Some schools had the six principles boldly displayed as a border around the college hallway ceilings. Perhaps the first prize goes to a campus where the female students renamed six of their dormitories using the names of the six principles. Colleges all across the country had faculty meetings to discuss how professors could benefit by using the six principles of community as a day-to-day formula for teaching and counseling students or when making other campus decisions.

Ready to Learn

I humbly want to tell you about my favorite report, *Ready to Learn: A Mandate for the Nation.* The words for this book seemed to come easily to my husband in 1991. The writing was the result of Ernie's interest and concern stemming from my work with the underprivileged mothers and their babies when I worked as a midwife in Washington DC. He sweetly writes in the acknowledgments for that book that "My wife, Kay, has been the inspiration that made it possible for this book to be completed."

Across the country, schools and universities began to provide parents with educational opportunities to help them prepare their children to be ready to learn from birth. The Corporation for Public Broadcasting (CPB) wrote a proposal to the Department of Education which was handsomely funded. This funding made it possible for the corporation, working in cooperation with PBS, to support a network of television programs called "Ready to Learn." These CPB-PBS educational programs are still running on PBS.

Moreover, since Ernie believed that no one entity could solve this intransigent problem in isolation, CPB funded "Ready to Learn" applicants to work collaboratively, bringing together early childhood institutions, precollegiate schools, experienced television producers and writers, and local PBS stations. Once developed, the programs aired nationally, hitting every small and large community that aired PBS programs. Studies have shown that the children who watched the *Ready to Learn* programs benefitted greatly from the experience and began school, whether preschool or first grade, indeed ready to learn.

The last two major books Ernie wrote, *Scholarship Reconsidered: Priorities of the Professoriate* and *The Basic School: A Community for Learning,* have been the best-sellers, and each was a culmination of his work and personal life and beliefs. Clearly, Ernie's fifteen years at the Carnegie Foundation for the Advancement of Teaching were defined by the seven major reports that he wrote, and the hundreds of speeches, articles, and interviews he offered.

Part III: Travels and Experiences

Ernie's wide-ranging work attracted attention from many people and places, and we were blessed with opportunities to spend time with some amazing people. One such chance came when Jimmy and Rosalyn Carter invited Ernie and me to come to Atlanta to have a private tour of the recently completed presidential library, the Carter Center, and to go to dinner with them.

When we arrived, President Carter was tied up with an interview, so Mrs. Carter took us on a tour of the Center. Her thorough knowledge of all the events and circumstances during her husband's tenure as president was very impressive, and she described many interesting personal details while we toured the remarkable library with her.

They wanted us to visit them in their small apartment next to the Carter Center and then go to dinner at their favorite restaurant. Before we left for dinner, they took us for a walk around the spectacular gardens in the masterfully designed setting at the center. It was pure beauty, enhanced by a lovely lake. The ride to the restaurant added an intriguing touch to our fascinating evening, and I love remembering the elaborate process—a process involving a number of particular steps.

As timed and directed by the security personnel, two large black presidential-looking limousines pulled up in front of the Carter's apartment. The right back door of the first vehicle was held open, and President Carter seated himself in the designated presidential seat. Ernie was escorted to the left side, behind the driver and beside the president.

Mrs. Carter and I stood waiting for the second limousine to move forward. Like her husband, she was helped to the same designated seat, and I was seated in the same position as my husband, next to Rosalyn. She apologized for sitting in the safest seat in the limousine, but said she was required to sit there. She wanted me to feel safe where I was sitting. Little did she know, I not only felt safe but also overwhelmed by the experience.

During the drive, as was her character, Mrs. Carter carried on an interesting and friendly conversation, beginning by complimenting me on what I was wearing, saying she wished she had been wearing a prettier dress. I always thought she dressed beautifully, and I certainly admired what she was wearing and told her so. After a little more chit-chat we arrived at the couple's favorite restaurant. Ernie and I had no clue as to what to expect, but soon realized that an eating place with peanut shells on the floor was a logical spot for a long-time peanut farmer!

We walked to the reserved table, crunching empty peanut shells with each step. We ordered what the Carters ordered—hamburgers and salads. The relaxed and fun atmosphere made for easy conversation, except we were continually interrupted by their friends who came by the table to give them a cheerful hello. We were introduced to many of their Georgia friends that evening, and Ernie and I realized just how fond people were of their neighbor and former president.

Our dinner discussion centered on their lives since leaving the White House and their developing plans. Both Ernie and I were amazed to observe their positive outlook. We wondered if we could have been so forward-thinking and optimistic after a defeat like President Carter suffered in his race for a second term.

All in all, Ernie and I enjoyed the evening and felt right at home being with President and Mrs. Carter. Of course, it was Jimmy Carter who had requested that Ernie serve as the United States Commissioner of Education during his presidency, and with whom we had shared some of our experiences in Washington. Furthermore, our friendship and shared respect were also based on our own mutual love for and commitment to God.

We returned to the Carter Center and their apartment after engaging in the same elaborate routine on our trip to the restaurant. The Carters politely invited us to come in and stay overnight, but Ernie knew how to graciously decline their Southern hospitality since it was getting late and we were sensitive to the many pressing demands on their time. After saying good-bye we drove our rental car to the hotel where we had reservations. The next day we flew back to Princeton.

Cultivating Friendship with China

Ever since our 1974 visit to China, Ernie and I had been eager to continue our friendship with the Chinese people. That friendship was rekindled in June 1987, when Ernie received an invitation from Madame Professor Hao Keming, whose title was Director-General of China's Most Important Arm on Education Policy-Making and Education Reform, to speak as the U.S. representative at the International Education Seminar in Beijing.

Ernie traveled to the seminar with our son Paul. After his speech, Ernie was approached by Mr. Li Tieying, China's "Top Education Authority" about a plan to partner with the Carnegie Foundation for the Advancement of Teaching. Ernie and Madame Professor Hao Keming enthusiastically supported a plan for China and the United States to be partners in education. Both nations shared the assumption that a nation's healthy social and economic development was strongly tied to education.

In November of 1988, Madame Professor Hao Keming traveled to Washington DC for a ceremony with Ernie held at the Library of Congress, where she signed an agreement of education collaboration between China and The Carnegie Foundation for the Advancement of Teaching. The formal ceremony was noteworthy as two people from different countries embraced the same goal for the future. It was the beginning of an important relationship lasting from 1987 until Ernie's death in December 1995. During those years, the partnership became an important part of our lives.

In 1989, Ernie and I traveled to China for the first of seven collaborative seminars with selected Chinese political and educational leaders and the CFAT. The foundation's delegation was led by Ernie. Every other year, Madame Professor Hao Keming would bring a delegation from China to meet with top universities and government officials in the United States. Ernie depended on his many friends in education to help arrange visits to various campuses for his Chinese friends.

Every time our U.S. delegation went anywhere in China, we were welcomed with amazing hospitality. Long-lasting friendships developed; I have particularly warm memories of our 1992 delegation trip to Guanghow and Dalian. The seminar presentations were on "How Higher Education Could Serve the Needs of the Local Economy and Social Development." Our sixteen-year-old grandson, Gabriel, traveled with us, and his youthful spirit added to our visits to high schools, factories, farms, villages, industrial zones, and research laboratories. He charmed everyone with his wonderful smile and his noble efforts to speak Chinese. Gabriel has continued to study Chinese, and now, more than two decades later, speaks fluent Chinese—keeping up with what he began on that trip with his grandparents.

I have many letters that remind me of Ernie's ongoing communication and relationship with Chinese education officials. Every time a delegation from the U.S. went to China or a Chinese delegation came to our country, there was always an elaborate gift-giving exchange. Once Ernie and I invited the delegation to be guests in our home for dinner, and before dinner was served, Madame Professor Hao Keming presented us with a beautiful Chinese tablecloth, which I still use.

We always felt our gifts to the Chinese were quite inferior to what they gave us, and so we struggled to decide what to give to Madame Professor Hao Keming when she and her delegation were guests in our Family Home Mansion. Ernie finally came up with the wonderful idea of asking my mother, Katie Tyson, to create one of her hand-stitched bed quilts, which would be a truly American gift. Ernie asked my mother to make the quilt with a Chinese red border and red-patch squares mixed in between other colorful patches. I have to say it turned out to be a very outstanding and unusual piece of art.

When Ernie and I presented this special quilt to Madame Professor Hao Keming, she was speechless. She was even too overwhelmed to eat her dinner, and the next day she told one of Ernie's staff members that her heart was so touched that she could not sleep a wink that night. My mother's quilt was taken to China and hung in the grand hall entrance of the "National Center for Education" building in Beijing. My dear mother never could have dreamed that one of her quilts would hang in a building of great distinction in China. In addition, Ernie and I marveled at how the heart of people and a nation can be touched by meaningful warm friendships and Christian love.

The Paradox of India

In the midst of all his writing and other important undertakings, Ernie was invited to India as a Distinguished Fulbright Professor under the direction of the United States Educational Foundation of India. It was an outstanding invitation, and it included travel for the two of us. We enthusiastically accepted their two-week opportunity and arrived in Delhi in January 1985. We found a land teaming with extremes ranging from the grandest of splendor and wealth to the poorest of the poor. It was what we had always heard about India, but the contrasts were immediately evident.

Mrs. Nayak, the U.S. personal representative for Fulbright, met us at the Delhi airport and was driving an Indian ambassadorial car along a four-lane highway to take us to the hotel, when suddenly the car broke down with some sort of engine problem. Ernie got out and pushed the car off the busy highway along with many men with turbans and flowing garments who came to help.

I also got out of the car and when I glanced down the road I saw what appeared to be a baby lying on the ground along the roadside. As I approached, two women appeared. Mrs. Nayak then came and spoke in Hindi to them so that she could translate for me. She explained to me that the mother of the two-month-old baby and her husband and his whole family were slum dwellers and migrant day-laborers, getting work wherever they could. This day they found work repairing the side of the roadway by piling on loose stones. The tiny infant was naked and was wrapped in burlap. It was a baby girl who appeared to be only five or six pounds. I lifted the baby and talked to her, but her eyes seemed to have a film over them, and I got no response.

The grandmother motioned to Ernie that she wanted money for the child. Mrs. Nayak told us not to give money to beggars, but when she was busy checking on the car, Ernie slipped the mother some rupees. The mother then sat on the dusty roadside ground and nursed her baby girl in the midst of heavy traffic from cars, carts, scooters, three-wheeled taxis, horses, donkeys, and bicycles. She had a big smile on her face while she clutched the rupees in her hand.

With the car at least partially repaired, we traveled from that shocking experience of confronting the life of the poorest of the poor, to the Delhi Hotel Oberoi Intercontinental where we had reservations. Judging by the uniformed doorman and the magnificent lobby, we immediately knew that this was a super deluxe hotel. The contrast between what we had just experienced on the highway and the Hotel Oberoi made it shockingly clear that we had just encountered India's societal contrasts at their most extreme.

Our schedule included travel to five cities and twenty lectures for Ernie at universities and higher education institutes. In between formal visits, Ernie spent his time preparing his next speech or meeting the people who had made appointments to speak with him. Our program planners thoughtfully arranged my schedule so that I could attend all of my husband's lectures. Then because of my background and interest, they arranged for me to travel and visit mother and child service programs in each city. These visits helped me to see and understand more about the depth of the economic inequality in this heavily populated and ancient society.

Although it may sound as if Ernie and I did not get to do much together, we had invitations every evening for dinners in lovely, spacious homes such as that of the United States Cultural Affairs Officer. We also had two special visits with U.S. Ambassador Harry Barnes, who was appointed by President Reagan to serve in India. All of these high-level, governmental events were hard to take in stride.

As we went from one opulent place to another, with all the upscale services, Ernie and I could not get thoughts of the mother and the precious tiny baby who we found lying along the road out of our minds. We could not help but think about the tiny baby girl's future or even the chances for her to survive. If she did survive, it seemed impossible for her to ever break free from the world into which she had been born.

Monument to Lost Love

The Fulbright program arranged for us to spend a day with a guide who was educated in the history of India and spoke excellent English. We rode with him on a train from Delhi to Agra to see the famous Taj Mahal mausoleum built in the 1600s. Our guide told us that it was erected by Shah Jahan as a love gift in memory for his favorite wife who died too young, and it is called "The monument to lost love."

We first saw it at a distance through arches. Then as we climbed steps we viewed it straight on but could not appreciate it as a whole because of its grand size. Finally, the entire scene unfolded before our eyes as we looked down from the high steps and saw it in its full magnitude. To add to the beauty, the Taj Mahal was built to be reflected in pools of water. The extravagant pure white marble structure against the blue sky with no background interference and reflected in pools of water was completely breathtaking, far more splendid than we could have imagined or even dreamed. To us, it felt like a gradual approach to heaven with a beauty beyond the human mind's comprehension. We wanted to stay there together and gaze at the unspeakable beauty, feeling unwilling to leave.

Being forced back to reality, the next morning we took a flight from Delhi to Calcutta. We were then driven from the airport to the Oberoi Grand Hotel. That name, that included the word "Grand," sounded like a boasting title for the hotel in the city of Calcutta. Ernie and I were self-conscious about the street people watching us go in and out of this costly hotel and asked each other why the program planners made all of our hotel reservations at the grandest places.

Calcutta

We were told in Delhi that Calcutta would offend our senses. We did not find that to be true but were more impressed by the busy activity of the mass of people. Everyone seemed to have a purposeful activity. The ladies, no matter if they were rich or poor, walked with stately dignity in their beautiful saris, usually carrying a basket on their head. Many men had a craft or product with which to barter. Right on the street was a barber cutting hair or shaving men; some were making shoes from pieces of old tires. We saw others who were making clay drinking cups for the price of half a penny. All this was taking place right along the street.

Ernie and I could not help but think about the industriousness and ingenuity of the people. They did what many older Americans had done before we became a highly industrial, technological society—making something out of nothing, using creativity and industry as their *modus operandi*. From our luxurious hotel window, the other world was immediately visible.

Ernie and I could hardly stop watching. The vendors, the constant flow of people, the human-drawn carts, and always the horn-blowing vehicles were an endless fascination and a reminder that all nations have their societal challenges. In India we saw how the press of humanity, from day to day, had become a way of life. We understood that 20 percent to 30 percent of the population in Calcutta were street people. We saw families who had set up housekeeping against the building directly across the street from our hotel window, and we saw beggars and mothers with babies pleading with other street people for a bite of rice. We deeply felt the agony and sadness of this place.

Before we left Calcutta, it was arranged for us to visit Mother Teresa's largest center for children, where she took in and cared for the sick and dying. When we arrived, the children reached to be picked up. Many were deformed from rickets and malnutrition and could only crawl or walk with support. Ernie carried a crippled child in each arm, and I picked up a darling little girl who was too crippled to walk. She laughed easily and wanted to embrace me. Those children clung to us and cried when we had to put them down.

Ernie's schedule was tightly planned with lectures, seminars, large luncheon affairs, and official meetings. When it was not necessary for me to focus on official business with Ernie, I would walk among the throngs on the street or go on a prearranged trip and report back to him with every detail.

I was sorry that Ernie could not be with me when I met with the professional service workers. He would have been as overcome as I was had he been with me at that hospital, which averaged fifty births a day. One room where the doctor took me was the ward with the mothers who had given birth to a baby that day. The crude beds that lined the room almost as far as I could see were filled with mothers and babies lying side-by-side. The doctor translated as we walked along the row of beds, and we talked to some of the mothers who were curious about me. I found almost no happiness during that visit. These were all very poor mothers, and a new baby made life for them even harder.

I noticed one mother who was not facing her child but had her back turned toward her baby. I stopped to talk to her though the language translation of the physician friend. The mother told me that her baby was a girl and that I should take her because she was not going to feed her. She said her husband told her she could not bring a baby girl home. She was being forced to let her baby girl die.

Here again I came face to face with the reality of poverty. I realized that from the husband's point of view, it was necessary for his wife to give birth to a boy. A father needed to be able to count on the manual labor of a male child. Girls were considered an economic burden to a family. The mother, needing the economic support of her husband, could not allow even the notion of defiance to creep into her mind. And so it was easier for this mother to turn her back on that baby girl, which also aided her in not forming an emotional bond to her female infant. Ernie and I suffered endlessly when we spoke about that precious soul.

"He Was the Star"

In my twenty-three page diary of our time in India, I did not speak modestly about my husband, as he had always asked me to do. However, I could talk to my diary as I wished, so I wrote, "He was the star." The *Indian Times* newspaper ran a long article and picture of Ernie, declaring that he had stunned everyone with his perceptions.

That would be a good ending for our India story, but I have one more story to offer from my diary, when I wrote:

> I stayed for Ernie's successful speech and then I walked out into the back streets and the open markets. The "street families" were everywhere and I noticed a grandmother squatting on the curb with a small child beside her. She had a fleet of tiny folded paper boats made from scraps of paper. As she and the child pushed the little boats back and forth, pretending that the street was a pool of water, they would rearrange the boat line-up and play some more as they both laughed. I wanted to take a picture but somehow it did not seem appropriate to single her out as being special because grandmothers give the same gentle love and attention to grandchildren everywhere in the world.

India, despite the poverty we encountered, proved to be no different.

Midnight Viewing

Ernie always had a great interest in international education. He believed educators around the world could learn from each other and thus took on the laborious responsibility of writing a monthly column for *The London Times Higher Education Supplement* from 1983 to 1991.

Ernie's monthly newspaper column attracted a wide range of readers around the world. To provide material for his column, he had to keep his mind alert for up-to-date education issues in the U.S. that would capture the interest and be helpful to foreign readers. He and I often discussed ideas that could be of interest, but my bigger task was helping him find the time to write the essays. I dreaded the final deadline hour. During those nine years there was an air of apprehension in our house the day before the article was due in London. It was not unusual for my husband to work late into the night before the due date, and as soon as the column was sent off, he needed to start thinking about what he would say in the next one. I have to confess that I started urging him to ask to be relieved of the responsibility, and I think that my urging reached the level of nagging, despite my efforts to not be a "nagging wife."

Finally, after nine years with the London paper, Ernie found another way to be engaged in international education causes by planning to convene a yearly Higher Education International Conference with the first being held in Princeton in 1991. After that, Ernie directed Higher Education International Conferences with sponsorship from education institutions in Mexico, the Netherlands, Australia, Kenya, Germany, and Sweden, and we traveled together to those events.

The Sweden-sponsored meeting turned out to be one of those once-in-a-lifetime adventures that can never be forgotten. Our son Ernie Jr. and his son Julian went with us. The twenty conference participants came from colleges and universities in Sweden, Denmark, Norway, Finland, and Iceland. The ten-day Sweden-sponsored conference ended with a special invitation to end the conference in Ivalo, Lapland.

Lapland is called "the land of the midnight sun" as it sits in the region of the Arctic Circle near the North Pole. At the time of our visit, it was daylight twenty-four hours a day. From the time we arrived, Ernie and I were captivated by the skies. One night the conference participants were invited to climb to the top of a high hill to enjoy a bright midnight panoramic view of one of the marvels of nature. The group stood together, holding hands on top of the world, or so it seemed, as we felt powerful awe for God's majestic creation while we seemingly viewed the whole world.

On a Mission for a Clinic

Another year the International Higher Education Conference was held in Ajijic, Jalisco, Mexico and was sponsored by the university in that city. Ernie again directed the conference and was a presenter in the sessions. When Ernie and I arrived, we were surprised by the opulence of the conference hotel, particularly since the immediate area was stricken by poverty.

The hotel was cut off from the real world by a high stone wall. However, as glorious as the hanging flower gardens were amidst the white tablecloth-covered luncheon tables in the enclosed hotel's outdoor restaurant, it seemed strange to be cut off from the many people who were beyond the wall who could only enter if they had enough money to pay the prices on the menu.

We were grateful for the blessing of the delightful meals provided by the conference, but I could not stop thinking about the people beyond the wall in the surrounding villages.

Through a contact I learned about a nearby village beyond the wall. Walking a mile or two down a dusty, narrow road, I found the village and spied a little clinic. Some might say I was led there by God's Spirit. I walked into the clinic and introduced myself to Dr. Montano, the village's only doctor. She invited me to stay with her that day as she worked with the many patients who came to the clinic, which was a very sparsely equipped medical resource that consisted of one small room for physical examinations and a tiny surgery room.

She told me she had set up the clinic using her own meager resources and was the only one to provide care. Dr. Montano was a middle-aged woman, small in height, but tall in her desire to serve the poor in the village where she grew up. She had a Christian heart and wanted to honor God and her own Ajijic neighbors by helping individuals in need who lived there. She had traveled all the way to Chicago to learn to be of service to her people, moving back to Ajijic after she completed medical school. Although Dr. Montano was dedicated to helping her own people, she was frustrated and concerned because she did not have funds to develop an adequate clinic.

As I walked with her around her poorly equipped clinic, she told me many stories about the medical needs in the village and the surrounding area. She said her biggest concern was for the newborn babies left to die in Ajijic's waste disposal areas because young, unwed mothers were too poor to provide for them. These mothers were disowned by their families and left all alone to give birth. When Dr. Montano finished telling me about her concerns, she told me she was praying for a way to help these mothers and babies.

That evening I told Ernie about my day. We talked about my visit to the clinic, my time with Dr. Montano, and that she was praying for the village's medical and social needs. Together we resolved that we had to think of a way to help. In particular, Ernie knew about a foundation in Washington DC whose special priority was helping the needy. After we returned home, Ernie was able to make an appointment so we could speak to the foundation program officer about the need back in Ajijic. In the meantime, I wrote a proposal outlining the problem and a budget for a plan that would provide help.

Together Ernie and I took the train from Princeton to DC and found our way to the offices of the Public Welfare Foundation, where we were seated at a table with the program officer, Anne Allen. From the start, we knew Anne was receptive to our proposal about the need in Ajijic. Ms. Allen then presented the urgent need to the Public Welfare Foundation Board of Trustees and within a short time called to tell us the trustees had approved a grant for the clinic in Ajijic.

The grant money was to be used to refurbish the clinic and build a house for unwed mothers and their babies. There was much interest in the help that the grant was providing, and soon other foundations got involved. Dr. Montano was even invited to come to the United States to receive recognition for her efforts to help destitute mothers. Soon, many American families wanted to support these mothers and babies. The project grew and grew until Dr. Montano's prayer was answered way beyond her expectations.

A Miracle at Birth

One of our most unusual and blessed events involving foreign travel did not involve strangers, but rather our son Craig and his wife and family. In late 1992, Ernie had just been diagnosed with cancer and begun chemotherapy, so we planned a much-needed vacation and family New Year's celebration for a time between his treatments in early 1993. Ernie chose a resort in Berkeley Springs, West Virginia. Craig and Flora and their three children would not be able to make the reunion because they were in Belize and Flora was expecting their fourth child. Ernie and I had reservations to fly to Belize after our one-week vacation at Berkeley Springs, planning to arrive in Belize two weeks before Flora was due to give birth so that I could serve as the midwife for the birth of their fourth child.

Then out of the blue, our plans suddenly changed in a way that radically shook up our family gathering. We were happily enjoying our New Year's Eve dinner, when I realized Ernie had become quiet and subdued. I even noticed that his facial expressions had changed with a look of worry.

When we finished dinner, he asked everyone to come to our hotel room. He took my arm as we hurried off ahead of the others to our room where he wanted me to help him gather enough chairs for everyone. I could not understand what was happening. Then, with a tone of urgency, he explained to me and all the seated family that he had a strange but strong prompting during the family dinner that he and I needed to leave and go to Washington DC to take the next flight to Miami that would connect to a flight to Belize City, to be with Craig and Flora as soon as possible. Ernie made it clear that the rest of the family should continue their vacation at the resort but that he and I would be immediately checking out of the hotel.

Paul and his wife, Hilary, volunteered to drive us to the airport in Washington, and we were able to get on the next plane to Miami, where we caught a flight to Belize City. We arrived there on New Year's Day 1993, and completely surprised Flora and Craig by arriving a week early. Fortunately, Craig had brought Flora to Belize City, making the long trip from their home near Punta Gorda in an old pickup truck. Craig's heart had also been prompted by the Spirit to arrive that day in Belize City.

Weeks earlier and at my request, Craig had been able to hire a medical doctor who would assist me with the delivery as I expected this would be another very large baby due to Flora's unusual weight gain. Five years earlier, Craig and Flora's third child, David, had weighed twelve pounds at birth, and his shoulders had been too large for a normal delivery, making it a very difficult birth.

Fortunately, before David's birth, I had enlisted a midwife friend from New Jersey to travel with me to Craig and Flora's home because I knew of Flora's weight gain. My friend and I had learned how to deal with David's shoulder problem during our midwifery education, and we knew how to quickly use a very special corkscrew turning maneuver until the shoulders were freed. With our help, David had a blessed and safe birth. However, it was a serious complication, and I wanted to make sure we had safe delivery plans for Craig and Flora's fourth child, which is why I had asked Craig to arrange to have a doctor available to help me for this birth.

After our hurried trip, Ernie and I arrived in Belize City and rushed to the hotel where we and Flora and Craig had reservations. They were very surprised and overjoyed to see us a week earlier than planned. When I examined Flora, I immediately understood why the Spirit had nudged Ernie, just twenty-four hours earlier, that we needed to arrive that night. Flora was large and uncomfortable and, without a doubt, she was going to have another extra large baby. Our dear Flora was showing signs of early labor, and Craig was enormously relieved and grateful that we had arrived when we did. He and his Father were thanking God for His watchful care, which had prompted all of us to arrive that evening, a week ahead of our well-laid plans.

A few hours later, in the wee hours of that morning, Craig knocked loudly on our hotel room door, saying that Flora was in hard labor. Craig and I rushed Flora to the doctor's house, where there was a well-equipped birthing room, while Ernie went to stay with our three sleeping grandchildren in the hotel room. He would watch over them and explain when they awoke in the morning that they would soon have a new brother or sister.

Craig and I frantically knocked and hollered to awaken the doctor, begging him to open the door and let us into his birthing room; I feared at one point that I would have to deliver the infant in the truck. Thankfully, the doctor finally heard us and let us into the birthing room just in time, and also notifying the pediatrician. Within a few minutes the head was delivered, but like with David, the shoulders were stuck. The doctor moved in to pull on the head, but I was prepared for the problem as I knew this was a high probability and had repeatedly reviewed the management of this emergency. I told the doctor not to pull as I moved in, and immediately began the corkscrew principle to release the baby's impacted shoulders.

But the problem was more serious than it had been with David, and it took four rotations, which took all my strength and seemed to be taking too long. I knew the lack of oxygen was turning this precious baby purple. Just then the shoulders cleared the pelvis, and our beautiful baby boy was delivered into my hands, although he was limp and not a good color. I immediately handed him to the pediatrician, who had just arrived. He reached to receive this limp and blue precious baby boy but said, "This baby is not going to make it."

The regular doctor was caring for Flora, so with a pounding heart, I ran from the room, dropped to my knees, and screamed, "Dear God, do not let this precious baby die!" I quickly got up and returned to the room to see the pediatrician breathing into the newborn's mouth and repeatedly giving oxygen. I kept praying and pleading to God for mercy when suddenly our precious grandson gasped for a breath of air and then gasped again and miraculously give out a cry. What tears of joy and praise to God filled that room!

Flora began recovering with amazing strength as she and Craig rejoiced over their fine baby boy—a miracle gift from heaven they named Andy. As I write, Andy is a strong, healthy twenty-year-old and a fine Christian young man who God has gifted for use in His kingdom.

As soon as I could, I called Ernie. He had been frantically waiting in that hotel room with the other three children but was trusting God for a good outcome. He was so relieved that we had arrived in time and was overwhelmed with gratitude that the Spirit clearly nudged him and that he responded.

He had been concerned because he understood my fears and knew how often I had reviewed the steps for managing problems that might arise during the delivery. In my heart I knew Ernie had been spending every minute that morning praying and waiting for my call. When he answered my phone call on the first ring, I was so full of relief and gratitude for the revived baby boy that I could not talk and could not stop crying for the joy in my heart.

Ernie tried to stay calm because sensitive eleven-year old Anna was awake and eagerly awaiting news of another brother or sister. Finally, I was able to stop crying enough to say he could tell the children that they had a baby brother. All the children were now awake, and I heard a happy cheer. They then asked their grandfather when they could see their baby brother and their mom and dad. I was still holding the phone when Ernie told them he would take them to the hotel dining room for breakfast after they slept some more, then he would take them for a swim in the pool before taking them to see their baby brother.

I was then able to answer all of Ernie's questions and tell him the whole remarkable and miraculous story. We both felt completely overwhelmed by God's leading and divine care. What a remarkable gift of caring and love from the heavenly father. We knew that God's presence and power had been with us throughout the whole experience. All was well, and we were overjoyed with gratitude for a new grandchild. Andy's birth was certainly a most precious gift given to us during the three years of Ernie's chemotherapy treatment.

Part IV: Honoring a Significant Life

Ernie's many accomplishments in the field of education did not go unnoticed, and we celebrated together many times as he was appointed to exciting positions and presented with honors for his outstanding work. Ernie was named by Secretary of State George Shultz to chair the National Council for American Overseas Schools for the U.S. Department of State. These schools were American-sponsored elementary and secondary schools in countries all around the world that served the children of U.S. government officials and private-company workers living abroad. Ernie was asked to lead a council of twenty-five outstanding American leaders to provide advice and policy guidance to these overseas schools.

Ernie and I both understood the uniqueness of the position, but we also knew that his time was already stretched beyond reasonable limits. However, because he was committed to pushing the envelope in the area of education both here and abroad and because he knew he could do the job with God's help, he accepted. In addition to being an honor to be chosen to head the council, the position allowed him to play a role in the international agenda he had envisioned many years earlier when he was the chancellor at the State University of New York.

I have to say that I was proud of the two well-deserved letters of praise and recognition he received from President Ronald Reagan related to his role on this council. In each letter, the president expressed profound appreciation to Ernie:

> You have helped to guide the formation of curricula, maintain high standards of teaching and implemented new programs. All this and more, has enabled our schools abroad to keep up with the best American standards. Many thanks for all you've done to ensure this.

Years later, Ernie received similar praise from President Bill Clinton, who wrote, "Thank you for your commitment to providing a world-class education to our students living abroad. I applaud your enthusiasm and dedication in carrying out the important tasks."

Hoods and a Very Special Quilt

In the late-1990s, I was proud to witness the opening of the Ernest L. Boyer Center at Messiah College, which was established in my husband's memory at his alma mater. According to the Center's website, the collection housed in Murray Library contains "more than 480 linear feet of manuscripts, audio and visual materials, correspondence, records of appointments, and other artifacts documenting the life and work of this American educational pioneer." In addition, the Boyer Center provides scholarships and implements other programs that seek to continue the work in education that Ernie valued so much during his lifetime.

Of all of my husband's memorabilia that are described in the six-page listing of the displays at the Boyer Center, several are extra special to me. The most eye-catching and precious display hangs on the large wall on the left as you enter the double-glass doors: a handmade quilt made by my precious mother with an extraordinary story behind it.

The quilt's story began when Ernie arrived home in 1986 after an event where he had been presented was another honorary doctorate. As I remember, it was his 128th honorary doctorate; he eventually received 141 in all. Each time an honorary degree is given, the recipient receives a flowing velvet or satin hood that is placed around the shoulders. That day he brought to our

Family Home Mansion another brightly colored hood that had been graciously placed around his shoulders earlier that day.

By this time, the closet where we stored the folded hoods was stacked very high in multiple rows. When he handed me another, I thoughtlessly did not marvel at its beauty or even congratulate my dear husband for receiving a special honor that day. Rather, I hastily said in a rather gruff way that many women who try to maintain order and organization in the house will surely understand, "You already have so many hoods, and I don't know where to find space for any more." He thought for a moment and then simply said that since we were running out of space, it was not necessary to keep all of them.

I was immediately horrified by the idea of disposing of the evidence of any of his honored accomplishments. I knew that he thought they were special, but I also knew that he was not one to hoard possessions or laud himself. I apologized for my rash comment and said we needed to think of a way to deal with the problem. I then suggested that we should ask my mother, Katie Tyson, which he agreed was a good idea because he knew my mother was very wise. We both knew we could trust her to think of a solution.

I called her and explained the situation. Without hesitation and with her usual enthusiasm, my mother told me to pack up all of those beautiful hoods and bring them to her where she lived at Messiah Village. She had an exciting plan and made a trip to the library to get information on the colors of the consecutive bands in a rainbow, saying the brilliant pure colors of the academic hoods matched those of the rainbow. She then gently removed all the stitching of the brightest colored hoods and transformed them into the large, prize-winning quilt that hangs in the Boyer Center at Messiah College. It is a spectacular display of a perfect rainbow and was a creative way to give honor to Ernie's academic hoods.

This quilt was my mother's special and unusual gift to her beloved son-in-law, and he offered her his heartfelt thanks many times over for saving his hoods. My mother then used more hoods to make beautiful wall hangings and quilts for our children, using all the different colors of the lovely fabrics. She was eighty-five years old when she took on the task of saving Ernie's academic hoods and still delighted in this kind of creative artistry, knowing how meaningful it was to her family. She had six children and many grandchildren and welcomed every chance to make something for any of us with her skilled hands and creative mind.

My precious mother died at the age of ninety-three. Family members were with her when she peacefully smiled, looked at us, and said, "I've always been faithful." She then slipped into eternity and the inconceivable delights of life with the heavenly Father. I will always greatly miss her and her nurturing and caring love. I remember telling her as a child that I could not live without her, and as I grew older I always depended on her advice and good judgment. In particular, I always trusted in her wisdom that was based on godly principles.

Signifying the Greatness of a Humble Man

No other display in the collection at the Boyer Center can compare to my mother's rainbow quilt, but another especially prized piece is a presidential award given to Ernie in 1994 by President Bill Clinton. It is the Charles Frankel Prize given to The National Endowment for the Humanities nominee. The prize is physically represented by a large, heavy obelisk standing twelve inches high with a base of over six inches.

The presentation was an overwhelming family event as we were invited to the White House and greeted by President Bill Clinton and First Lady Hillary Clinton. The beautiful ceremony took place on the West Wing lawn, where guests sat in rows of chairs in the shade of the trees on the manicured White House grounds.

President and Mrs. Clinton together lifted the large crystal obelisk described as "signifying greatness" and handed it to Ernie. I was so nervous and excited for Ernie that it was hard for me to appreciate all that was happening. That evening Ernie and I were invited with other guests to have dinner in the White House dining room with the Clintons and then to a concert in the East Room with Itzhak Perlman, the Israeli-American violinist who played with such passion and purity that evening.

Each award on display at the Boyer Center touched Ernie's heart, and he was always grateful for the honors bestowed on him. At the same time he felt conflicted whenever he was singled out for his accomplishments. His feelings were in tune with Mother Teresa when she said, "We are not called to be successful, but to be faithful."

Ernie had God's kind of love that was directed toward others, not toward himself. There was a divine glory that pervaded his life and needed no public recognition. His love was absolutely unselfish, and he worked and gave while expecting nothing in return. The awards are on display because they tell interesting stories about the facts and the breadth of Ernie's work. In addition, many of the awards are masterful works of art, which he always recognized with great appreciation.

A Very Special Hooding Ceremony

I was always proud of Ernie when he received an honorary degree, and I know he was especially proud of me the day I received an honorary degree from Hood College in Frederick, Maryland. The ceremony was in June 1995—just five months before Ernie's death, although we did not suspect we had so little time left on that June graduation day.

My whole family was there to see Ernie, my dear husband, place the doctoral hood on me, a beautiful act that had been thoughtfully arranged by Hood College President Martha Church. At that special moment, when we looked into each other's eyes, we both experienced a deep joy at being able to share that experience.

You can be sure that I have carefully preserved my hood that carries with it those sweet and treasured memories. Nary a word of concern did I express to Ernie about where on earth we could find room to store one more honorary doctoral hood.

Heartwarming Words to Mark Forty Years

Five years prior to the small moment at that graduation event, we had enjoyed together a momentous celebration in honor of our fortieth wedding anniversary. It was almost as emotional as our twenty-fifth anniversary when we had repeated our wedding vows at the Chancellor House Mansion. I guess Ernie and I were both sentimental, and we cherished these events that brought the family back together and honored our past.

Ernie had made reservations for all the family to gather at the Lake George Inn in New York State to help us celebrate our anniversary. On the last night of our weeklong reunion and anniversary celebration, he asked everyone to get dressed up for a family photograph and a special dinner. I have that reunion picture hanging on my wall, and when I look at the twenty of us in that photograph, sweet memories flood my heart as I look at the happy faces of all our family.

That evening, our four children made plans to surprise Ernie and me by presenting us two exquisite red amber vases along with a beautifully framed and signed heartfelt statement of love that they had written together. Their affectionate words were the best gift they could ever have given us, and our hearts were very deeply touched. They wrote:

Parents live as models for their children.
The values, vision, and love of one generation
are given as a gift to the next.
We have spent our lives watching and
learning from you both,
trying to capture and understand the special gifts
you have to offer us.
We have repeatedly drawn on the vast reservoir of love
you have created, and for this we are especially grateful.
We all now have children of our own.
And growing among us is an understanding that
the lessons you taught us have been learned—
however imperfectly—and continue to be shared.
The simple threads that once connected you to your
four children have stretched and multiplied,
becoming a strong web that holds and supports all of us together with a complexity that defies understanding. It is a web that began and is renewed with each acknowledgment of love.

With profound respect, gratitude and love,
—Ernie Jr., Beverly, Craig, S. Paul, and their spouses

We did not know it at the time, but in the coming years, Ernie and I would draw deeply from the reservoir of love and strength we had built over the years and celebrated on that fortieth anniversary.

Part V: A Three-Year Battle and the Final Victory

In 1992, Ernie and I traveled to the University of Oxford, where he was the keynote speaker at a higher education conference. He spoke about the four areas of scholarship he had spent many years examining and writing about in *Scholarship Reconsidered.*

We invited our grandson Nathan, who was studying in England that year, to come to Oxford and spend several days with us. We had a wonderful time with Nathan, spending a long afternoon hiking through Cotswold villages with their red-roofed, ninth-century, vine-covered cottages along the winding narrow roads. We admired the picturesque quaintness of the villages as we walked along, talking with delight to Nathan about his exciting plans for when he finished college. Although I enjoyed the time with our grandson, I couldn't help remembering the months Ernie and Paul and I had lived in England. I had the feeling that time was moving too rapidly, and I wanted it to move backward.

I did not know until we were on the long flight home from England that Ernie had been putting on a very bold front in spite of a grave fear he was harboring because he did not want to spoil our precious time with Nathan. His fearful suspicion had begun during our long hike when he discovered a lump in his neck. It concerned him, but he said nothing until we said good-bye to

Nathan and boarded the plane for our flight home. When he told me about the lump, I examined it and tried to console him (and myself) that it was just a swollen gland. But we both knew that as soon as we got home we were going to find the best doctor.

Devastating News

Sheldon Hackney, the president of the University of Pennsylvania at that time, was chair of the board of trustees at the Carnegie Foundation for the Advancement of Teaching. He and Ernie were special friends, and Ernie and I decided he should confide in Sheldon about his health concern. The campus of the University of Pennsylvania included a large medical center with world-renowned doctors and medical facilities. Dr. Hackney often told Ernie about the excellent reputation of the center's medical staff, and Ernie gave him credit for attracting the best medical team, so it is easy to understand why he wanted to confide in his friend.

After they talked, Dr. Hackney immediately contacted Dr. John Glick who was listed among the country's top oncologists and taught at the University. Although Dr. Glick was not accepting new patients, he willingly agreed to see Ernie and perform a biopsy to obtain a diagnosis. We went to his office with great hope but also aware that our prayer for full health might not be answered.

When we returned to Dr. Glick's office to receive the biopsy report, Ernie and I sat side-by-side, holding hands. My heart was pounding, and I could tell by the expression on Ernie's face and his tight grip on my hand that he was afraid to hear the results of the biopsy. The good doctor chose his words carefully, taking pains to express concern, but without beating around the bush informed us that the test results showed Ernie had lymphoma—a cancer that was in his lymphatic system. Despite Dr. Glick's thoughtful and caring style and his carefully chosen words, we were devastated. While the doctor did not say chemotherapy would cure Ernie's problem, he did say that he expected the cancer cells would be destroyed with treatment.

We left his office shocked and shaken. We did not know how to deal with the news that Ernie's body had been invaded by growing cells that had the potential to take his life. What were we to do? Along one of the hallways in the large medical center, we saw signs for a chapel and were drawn to enter. The small chapel was empty, and we knelt at one of the pews and told God we desperately needed His help. Then we committed everything to Him and asked for courage to move forward with strength.

We left that chapel with a determination to trust God and fully depend on Him for what was ahead. We did not know about the intense hardships we would soon experience, but we did know that we longed for God's grace and care.

Too Much Work

In 1992, when we learned of the lymphoma, Ernie was sixty-four years old. His work had reached its zenith, and he was finding even greater desire to see his endeavors come to fruition. In retrospect, I realize just how determined he was not to give up after he had been told he had cancer.

In fact, Ernie took on new challenges, and his schedule was replete with speaking, traveling, and writing commitments. He resumed his hectic pace; in many ways, he really did not know any other way to live. He was determined to adhere to his normal schedule and continue to work with his staff on major writing commitments. He continued to strive for perfection in his work, and he expected the same from his colleagues.

As his wife of forty-two years, I made every effort to support him and tried hard not to nag about pushing himself too hard. However, there were occasional moments when I was moved to gently caution restraint. I knew my husband was fighting for his life, and I did not want him to ignore his special health needs.

Our children knew everything we knew about their father's illness. In fact, Dr. Glick had a session with the children, explaining to them what he had told us. Of course, they were extremely troubled and alarmed by the diagnosis, and they also worried because their father kept working as hard as ever and taking on new challenges. They were determined to see him get well and felt it was important for him not to have so many demands on his time.

We all prayed that he would completely recover from his illness; however, we all knew that he was working much too hard.

One Saturday when Beverly was at our house she heard her dad talking on the phone, making a commitment to speak at another conference "as a favor" to someone who in my judgment should not have called our home on a Saturday to ask. She motioned for me to step outside with her. As we headed down the walkway she started to cry and said we somehow needed to help him not to accept so many demands. We both cried since we felt like we didn't have an answer to this problem. People were very loving toward my husband and yet were very demanding of his time.

'Til We Meet Again

Ernie continued his work for the next three years, even while he took chemotherapy and other treatments for his cancer. As the autumn months of 1995 arrived, he continued to deal with the reality of his lymphoma with unwavering faith in God. He worked every day, meaning that he went to his office or traveled to speak at some education event. He was also deeply involved in the details of our family life.

On November 6, 1995, he wrote in his journal, "What a day of rejoicing! Ernie Jr. passed his doctoral examination and I thank God for this great victory. I admire beyond words the talent and discipline and courage he brought to this truly awesome assignment." Sadly, Ernie did not live to rejoice when our son Paul also completed the work for his doctor of education degree.

Ernie's journal entry for that day continued, "Now, I pray for God's continued healing in my life, and as always I feel such love for Kay and for all of our children—each of whom is doing such remarkable things to make a better world."

The next day he wrote in his journal that he was thankful for the renewal effect of his first blood transfusion and was grateful that medical science had discovered how blood can be shared. He went on writing, directing a prayer to God: "I feel overwhelmed by your blessings. Bring healing to my body—to honor you. And may Kay and I walk hand in hand all our days on earth and for all eternity. Praise the name of the Lord!"

That evening during our regular Bible devotions, Ernie read from Mark 9, the account of a father coming to Jesus on behalf of his son's illness. The father said, "'If you can do anything, take pity on us and help us.' Jesus said, "'Everything is possible for him who believes.' The father exclaimed, 'I do believe; help me overcome my unbelief.'" As our devotions continued, Ernie prayed for our heavenly Father to strengthen our faith, telling God we were committed to His will. I recall that I found it difficult to fully commit to God's will as I was too fearful about what lay ahead.

The very next day, November 8, 1995, Ernie had a CAT scan and we learned that the cancer was spreading rapidly throughout his body. Dr. Glick said his condition was very serious and advised that Ernie should be hospitalized for a week to receive very powerful chemotherapy. After hearing this report, Ernie wrote in his journal:

> I thank God for family love and bonding. I do not know the future. The path seems so uncertain. But I do know that God heals and I trust him and I pray His will be done. I also pray that these days of trial will deepen me spiritually. I open myself to the divine, with God at the very center of my life. I pray that you, heavenly Father, will give Kay and me the strength and steady faith we need and that throughout eternity we will be wrapped as one in the warm embrace of your divine love.

Two weeks later, on the Wednesday before Thanksgiving, Ernie and I were driven to the Philadelphia hospital so he could receive a blood transfusion. This treatment gave him new energy to more fully enjoy the large family gathering for a festive Thanksgiving at Beverly and Dale's house, which was just around the corner from our Family Home Mansion. Dale's family, our family, and a young student couple who had just arrived from China were all there. Ernie always enjoyed being with family and new acquaintances.

On that Thanksgiving, we enjoyed typical holiday food and a lot of happy talk with friendly fellowship. Best of all, the transfusion helped Ernie to feel stronger so he could enjoy this special time of being together. When the tables were cleared and the dishes all washed, we joined together for a wonderful sing-a-long; Dale played the piano as we sang folk songs, hymns, and spirituals. Ernie sang along joyfully. When it began to get late and he was getting tired, he asked if we could end with the song written in 1880 by Jeremiah Rankin, the president of Howard University. It is the good-bye hymn, "God be With You." The chorus reads "'til we meet, 'til we meet, 'til we meet at Jesus' feet, God be with you 'til me meet again." Everyone knew of Ernie's grave illness, and this song led to many tearful embraces.

Requesting that we sing this song together was Ernie's way to say a sweet good-bye because he knew God was pacing his days and giving him that sweet Thanksgiving Day as a gift. Then Ernie asked Dale to play some familiar, happy children's songs to lift the mood and allow everyone to feel happy and blessed on this—his last—Thanksgiving Day.

Prayers for Healing

Before leaving for the hospital to receive the week-long aggressive chemotherapy, we asked George Gallup to come to our house and pray with us. George was a colleague of Ernie's in a large education survey project that the Carnegie Foundation for the Advancement of Teaching was conducting with the Gallup Foundation. While working together, George and Ernie often acknowledged their faith, and George told Ernie he and some of his friends were praying for Ernie's healing, so we invited George to come to our house to pray just before we left for the hospital.

We were feeling very fearful and needed encouragement. George came with his friend, Bill Hayes, a local physician. Ernie Jr. and Beverly were there as well, and we all joined hands. Ernie described this powerful prayer period by writing, "We joined hands and the Spirit flooded in."

Dr. Hayes began, "Prayer heals!" In his journal, Ernie wrote, "I claimed that healing promise in my heart that moment and throughout that week in the hospital." Then Ernie continued, writing this prayer: "My Father, I do not know the future. But I know you have a divine plan for my life, and I will, with confidence, follow you to the end." Ernie knew that he could not will his death away.

A Week of Treatment

Dr. Glick arranged for me to have room adjoining Ernie's for the week he was in the hospital. The treatments were extremely rigorous, and I was fully occupied caring for my husband. However, I was also able to take some time to write in my journal about some easier and happy moments that took place that week. For example I wrote:

> Hilary, S.Paul, and two-year old Avery drove all the way from Chestertown, Maryland to be with us in the hospital room for several hours. When they were ready to leave, S.Paul was hugging his Dad, who was sitting in a reclining chair, when little toddler, Avery, walked over and stood beside his Papa, as he called him, and took his big hand into his little hand and smiled lovingly at his grandfather. No one had prompted him. It was just about the sweetest scene on this side of heaven. It so thrilled Ernie because it felt like a tender healing touch of love.

I still value the thoughtfulness of many friends during that period, and I especially treasure my conversations with my best friend, Francis Harmon. She called from California and gave me a special verse from 2 Timothy 4:17: "But the Lord stood at my side and gave me strength." It was the exact encouragement that Ernie and I needed at that very moment.

Near the end of that week, Ernie and I had a momentous evening together. The treatment seemed to give him some appetite, so I ordered his favorite foods from the hospital kitchen. I used a folded sheet as a table cloth for a table stand that was in his room. I found a small bouquet of fresh flowers on a hallway table and "borrowed" the bouquet for our evening. Ernie happily helped with the planning of our romantic evening dinner in his room at the University of Pennsylvania Hospital.

I was keenly aware during this week of strenuous treatment that Ernie was intent on hanging on to the life he loved. After we ate and enjoyed the romantic atmosphere, he tearfully said he just could not leave me and his precious family—he wanted to live. He talked about everyone's bright future and said he did not want to miss out on any of it. He also told me that if he died, the separation would be hardest for me, and that it would be better if I died first so that he would then be the one left to do the painful grieving. He said staying would be the hardest to endure because the other one of us would not be there to share and understand.

However, he then said I needed to stay because the family needed me. I remember thinking then that it was their dad that they needed because he was the one who best knew how to help and counsel the family. But Ernie went on to tell me that my trust in God would give me an abundant life until he and I were together again. He pointed out that the one who dies first gets to go to heaven and into the arms of Jesus and explained that the separation would be short, even though it would seem long to me. In heaven there would be no measurement of time for him.

I told Ernie that I desperately wanted to go with him, but he gently told me I would have to stay here because my work on earth must not be finished, indicating it seemed like that was in God's plan. He said his service on earth was finished but that my time was not. I let him know I would work hard to finish my work here and hurry to him.

It was unusual for me to let him talk as I had always stopped him when he had tried to speak about his dying. I believed it would show a lack of faith in what I believed would be a complete healing. Thankfully, I did not stop him this time because he seemed comforted by his own words. His loving concern and assurance that our separation will end when my work here is finished has kept me going day after day.

Ernie was feeling stronger when he was discharged after the week of intensive treatment. Within a day he met with members of the board of trustees for a regularly scheduled, two-day session. He was eager to get back to work, but clearly his body was weakened.

I remember how at that evening dinner with the trustees, he thanked them and said they were part of his loving and caring family of friends that his loving God had given him. The next day he led them through the business sessions. He felt peaceful and wrote in his journal that he had a deep awareness of the Spirit of God's presence during the long and tiring hours he spent with them.

Wrapping Up His Work

I need to say that several months before the one-week hospitalization, Ernie had experienced a strong urgency to complete the fine tuning of a report called *The Basic School: A Community for Learning.* He felt this book had a special mission for the sake of all children and somehow knew he had to rework the chapters without delay.

In the book's Acknowledgments, he wrote how he and I had spent endless hours in manuscript review, which was very true. We found a small bed and breakfast in Delaware that was an easy drive from Princeton and kept returning there to be alone and away from distractions. In a quiet and cozy sitting room we sat and concentrated on every sentence until he was satisfied. He completed his goal, and that book was published in 1995, shortly before his death. Our son Paul later wrote, "It was without question my father's most important book, because in it all the pieces that shaped his work and personal life came together."

There was another deadline with which Ernie's spirit was wrestling. He had reluctantly made a promise to Norman Koonce, president of the American Architecture Foundation, to write a report on architecture education and practice. It was a huge undertaking, and Ernie knew it would require a large and skilled team to do the background research. He worked diligently to hire the best group and as their findings came back, he wrote the text. It was a labor of love and friendship for his dear friend, Norman, but as his body weakened, he feared he was running out of time and worked with a good writer, Lee Mitgang, who could assist him. Ernie did not get to write the last chapter, and I knew the unfinished book was a stress on his mind.

"The Hardest Day that There Could Ever Be"

On December 6, 1995, I wrote in my journal, "This is the hardest day that there could ever be." Earlier that day, Dr. Glick had told me and Ernie that the intense treatments were not working and that his time was short—weeks or even days. Sitting in that room with Dr. Glick and Ernie, my heart started pounding, and the walls of the room seemed to be receding. Everything seemed unreal. I wrote, "God, please help us to be strong and courageous while we wait for your gift of healing."

That same day Ernie had scheduled a 4 p.m. meeting in his office with State Education Commissioner Mary Lee Fitzgerald and seven New Jersey school principals. However, Dr. Glick kept him at the hospital all day for a platelets transfusion in the hope of helping him to feel better. Ernie told Robert, his driver, the shocking news, and Robert, in deep distress, immediately took off for Princeton to bring Ernie Jr. and Beverly to the hospital. I was in such a state of shock I could barely move, and I refused to listen or speak to anyone. How could I live with such news?

We were finally able to leave the hospital at 4:15 p.m. From the car, Ernie called his office and calmly asked his assistant, Louise, to arrange a car speaker phone for a conversation with the principals who were waiting for him at his office. He then conversed with them for the whole hour it took for us to drive from the hospital to our Family Home Mansion. He talked and carried on as if nothing had happened and that nothing was wrong.

I will always remember the terrible pain in my mind and heart during that drive home from the hospital. I would not let my mind think. If my mind was blank, there was no reality in Dr. Glick's words. With Ernie carrying on his discussions with the school administrators, I decided that there was no bad news. I was in complete denial of the actual situation.

But the next day, I could see what I did not want to believe. Although Ernie had not given up, his body had given out. He asked Lee Mitgang to come to our house, and all morning they sat side-by-side on chairs in our bedroom, working on the last chapter of the unfinished architecture report until Ernie was satisfied that he had fulfilled his promise. The book was published in 1996 with the title, *Building Community: A Future for Architecture Education and Practice,* by Ernest L. Boyer and Lee D. Mitgang.

The Touch of an Angel

Several days earlier, our son-in-law Dale had sent a message to Belize that Ernie's time with us was nearing the end. Broken-hearted, Craig traveled to the distant telephone center in Punta Gorda and placed a call to our house, and he and Ernie were able to talk on the phone a long time. Craig recalls that his father spoke in a bright, upbeat manner, telling him that the three years of his illness were wonderful years that he would not trade as they had drawn him closer to God, which allowed Ernie and Craig to rejoice together.

Then Ernie told Craig that there was no need to come home and that he should stay there to continue his missionary work because Ernie said he was feeling sustained. Craig's mind was in turmoil about what to do. Ernie Jr., Paul, and Beverly told Craig to bring his family and come home. I was too broken to talk to Craig, but I felt assured he and the family would come home to Princeton as fast as they could. I needed them along with the rest of the family.

When I heard Ernie tell Craig that he was feeling sustained, my mind flashed back to Ernie's experience when he was receiving his first chemotherapy treatment. He was very apprehensive about what the procedure would be like and was also worried about the side effects. The treatment had just begun when I was called out of the room for a moment to receive some pills that I was to give him later to prevent nausea. When I stepped back into the room, I found him very pale, stunned, and unable to speak.

It was some time before he could put into words what he had experienced when I had stepped out of the room. Then, filled with utter amazement, he told me that after I left the room he saw the wing of an angel come from behind him and gently cover him. He had a deep awareness of a loving divine presence enveloping him in a canopy from heaven. He said it all happened in an instant. It was an overwhelming experience, and for the next three years of his illness, he frequently used that moment to sustain him, knowing that same loving presence was with him.

> *"Because you are my help, I will sing in the shadow of your wings."*—Psalm 63:7

> *"The angel of the Lord encamps round about them that fear Him, and He delivers them."*—Psalm 34:7

Ernie was very deeply touched by the experience of the angel's presence and kept it close to his heart although he felt it was too sacred to talk about openly, partly because he also thought it could be hard for some people to understand or to believe. He was quietly resting in God's goodness, love and perfect plan—regardless of whether or not he would be healed. He was drawn near to God's loving heart and placed his life in His hands.

The Final Day

The night of December 7, 1995, one day after we had received the dreadful medical report from Dr. Glick, I wrote in my journal:

> Ernie slept well all night—but I could not sleep as I listened to his breathing—trying to believe that I wasn't hearing sounds of his lungs filling with fluid. He awoke feeling refreshed and rejoicing at another "beautiful day," as he called it. He was very weak but he wanted to dress with a shirt and tie and dress trousers for a videotaped interview with Ernie Jr.

For some time, Ernie and Ernie Jr. had been working together on the writing of a book on leadership—a different sort of a biography. They gave it the title *Everyone Can Lead.* That morning, December 8, 1995, Ernie Jr. set up a microphone and taping system. Everything was ready in Ernie's large office and lounge room upstairs. Using what little strength he had, Ernie very slowly climbed the stairs as two of his children supported and lifted him up each step. They helped him get seated in his comfortable lounge chair.

Ernie was short of breath, but he was eager to express his views on the tape, thoughtfully answering Ernie Jr.'s questions for about two hours. He forgot himself and any illness and got very involved in the stories of student leadership during the riots of the late-1960s and early-1970s and other experiences he wanted to share. Ernie Jr. has kept that tape in his loving care, but has never been able to listen to it.

The interview ended as all the family gathered in that room, except for Craig and his family who were still on their way from Belize. I so hoped they would arrive soon. The room was filled with family sitting on chairs or on the floor making a circle around their father and grandfather. I was sitting close beside Ernie. The room was hushed.

Ernie had everyone's rapt attention and he began talking gently about the love of Jesus. He spoke about the reasons why Jesus loved children. All the family knew that their father had a special place in his heart for children and that his love was patterned after Jesus' own love. Jesus told His disciples to never turn children away but to reach out to them. Ernie said Jesus loved children because they were very teachable and did not have their minds already made up.

He told us that we need to be open, with receptive minds about the teachings of Jesus and believe in him with childlike faith and sincerity, explaining that children can see God in everything and accept His love and the gift of Jesus that was offered to each of us. With deep feelings, he said the unencumbered faith that children have is what God wants from us, and that we will find peace, happiness, and eternal life in this kind of faith. To me, and all the family seated around him, these gentle and profoundly moving words were what God's Spirit gave him to leave with each of us.

At this same moment, I was in such a state of grief and perplexity about what was happening. Was my husband in the state of dying while I was fully depending on God for his complete healing? I did not want to think my prayers could go unanswered by a loving God and refused to believe God would overrule my prayers because my timing was not His timing. I was too afraid to pray the prayer that Jesus prayed when He was about to die: "Nevertheless, not my will, but Yours be done" (Luke 22:42). I could not comprehend what was happening, and I looked on with intense fear and grief.

The phone kept ringing even as Ernie's body was failing. Senator Paul Simon from Illinois, who sat with Ernie on the National Education Commission, called. Hillary Clinton called to thank Ernie for the time he had responded to her request to evaluate and make recommendations to improve the Arkansas state school system when Bill Clinton had been governor of that state.

Next, President Jimmy Carter called to thank Ernie one more time for his contribution to education when he was the United States Commissioner of Education. The president was praying for him, but Ernie could barely catch his breath. He listened to President Carter's kind words and then breathed out a labored "Thank you." I took the phone and told President Carter that Ernie was too short of breath to say more. I thanked him for his words of thanks and said his call meant very much to Ernie and to the family.

Bob Hochstein, Ernie's closest colleague and dearest friend, took the morning train from Washington DC to sit with Ernie. It was too heart-wrenching for Bob to see his friend slipping away. Even though Ernie was so short of breath, he tried to make Bob feel welcome. After about thirty minutes, Bob left, brokenhearted, taking the next train back to Washington.

Ernie's oxygen supply was so low that he started to have pain in his legs that soon became intolerable. Beverly and Paul's wife, Hilary, said we needed to call an ambulance. Ernie was relieved to think he would get relief at the Princeton Hospital emergency room. I called George Gallup and asked him to meet us at the hospital to come and pray for healing. George indeed met us in a private side room immediately adjacent to the emergency room. When Ernie's friend, George, prayed for complete healing, Ernie reached out for his hand and said, "Thank you, George, for that wonderful prayer." Beverly and I were close beside him, and we kept reassuring each other that he was getting better after the prayer.

I sat next to my Ernie, holding his hand, praying and reassuring him that he was going to be feeling better soon. They gave him intravenous Demerol for pain relief. I was glad for the pain relief, but I wanted them to treat Ernie for the problem, so I asked Paul to take my place and sit next to his father and hold his hand while I talked to the doctor.

When I asked the doctor about the treatment plan, she told me to sit down on the chair that she was holding out to me. Then she said to me, "Mrs. Boyer, your husband is dying." All of a sudden, I had to face the impossible—but where was God? I thought, if God has the power to heal, why isn't He doing it for Ernie now? I tried to get up to walk back to our children and to my one and only love. Ernie Jr. helped me take those heavy, weary steps back to my beloved husband's side. I needed to be there to help him leave this life that he so loved. I needed to help my Ernie leave his family and be transported to his heavenly mansion.

The heartbreak was beyond description. I wanted to hold Ernie in my arms. I tried to embrace him, and I told him over and over that I wanted to go with him. How could I let him go without me? We always believed we were matched by God. Our lives were very deeply connected. How could we now be separated?

However, I was being told that he was truly dying—that I would soon be left alone, without my best friend, my love, my happiness, my daily joy, my husband for forty-five years, three months, and twelve days.

At that moment, I realized I had to let him go to Jesus. I was then able to tell him it was all right to go. I told him that the angels were singing a beautiful welcome song to usher him into heaven—that Mother and Daddy, Grandfather and Grandmother, Ma and even my father, who died when I was three months old, were all so happy for his soon-to-be arrival. Jesus was standing ready to receive him with a grand welcome.

Beverly helped me as I tried to sing and to recite the 23rd Psalm and the Lord's Prayer. Many more family members had arrived, and everyone moved in close to say how much he meant to each of them. Beverly's four children were all there and were suffering the depth of grief along with Ernie Jr., Beverly, Dale, and Paul and Hilary, who were holding their two-year-old Avery. Tears and sobs went on unrestrained although I knew that Ernie did not want to make us feel sad and lonely and that he still had much he wanted to get done. I said, "My sweetheart, we will carry on your work for you."

We were all together in that room from 8:30 p.m. on December 7 to 1:30 a.m. on December 8, 1995, to give him our final words of love and promise to have the family joined together again in heaven for all eternity. His breaths came less and less frequently, and I told him I would help him breathe his last breath. I put my lips to his sweet lips, and we breathed his last two breaths together. Everyone sobbed with me for a long time. I thought I could not walk away and leave him in that room alone. In unbearable grief, we helped each other walk away, but I went back again. I told him I wanted to come with him because grief is so weary, so heavy, so alone.

I had asked God for a complete healing, and I thought that meant healing here. Gradually, I realized, however, that it was not God's plan for Ernie's earthly healing. God had His own way of healing my husband—by taking him to his beautiful heavenly mansion where there is no more sickness, pain, or death.

> *Surely goodness and mercy will follow me all the days of my life and I will dwell in the house of the Lord forever.*
> —Psalm 23:6

Conclusion

I made a promise to Ernie on those painful days in the hospital shortly before he died that I would carry on the work he loved so much and that God had placed upon his heart. This book is but a small testament to my desire to keep that promise.

Faith, family, and public service know of no easy, predefined relationship. We all have to figure out how they relate to one another in our own ways. God places a special calling on each one of our hearts. I was called to be an advocate on behalf of children preparing to enter the world. Ernie was called to provide those children with ways by which they could take their place as rightful leaders in our society. Days were long, and the pain that comes with being open to the world's deepest needs often brought us to the brink of despair. Thinking back to the time we spent in India, how could a mother turn her back on her newborn child? Or, how could a nation turn its back on its children it so desperately needed to educate?

At the brink of such despair is where we find Jesus' hand being pressed into our own more intently than at any other time. His hand is always outstretched, but in those moments, when the pain of the poorest of the poor becomes our own, His will becomes our will. Grace becomes that strength we cannot summon but that finds us in mysterious ways that can only flow from God.

As I write these words, I realize that Ernie passed away almost nineteen years ago. On December 8, 1995, I did not think I could continue, but alas here I am—hoping and praying that I continue to do God's work in what time I have left. I am eager to see my Ernie again and to meet our heavenly Father. In the meantime, I must still have some work to do.

If nothing else, I hope the story I have shared raises questions in your mind about what you are called to do and who you are called to love. My husband and I were fortunate enough to meet leaders of nations, universities, foundations, and a host of other influential entities. However, please remember that the time we loved the most was the time we lived in Upland, California, surrounded by family members and friends. The work was hard, the pay was low, and Upland College was not even accredited when we arrived at our first of many California mansions. However, lives of faith, family, and public service are far better measured by the quality of influence, not the quantity.

To know Jesus Christ is to also know who you are called to love. I saw those answers in the eyes of each mother and child I helped to meet for the first time this side of the womb. Ernie saw those answers in the eyes of each child who stepped into a school building. Together, we saw those answers in the eyes of our own children and grandchildren. Where do you see them? Lives of faith, family, and public service are at times hard, but the rewards on both sides of eternity are immeasurable.

Index

Name Index

Subject Index

Biblical Passage Index

Many Mansions: Lessons of Faith, Family, and Public Service

by Kathryn Boyer

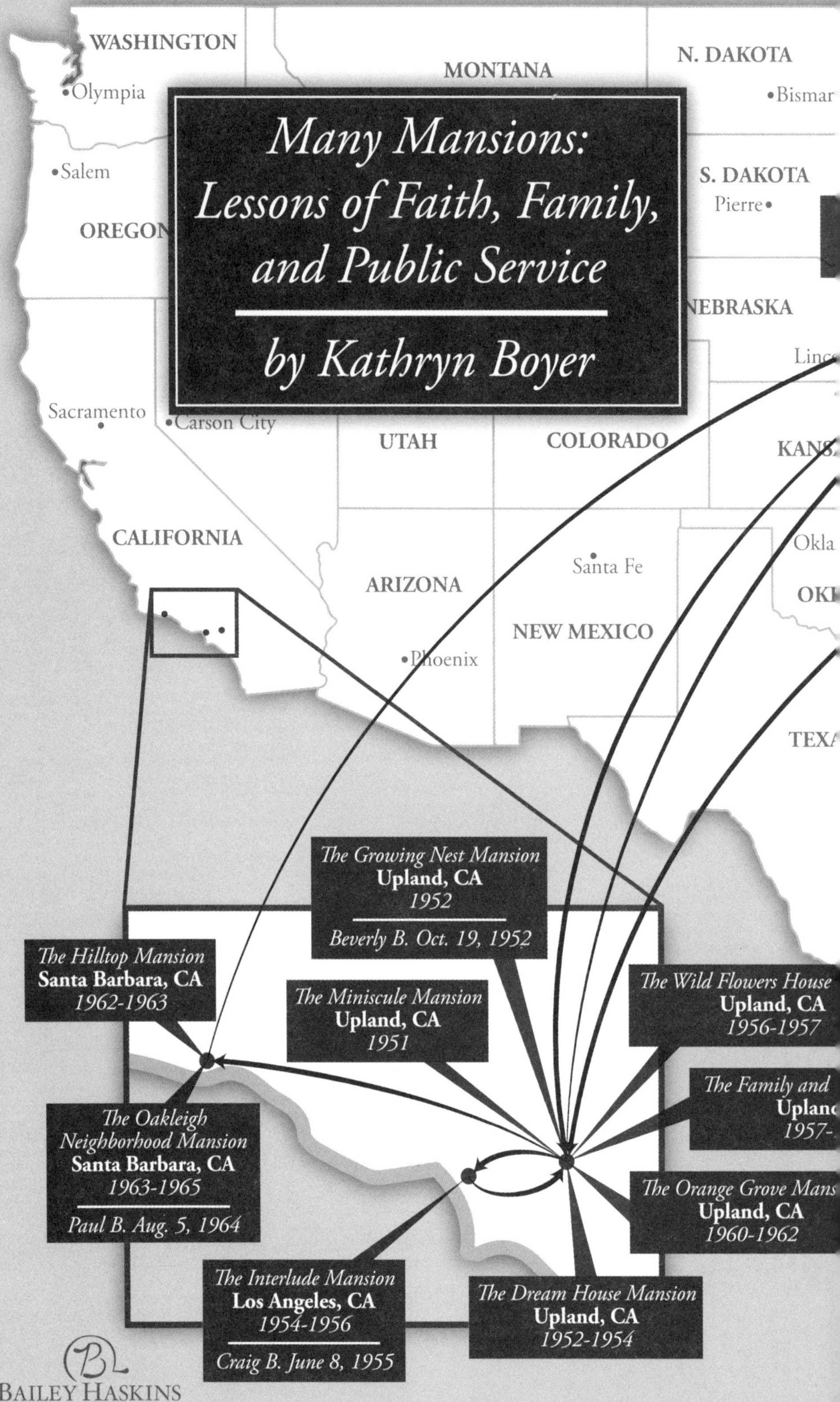

BAILEY HASKINS DESIGN